AMERICAN LIFE AND INSTITUTIONS

GENERAL EDITOR: E. A. BENIANS, M.A.
MASTER OF ST JOHN'S COLLEGE, CAMBRIDGE

I

RELIGION IN AMERICA

In Grateful Memory of

B. H. STREETER

Who was my tutor at
Queen's College, Oxford

1904–7

RELIGION IN AMERICA

BY

WILLARD L. SPERRY

Dean of the Harvard Divinity School

Appendices compiled by
RALPH LAZZARO
Instructor in Church History
Harvard Divinity School

CAMBRIDGE: AT THE UNIVERSITY PRESS
NEW YORK: THE MACMILLAN COMPANY
1946

LITHOGRAPHED IN THE UNITED STATES OF AMERICA

CONTENTS

CONTENTS

FOREWORD

This book was written, in response to an invitation from the Cambridge University Press, for readers in England. It is to be one of a series which the University Press is issuing in a friendly attempt to present contemporary America to the public on that side of the Atlantic. By the time it appears here, it will already be out over there.

The original text stands without alteration on these pages of an American edition. I might have revised it or rewritten it altogether for the local public. For such uses it has certain patent defects. Some of its pages will be so familiar as to seem little less than platitudinous. One needs to remember, however, how little America in its totality is known in England. More particularly, members of one denomination or another will feel that they have been overlooked altogether or given scant recognition. I admit that fact, but may say in self-defence that I have made only the briefest mention of the particular denomination to which I happen to belong.

The book must be read here as an effort at interpretation or translation. Therefore, I have dwelt less on such aspects of the religious life as are common to both England and America, than on those which are peculiar to us and at the same time characteristic of our culture as a whole. To this extent the near-to perspective of the book is false, since it was originally meant to be read at a distance. From first to last I was concerned to try to give our friends in England some idea of the religious situation here in its complexity and prodigal variety.

Even such Englishmen as think they know us well cannot realize fully the restrictions imposed upon us and the liberties accorded us by the separation of church and state. And we ourselves, having taken that separation as a matter of course for a century and a half, do not always make conscious reckoning with the consequences of this major premise of our religious life. Given the history of Christianity as a whole it is a recent fact and many of its first promises still remain to be redeemed. If the separation of church and state has spared us some of the stubborn, unhappy issues with which the Old World was for centuries only too familiar, in that it forbids the question ever being stated here in its classical form, it has not yet solved to our entire satisfaction the problem of the relation of the sacred and secular orders, of religion to the world of affairs.

One more word. Two or three friends who kindly read the manuscript while it was in preparation felt that I was rather too deferential in my style, and were inclined to urge a little more manly independence, if not truculence, on my part. To this charge of an undue Anglophile temper I plead not guilty. The tone of the book merely seeks to perpetuate the spirit of courteous charity which prevailed at the Oxford and Edinburgh Conferences, and runs true to that form. But beyond all this, our friends in England have been hard pressed these last years. They have suffered more than we have. It is to be hoped that thoughtful persons on both sides of the water will meet hereafter with new generosity of mind and heart. Overstatement is a familiar American vice, from which, I fear, our churches are not wholly free. Perhaps English culture errs on the side of understatement. Of the two vices or errors I have, for the original purpose of these pages, preferred the latter. I hope that I am not thereby self-exiled from the goodly fellowship of American Christians.

WILLARD L. SPERRY

PREFACE

I have found it a little difficult to decide on a pattern for this book, which might be, variously, a history, a volume of statistics, a social study, an apologia. No single one of these possible plans for its organization seemed promising. Therefore the reader who is concerned solely with history or theology or sociology or apologetics will feel that his concern is not given full recognition here.

I finally decided that the book had best be an implied conversation between myself here in America and you in England. At the risk of seeming at times to understand the English situation better than is possible for one who is not himself an Englishman, I have assumed that we are more or less acquainted and ought to be still further acquainted. Therefore I have made constant use of the gambits 'you' and 'we', 'yours' and 'ours', in introducing one subject after another.

The book is, therefore, informal in its style, and its faults of style are to this extent deliberate. If, at times, serious matters seem to be treated lightly, that impression must be charged against my desire to avoid pedantry or a dispassionateness so studied that it might seem to suggest a lack of personal identification with the subject. I do not profess to be a disinterested observer and critic of the facts which are my theme. And I have assumed that those who have spent a lifetime with churches and religious movements will not misunderstand the rather intimate tone in which one speaks of matters for which one has a deep affection. Moreover, America is an informal country, and these pages would be a wholly false transcript of our life if they were too formally dressed up to 'go abroad'. I have come to you therefore in our everyday clothes, rather than in Sabbath-day garb.

One other note of explanation should be added by way of warning. A disproportionate amount of space in the pages which follow has been given to the small sects in America. They do not in fact bulk as large as their mention here might seem to suggest. They are, however, within their rather meagre limits characteristic of us. It was in just such modest terms that the older churches of Europe, once they had migrated here, began their life on this new soil. To this extent our small sects, however recent they may be, run true to historical precedents. Furthermore, the formal separation of church and state has allowed, and indeed has encouraged, the birth of new religious movements among us. This perennial process, which has gone on ever since the beginnings of organized religion, offers the student of theology and the social sciences contemporary source material here in America which cannot always be found in the Old World. It should be understood, therefore, that my failure to dwell at much greater length upon the more familiar types of church life, which we share with you, is not an attempt to minimize the dimensions or the major importance of such churches. But I have thought that you would be more interested to know about religious movements and institutions which are not paralleled in England, than to be told about denominations with which you are already familiar, and which differ from yours only in their local nuances.

Some of the material in the first chapters of this book was used in a series of lectures delivered at King's Chapel, Boston, in 1943, under the auspices of the Lowell Institute.

I am indebted to the Committee which administers the Milton Fund in Harvard University for a generous grant which has enabled me not merely to prepare my manuscript, but to have the help of Mr Ralph Lazzaro, a graduate student in Harvard Divinity School, in the verification of many references and citations of fact, and more particularly in the preparation of a series of appendixes. The material which he has gathered for these appendixes represents much searching in many scattered sources, and his resultant tables give to my text a warrant which otherwise would be wanting.

I am further indebted to many friends who read a first draft of the manuscript and offered both needed corrections and valuable suggestions. In particular I have drawn freely on the many books on American religious life written by Professor William Warren Sweet, of the University of Chicago. He has

PREFACE

graciously given me the freedom of his pages. Dr Theodore Maynard and his American publisher, the Macmillan Company, have generously allowed me to use his recent book on *The Story of American Catholicism* as the basis of my chapter on that subject. For the rest I am most grateful to my colleagues in Harvard, Professor Arthur Meier Schlesinger and Professor Arthur Darby Nock; to Dr H. Paul Douglass of the Federal Council of Churches; and to Mr Eugene Exman of Harper and Brothers, for wise and friendly criticism.

Finally my thanks are due to Mrs Horace Reynolds for much patient help in seeing the manuscript through a first draft and a subsequent revision.

WILLARD L. SPERRY

Cambridge, Massachusetts

24 *May* 1944

CHAPTER I. *PRESUPPOSITIONS*

These pages have been written in response to a generous invitation from the Cambridge University Press. I have been asked to try to give English readers some idea of the present state of religion in America. The invitation is gracious; the assignment difficult. America lacks the homogeneity of England, and generalizations about so mixed a people and so complex a society are always open to exceptions. Comprehensive precision will be impossible, and pedantry should require a battery of footnotes at the bottom of every page, if the text is to be faithful to the many diverse facts.

Moreover, no American can pretend to know his land intimately in its length and breadth. Residentially he is the citizen of a single state. The Declaration of Independence, referring to the thirteen rebel colonies of 1776, mentions not the nation, but 'these States'. The resultant doctrine of states' rights was for ninety years thereafter vigorously defended in theory. This right was held to involve ultimately that of secession from the Union. The issue, so long open to equivocal interpretation, was settled only with the conclusion of the Civil War. Since then it has been inconceivable that any single state or group of states should reassert what was once held to be the right to secede from the Union. For political purposes the nation is, in words taught to every school child in the land, 'one and indivisible'.

Nevertheless, old sentiments and affections linger on, though shorn of their one-time menace to the federal government. Pride of state and pride in one's own state are still familiar and powerful forces in American life. It is with us very much as it is with the members of the Universities of Oxford and Cambridge. A single college is the dwelling place for its fellows and students, who meet the university only in its 'federal' capacity. So it is with the American. For many of the purposes of his daily life he is primarily a citizen of Massachusetts or Missouri. Most of the laws which prescribe the pattern within which his life has been lived thus far are state rather than federal laws. Not only do the codes of these states, both civil and criminal, vary; their *mores* vary even more. The senator from Kentucky would not wish to be confused with the senator from Connecticut. Even the way-faring man must have his wits about him on his transcontinental journey. The Sabbath laws and the sumptuary laws change from state to state, and the traveller's mild indulgences *en route* must be accommodated to the practice of the state through which he may happen to be passing.

Such parochialism is not to be wholly deplored. England knows it well, and treasures it. The Cornish fisherman and the Lancashire weaver are not indistinguishable, the one from the other. It would be an unhappy thing for England were they ever to become identical. Reflecting on the Revolution in France, and pleading against the vague abstractions of the social contract, Edmund Burke defended the provincial loyalties of the Anglo-Saxon: 'To be attached to the sub-division, to love the little platoon we belong to in society, is the first principle (the germ as it were) of publick affections. It is the first link in the series by which we proceed towards a love to our country and to mankind.'

Much of the best recent writing in America, as English readers well enough know, has been prompted by a penetrating and affectionate sectionalism. The old hymn 'America' professed a love for the country's 'rocks and rills, its woods and templed hills'. Such sentiments served well enough as long as America still lay to the east of the Appalachian Mountains. They lost their relevance as people went west. There are no templed hills in the plains, nor any rills in the dust bowls. Another medium has had to be found to express the folkways of Kansas and Texas. We have even welcomed the help of sensitive visitors like Mr Priestley in making Santa Fé and Taos vocal after their long, mute years. If the mechanical progress and the political drift of the times seem to be standardizing the country, much of our contemporary art is moving in the other direction toward a meticulous particularity. Willa Cather's *Death Comes to the Archbishop* is thus, in new and non-political terms, an affirmation of the state's rights of New Mexico.

As no American who knows and loves England would wish to see the rich variety of its local dialects overlaid and finally obliterated by the passionless neutrality of a BBC broadcaster's voice, so, we may hope, no Englishman would ask, for the sake of easy generalities about America, that the ways of New Orleans should be accommodated to those of Duluth, or the mind of a Wyoming cattle ranger merged with that of a Maine fisherman, to yield some single synthetic American mentality. Given a national crisis all Americans are now aware of their community of interest. But, as with 'the Solid South', so with other parts of the country, sectionalism is a stubborn fact both politically and culturally.

This fact conditions, and in a measure defeats, all attempts to generalize as to American religion. The country was in colonial times diverse in its origins, and immigration during the subsequent years of our national independence, so far from clarifying the situation, has only complicated it. Statements as to the predominant type of Church life and moral custom which might be true 'at the North' have less relevance in the South. The historic Congregationalism of New England, one of the major religious traditions in American life, means almost nothing below the Mason and Dixon line. Baptists are in the ascendancy there. The Episcopal Church flourishes in the cities, but, save in states like Virginia, it is not a convention in the country districts. The Society of Friends, a body influential and honoured among us as with you, is intensely local in its meetings, being concentrated in a few areas rather than spread thin over the whole land. The Mormons have made Utah their homeland: for five hundred parishes in that state they have only five in Massachusetts. Scandinavian Lutheranism which is a commonplace in Minnesota is all but unknown in Maryland, one solitary church of the Augustana Synod defending the faith in that state. These facts are not an accident, save as all history is accidental; they have their origins in the arrival and the subsequent movement of immigrant groups from the days of the *Mayflower* to the days of the 'ram-you-damn-you-liner' with its crowded steerage. No single consistent account of the total situation can be given; no one pass-key to its elusive meaning can be found.

Likewise, no single writer can hope to be fair to all concerned. As it is the nature of every religion to seek to universalize itself, so it is the habit of the individual believer to impute to others the

3

forms of his own faith and practice. These pages cannot hope to be free of that tendency of the human mind. Furthermore, familiarity with some one scene native and most familiar to him makes it difficult for a man to deny his mental second nature and enter fully into the religious life of some distant part of the country. We are a mobile and migrant people, dwellers in flats and apartments. 'Moving Day' is a recognized national festival, but the day of long moves is over. Our moves are from one block in the city to another, or from this farm to the next but one. (Exception must be made to allow for the temporary dislocation of our population, due to the industrial needs of war-time.) Therefore, what can he know of Oklahoma who only Vermont knows? It is a bold venture for a writer sitting at a desk in a college town in Massachusetts to attempt to interpret the religion or the irreligion of a mining community in Montana. The genteel practices of his church, with their cultural presuppositions, unfit him for that task. Therefore, what is said hereafter in these pages may deceive and in some measure satisfy readers in another land who think of America as a uniformly consistent whole; it can neither deceive nor satisfy those whose intimate knowledge of other places and other ways within the land prompts an instinctive feeling of resentment because they feel themselves either ignored or misrepresented. With the best will in the world any attempt such as this is doomed to failure from the start. It will be provincial and partisan. How shall a New England Congregationalist feel the inwardness of the life of the Amish Mennonites in Pennsylvania, who for religious reasons fasten their garments with hooks and eyes rather than with buttons, or hope to convey the profound intimations of the *mysterium tremendum* suggested by the sight of a Dunker foot-washing in some cloistered community in Kansas?

Nevertheless, when these reservations have been made and duly entered, it remains true that the total fact of America has done something to every one of the religions which have migrated here. No one of them now is the exact counterpart of its parent body in Europe. Be it the climate or the Constitution, some subtle change has taken place. The text of creeds, confessions, and liturgies may still be the same, but the accent with which they are spoken is not that of the Old World. The characteristic nasal twang may now be heard.

Non-English languages of continental origin survive in our churches longer than they survive anywhere else, but they hardly outlast two generations. Grandparents may still use in church the native tongue of their fatherland; the grandchildren in a Sunday School are contemptuous of their non-assimilated elders and clamour for that English which makes and marks them citizens of their own country. With one or two exceptions, all of the major forms of organized religious life in America are of European origin. Yet they are not literal transcripts of that past. They represent subtle restatements of the elder faith and practice, occasioned and in some measure required by the process of their transplanting. The most universal church in the Western World is, by common confession, the Roman Catholic. Its universality rests upon its *quod ubique, quod semper, quod ab omnibus*. Yet this ancient canon, still theoretically in force, has not saved our Catholicism from American restatement. This great Church, numerically the strongest single religious body in the States, is in some ways the most vocally American of all our many denominations. The Irish priest with us, despite his age-old Missal and his unvarying Mass, is not the same man as the parish priest back home. He may remain consciously and devoutly Catholic, but he does not hesitate to speak boldly of 'American Catholicism', even though the words theoretically imply a contradiction in terms.

The slow process of assimilation and accommodation is still unfinished, indeed so unfinished that a British visitor not long ago was prompted to say that America is not a melting-pot at all, she is merely a varnishing pot, from which a thin veneer of seventeenth-century English Puritanism has been laid over the most diverse religious traditions. Nevertheless, the process goes on. It has already gone so far that when an ecumenical religious conference is convened, American delegates from our many local denominations find that, despite their differences, they are strangely nearer to one another than they are to the communions with which, by origin, they are severally identified in the Old World. The fact of their common Americanism is more strongly felt than are the ecclesiastical ties which bind them severally to their parent bodies in Europe. Whether this common quality has any religious meanings is an open question. It may be nothing more than a subtly pervasive secularity; it may be the portent of some new thing. Of the felt fact, however, felt by us most strongly when we forgather in some other land, there is no doubt.

These things being so, it is possible to make certain preliminary generalizations as to the religion of America, which will not do violence to the prodigality of the facts. These generalizations, which will be taken up and developed one by one as the record progresses, furnish our immediate point of departure.

I

The most important difference between the religious life of England and that of America is the continued existence in England of the Established Church, and the total absence in America of anything like an establishment. Let it be granted at once that in this respect the temper of English life is changing rapidly, and that what Henry James once called 'the fine old ecclesiastical arrogance' of all European establishments is now in England largely ancient history. Americans are well aware of the present relations between official Anglicanism and the non-Anglican bodies. The steps which England has taken in the field of inter-church action, and the lead which she has given—an action and a lead which the present crisis has perhaps compelled her to take in the interest of all that is meant by Christianity—are matters of common knowledge on this side of the Atlantic.

Nevertheless, it remains true that church and chapel are not culturally the same thing in England, and even were disestablishment to come to-morrow, the distinction would persist in memory and usage. The bishops entitled to sit in the House of Lords may not be in constant and faithful attendance at its sessions, yet the right remains. No American ecclesiastic has by virtue of his office any right whatsoever to a seat in the Senate of the United States. The parish church in an English village often carries on its walls a tablet bearing the names of all members of the parish, whatever their religious profession, who died in the first World War. That is the fit and recognized place for their corporate remembrance, even though individual memorials may also be accorded some of them in their own dissenting chapels. An American Unitarian visiting the little country churches in England twenty years ago said that he felt, in the presence of these memorials, as he had never felt before, the validity and the effectualness of an establishment, and thus the historic appeal of the Church of England to a whole people. There is no denominational church in any American community which may properly erect any such memorial for the young men of village or town. Each may memorialize only its own particular members. The slightest attempt on the part of any one parish church to seem to represent the community as a whole would be instantly repudiated as an unwarranted assumption of rights, wholly un-American. Any such total roster is therefore self-exiled from the churches and relegated to the town hall or to a plaque in some central square.

Hence the words Nonconformity and Dissent are meaningless in America. There is no politically privileged church to dissent from and no one body to which the sectarian may fail to conform. Granted that the last of the secular grievances of English Nonconformists are now gone, it is impossible to deny the background of the Establishment before which the action still takes place. The City Temple, before its sad destruction, was not the Abbey, and the difference, felt even by the uninitiated American visitor, was not a mere matter of architecture. The serene self-assurance, in the best sense of that word, of the Abbey is unlike the baffling compound of modesty and self-assertiveness in a Nonconformist chapel. There still is, unless a visitor's impressions are wholly in error, a cultural rather than a doctrinal or liturgical gulf between the offices in a parish church of the English Establishment, and the ceremonies, or deliberate lack of ceremony, in a Dissenting meeting house. Theology may be less able than once it was to describe, define and validate the doctrinal distinctions between church and chapel, but the words still have different connotations.

Be these matters as they may, and it is perhaps rash of the foreigner to còmment on them, no Englishman can hope to understand religion in America, unless he rids his mind of the idea of an Established Church and of the consequent distinction between the church and the sect, and then tries to remake his thinking after another pattern. The truth is that America has little idea of 'the Church' in anything like its actual or its ideal catholicity; we know only churches. It is of these churches that Henry James was speaking in the passage from his *American Scene* which yielded the phrase just quoted.

Looking for the moment no more established or seated than a stopped omnibus, they are reduced to the inveterate bourgeois level, and fatally despoiled of the fine old ecclesiastical arrogance. The field of American life is as bare of the Church as a billiard table of a centerpiece; a truth that the myriad little structures 'attended' on Sundays and on the 'off' evenings of their 'sociables' proclaims as with the audible sound of the roaring of a million mice. When an ancient treasure of precious vessels, overscored with glowing gems and wrought artistically into wondrous shapes, has, by a prodigious process, been converted into a vast community of small change, the simple circulating medium of dollars and 'nickels', we can only say that the consequent permeation will be of values of a new order. Of *what* order we must wait to see.[1]

By inference one may read out of these words Henry James's personal preference for the finer forms of the elder arrogance. His words sound, on our side of the Atlantic, a little ungenerous, too afraid of what Henry Adams once called 'the degradation of the democratic dogma'. For our present purpose his picturesque over-statement may be conceded. America is naked of 'the Church' in the historic sense of that word, as Europe has known it and used it. The place of the church is taken by 'denominations'.

Lord Bryce in his *American Commonwealth*, a generous and accurate book on which we still depend for an understanding of ourselves, cites the separation of church and state as being the distinguishing feature of American religious life. Not merely does he enter the fact; he evidently approves of its effects:

[1] *The American Scene*, by Henry James, p. 327. Harper & Brothers, New York, 1907.

Of all the differences between the Old World and the New this is perhaps the most salient. Half the wars of Europe, half the internal troubles that have vexed European States, from the Monophysite controversies in the Roman Empire of the fifth century down to the Kulturkampf in the German Empire of the nineteenth, have arisen from theological differences or from the rival claims of church and state. This whole vast chapter of debate and strife has remained virtually unopened in the United States. There is no Established Church. All religious bodies are absolutely equal before the law, and unrecognized by the law, except as voluntary associations of private citizens....So far from suffering from the want of State support, religion seems in the United States to stand all the firmer because, standing alone, she is seen to stand by her own strength.[1]

II

The next thing to be said of American religious life as a whole is that, in contrast to that of the Old World, it is rankly individualistic. According to the polity of Congregationalism (i.e. Independency), which was the pattern for church life in the New England colonies, any group of like-minded and professed believers have the right to organize themselves into a church, which is in matters of both faith and practice a law unto itself. The Bishop of Gloucester, a candid though not unfriendly critic of America, has often said in the spoken word and in print that, from the standpoint of church life in England, all churches in America, whatever their polity, are congregational. Once again there is an element of deliberate overstatement in this judgment, but there is also an element of truth. We shall have occasion later to comment on the actual number of Americans organized into churches on this polity, as of their effect upon churches theoretically organized upon a wider and more comprehensive basis.

Meanwhile, it is true that when the average American thinks of his church, he thinks not of the communion to which that church belongs, much less of any Holy Church Universal, but of the four walls of the building where he worships on Sunday and of the group of familiar friends and neighbours whom he

[1] *The American Commonwealth*, by James Bryce, vol. II, pp. 763–78. The Macmillan Company, New York, 1913.

meets there. The idea of the church has for him an intensely 'local habitation'. Even his denomination, which must constantly be preached to him as a larger truth, means less to him than the particular parish which for him represents that truth. It is only by a deliberate act of the imagination, bringing some kind of order and common concern out of the chaos of denominationalism, that he is able to envisage, even remotely, what is meant by the Church Universal. In America the seamless robe seems to have been shredded into so many rags and tatters that it is beyond recovery. A Christian must make shift with the particular fragment which has fallen to his lot. The great ecumenical conferences of recent years have made constant use of the majestic term *Una Sancta*. Even though the American delegate to such gatherings may be able to muster enough far-off Latin to understand the reference, the words sound remote. They are an abstraction, a vague hypothesis. There is nothing in his American experience to correspond to them. His heart does not kindle at the thought, and he is sceptical as to the possibility either of recovering an ancient reality now lost or of creating some fresh reality never as yet achieved.

This intense individualism of American life must not be identified as an excess of personal piety. We are probably neither more pious nor less pious than church members elsewhere in the modern world. Nor is there among us anything of the solitariness of the mystic, with his 'flight of the alone to the Alone'. The American is sociable and gregarious. He does not like solitariness or the solitudes. Therefore the strong strain of individualism in his religion is not, in the first instance, religiously conditioned. It is merely a transcript of what has been until most recent times an accepted phase of American life as a whole, to be understood and interpreted not in the authentic terms of the hermit tempers, but in the terms of the self-reliance of single individuals who have been pioneering for three centuries on a frontier. Rufus Jones, the beloved and honoured American Quaker, likes to tell of the farmer who was showing a visitor his well-tilled acres. The visitor said, 'It is wonderful what God and man can do together when running a farm.' 'Yes', said his host, 'but you should have seen this farm when God was running it alone.'

Not only so, but the political traditions of the country have encouraged the habit of self-assertion. The eighteenth-century struggle for rights survives as a recognized heritage among us, and its processes have become our mental habit. The result has been, in history of both church and state, certain grave defects in American life. At this point the contemporary American is now remaking his mind after a more adequate pattern for the conduct of life hereafter. Meanwhile, the doctrine of the rights of man, supplementing the Reformation vote of confidence in the private conscience, has made of our people as a whole a society of religiously self-assertive individuals. The single individual habitually accords to his opinions, to say nothing of his convictions, an importance which the total truth of things by no means always warrants. The inbred passion for the rights of the individual still survives and expresses itself in the life of the average church. At the turn of the eighteenth century, as we shall see hereafter, it threatened even the corporateness and catholicity of the Roman Church.

This trait in the American temperament is still served by the popular cult of personalities. The American newspaper, as against the classic type of the European press, is made up of columns given over, in an inordinate measure and at the cost of space devoted to larger and more impersonal issues, to the vivid reporting of the fortunes and misfortunes of single individuals. Trends, movements, social drifts may be observed and studied by intellectuals; they are not front-page news in the average daily paper, save in the larger and more sophisticated centres. The *New York Times* is a great newspaper, but it is not typical of the press of the country as a whole; it is too world-wide and impersonal.

Hence the prominence in American religious life of the single picturesque or vivid figure, more often than otherwise the popular preacher. The normal denominational church history of any given religious body in the country is more often than otherwise merely a dictionary of ecclesiastical biography. It may well be that the time ought never to come when religion is to be relegated to what Thomas Huxley once called 'the passionless impersonality of the unknown and the unknowable'. It may further be that our only human salvation from such impersonality is to be found now in one man and now in another who incarnates for the many the very idea of religion. The crowd can comprehend him and follow him. But so much has this been true of American religion that the great preacher, of whom we have had many, seems often to be a liability to the institution rather than an asset. One of the major unsolved problems of American religious life is that of provision for the successor to such a man. So also, the history of most of our smaller sects is that of relatively short-lived movements which flourish under the leadership of a captivating founder, but languish under his dull successors. Thus, so long as Father Divine lives he can keep his angels in charge and in order, but who is to take over and carry on when he must forsake his Harlem heaven for the ultimate reality? The recurrence of this problem in the record of the small sect in America is a familiar phenomenon.

At more sober, if not higher, levels the same situation obtains through the major and more permanent religious bodies. He is the very rare leader in American religious life who shares to the full Tolstoi's fear of disciples, or can transmute their personal devotion to him into loyalty to the longer-lived society as a whole. These personal followings of single gifted individuals are probably inevitable and perhaps necessary. But in America the ordering of such matters has been carried so far that our corporate religious life, which seems at first to have been served so well by the presence of the pulpit orator, has also suffered from that fact a paradoxical disservice. This whole situation is by no means unique or confined to America, but it is so characteristic of our people and our culture as to find here perhaps its most extreme statement.

III

A third characteristic of American religion, to quote one of our historians, is its 'immense and indomitable optimism'. This quality of the national spirit derives directly from the whole history of the country thus far. Mr Churchill, in welcoming America as an ally, lifted two lines from Clough's familiar poem and gave them just such an interpretation,

> In front, the sun climbs slow, how slowly,
> But westward, look, the land is bright.

Successive generations of emigrants from Europe have been lured westward by that brightness. Those who have stayed behind in the Old World have followed the movement with mixed emotions of envy and scepticism. There has always been the possibility that the *émigré* might find the pot of gold at the far end of the rainbow. There has been, also, the suspicion that he might find himself the deluded follower of some will-o'-the-wisp, in which case those who stayed behind were proved to have chosen the better part. Our text-books have abounded with detailed records of the many waves of immigration which have washed up on these shores. The ongoing fact is celebrated as being a warrant for the hope which the Old World has vested in the possibilities of life in the New World.

Many an American schoolboy has had to go to England to learn to his surprise that in the 1770s some 80,000 to 100,000 Tories or Loyalists left the Colonies to go to Canada, or to return to England. Until most recent times this fact was omitted from American school books. So, even at this day, such books usually fail to tell of the backwash of the immigration movement, which in many a recent year has carried home again to Europe disappointed would-be settlers more in number than the new arrivals. This reversal of the tide is due not merely to the passage of stricter immigration laws. It is itself the sad sign of much suffering and disillusionment. To concede the existence of such persons in such numbers is, however, still treason to a major article in the national faith, which continues to pronounce our country the 'Land of Promise'. The myth long ago became legend, a legend which for at least two centuries and a half had its warrant in the event, and the legend in turn has become dogma. To deny the warrant for the hope or to question the validity of the promise is even at this late date little short of heresy. No public official, relying for his position upon popular suffrage, can as yet afford to indulge openly in sober second thoughts as to the full and final warrant for the traditional optimism of American life. He must continue subscription to the orthodox creed.

This temper has been, of course, much fortified by the doctrine of political perfectionism which was abroad in the world in the mid-eighteenth century and which was given in America an unparalleled opportunity to vindicate itself in fact. That doctrine had in America a free field which at the time could not be found anywhere in Europe. It has had here a less stormy and more consistent history than in the one other country where it sought to realize itself by revolution, France.

When he first visited America many years ago, Mr H. G. Wells said that curiously he felt himself to be in a culture older than that of England, for the simple reason that in America the political consciousness of the country went back uninterruptedly to the 1770s, while in England no man's mind antedates, politically, the reforms of the 1830s. Washington still lives in the American mind as a contemporary; in England the Georges are ancient history. The Englishman has to go back of them to an earlier time, the sixteenth and seventeenth centuries, to recover contemporaries. Until the first World War the only interruption in America of this unbroken political consciousness was the Civil War, and, grave as that crisis was, it proved to be only an interruption of the direct development of the national mind, not a radical diversion. Dogmas are tenacious of their life; they give way only slowly and long after the event to happenings which require their re-vision. So it is with the dogma of the Land of Promise and the hopes begotten by the prospect of such a land. Present facts may no longer warrant that dogma in its original naïve forms, but the words continue to be said as a stubborn profession of faith.

This immense and indomitable optimism has been, and still is, curiously at variance with the theological axioms of the historic faiths which the succession of immigrants brought with them. Those faiths have uniformly taken a pessimistic view of human nature as their point of departure. Man, as we meet him in our fellows and know him in our own members is, they assert, a fallen and sinful creature, dependent upon divine grace for his salvation. Orthodox religion has never professed or pretended otherwise. Not that religion, so construed, is without final hope in the world; but rather that, as with Saint Paul, such hope lies on the far side of a preliminary discipline in tribulation, patience and much stern experience. George Tyrrell once said that Christianity is an ultimate optimism, but an optimism which is founded upon a provisional pessimism. So construed, the religion of America has been premature and inexpert. It has struck straight for the ultimate optimism in neglect of that preliminary pessimism which the great religions of the world have all presupposed as their premise.

The result has been that the average American, the child of a geographical pioneer and a political perfectionist, has been impatient of any mention or recognition of the more sombre aspects of human nature and human history. For three hundred years he found in the history of his country no occasion to concede any such disquieting facts and no need to doubt his own resilience in the presence of trouble. Therefore, the old grim·words which, in varying forms, he has used on Sundays to confess his sins, have had little relation to the cheerful self-confidence with which he has gone about his business for the rest of the week. William James in his *Varieties of Religious Experience* soberly reminded his fellow countrymen a generation ago that 'the completest religions would seem to be those in which the pessimistic elements are best developed'. So far as most Americans are concerned his words fall on deaf ears. They know themselves to be the happy 'once-born souls' whom James had previously described with such fidelity to the national character; they do not identify themselves as the 'sick souls' and the 'twice-born souls' in whom he goes on to vest his final confidence.

There is, thus, an unresolved contradiction at the heart of American religion. The old sombre theological words are still said, but daily life is conducted on another assumption. This contradiction is, of course, met wherever the modern world exists, but it is most perversely present in the land where the record thus far seems to have given the lie to ancient creeds. The authentic religion of America has been, thus far, that of the premature and provisional optimism to which youth is always liable; which, indeed, no generous-minded person would deny to youth. This inexpertness of ours should probably be understood and patiently borne with as the normal mood of a country which has been until most recently still in its adolescence.

How the grim hereditary Calvinism of New England could survive so complacently beside the resolute cheerfulness of daily life is a riddle which remains to be read. That it did so is, however, a fact that cannot be denied. In his memorable essay on Jonathan Edwards, Leslie Stephen hit off the situation in a single illuminating and devastating sentence. He is talking about Edwards's familiar thesis, elaborated in more than one of his terrifying sermons, that, if children are 'out of Christ', they are but 'young vipers, and are infinitely more hateful than vipers'. Stephen then goes on to say, 'That Edwards should have been a gentle, meditative creature, around whose knees had clung eleven "young vipers" of his own begetting, is certainly an astonishing reflection.' The paradox may suggest that men are often better than their creeds. Perhaps this is the truth of the American situation. Be these abstruse matters as they may, the average American has not been deterred from peopling the land with young vipers of his own begetting by a prudential theological dread of the result.

At this point, however, a radical change is already taking place in American life. Uncritical and uncriticised optimism is no longer possible in its traditional forms. A strange and hitherto unknown sobriety has come over the national mind. What this soberness implies, as a reflection on the past and as a portent for the future, remains to be seen. Perhaps the religion of America is to be hereafter less incomplete than it has hitherto been, and thus more akin to the elder historic faiths which Christendom as a whole has professed.

IV

A final generalization remains to be made. These pages assume, as a matter of course, that the religion of America is in the first instance that expressed through its churches. It is difficult to estimate the hold which the churches of Christendom have upon their peoples as a whole. · Statistics are proverbially untrustworthy. In most nominally Christian countries the number of parishes, members, communicants, and adherents still remains considerable. Yet there has been in all countries the suspicion, the lurking fear, that these churches and what goes on in them are no longer directly related to the realities of common life round about.

In a famous bit of American doggerel about the deacon's

'Wonderful One-Hoss Shay' (one-horse chaise) Oliver Wendell Holmes subtly satirized years ago the nature and probable fate of the New England orthodoxy. His verses are a description of a two-wheeled gig built of the best materials, honestly put together, and intended to last indefinitely, if not for ever. Occasion for the satire was not wanting. The author had in mind the bold ascription of eternal life to its creed and to its articles of incorporation made by a well-known Calvinist theological seminary. The founders of the institution declared that their creed should 'forever remain entirely and identically the same' and that its governance should 'continue as the Sun and Moon, forever'. That was in 1808. From 1886 to 1892 and again in 1925–6 this institution was before the Supreme Judicial Court of the Commonwealth of Massachusetts involved in litigation necessitated by the theological strait-jacket in which the founders had so presumptuously confined it. The certain prospect of just such an eventuality had, in the meantime, prompted the lines in question. The deacon's one-hoss shay did run for years, truly and well, until in one sudden catastrophic moment the whole affair went to pieces altogether and vanished in a cloud of dust. The wry humour of the poem has never been lost on thoughtful churchmen in America. Churches, behind their bland self-confidence, are uneasy and apprehensive. Their dissolution may be nearer and more total than they know. There is always the sober warning of the Gospel that the kingdom of God may be taken from ecclesiasticism and given to some other order nearer the spiritual and moral realities of things. No reflective churchman can wholly safeguard himself against these salutary fears.

I hesitate to hazard any appraisal of the present situation in nominally Christian lands. My strong impression is, however, that churches, church members, church attendants are still relatively more numerous in America than in most other countries. If this be true, there remains the uneasy suspicion that we may have here, as in so many other respects in America, a survival form of life rather than a transcript of contemporary facts. It is an accepted commonplace among us that the rigors of life in Europe have forced many of your conventions either to succumb to a new situation or to come up to it. If they still have vitality, they come abreast the issues of the day; if they survive merely as habit which has lost its warrant, they eventually drop away unnoticed and unregretted. One sometimes suspects that the still appreciable church-going in America may be merely a matter of unspent momentum from the past. It is true that the ship still has steerageway, but she may be losing the breeze.

There is a recognized 'lag' between the social changes which go on in Europe and those in America. A shrewd English bishop, asked to give his dominant impression of American life, replied not long since, 'The thing that strikes me most is the backwardness of your labor movement.' His comment, it is true, antedated the days of John L. Lewis and the CIO, yet there was much incisive truth in it. So one may read out of the statistics of American church life a suggestion of some cultural backwardness in the formal religion of the nation. If our present church figures represent merely a lag rather than a contemporary reality, one can only say that it is a happy thing that this lag has lasted on to a time when Christendom has much warrant for thinking better rather than worse of its churches. However recreant and culpable our churches may have been in the past, there is abroad in them to-day a new moral earnestness, prompted for the most part by the heroic resistance of parent bodies in occupied lands. The admiration bred by that example is not confined to churchmen. Writing from the safe seclusion of his shelter in Princeton, Professor Einstein said not long since:

Being a lover of freedom, when the revolution came in Germany, I looked to the universities to defend it, knowing that they had always boasted of their devotion to the cause of truth; but, no, the universities were immediately silenced. Then I looked to the great editors of the newspapers, whose flaming editorials in days gone by had proclaimed their love of freedom; but they, like the universities, were silenced in a few short weeks....

Only the church stood squarely across the path of Hitler's campaign for suppressing truth. I never had any special interest in the Church before, but now I feel a great affection and admiration for it because the Church alone has had the courage and persistence to stand for intellectual truth and moral freedom.

I am forced to confess that what I once despised I now praise unreservedly.[1]

Such testimony is to-day becoming a reassuring commonplace. There is outside the churches a new fund of good will toward churches which will make the conventional prophecy of an imminent collapse of the church less likely of fulfilment than may have been the expectation in the past. Should such renewed interest in institutional Christianity survive the war, it will certainly find in the American churches an appreciable number of persons who represent the lag we have mentioned. But, if so, the interest and confidence of these persons in their churches may well be greatly stimulated. There is much fallow ground in our American church life that can be recovered and recultivated, not yet 'gone back to nature'.

Quite apart from all church matters, there remains the question whether or not conventional ecclesiasticism ever represents the living religion of a people. If we use the word 'religion' to indicate the major loyalty of a society, we must accept the fact that in recent times and in more than one land religions of state and race and class have replaced that of our traditional faiths. These religions are reversions to more primitive types of life, but to the degree that they are fanatically sincere they are also alarmingly effective.

The honest critic of American affairs must therefore face the possibility that the true religion of his land is not that of Protestant, Catholic or Jew, but is rather that of some secular idolatry. Thus, it is commonly said that the American worships 'the Almighty Dollar'. Thus, again, John Ruskin, writing to Charles Eliot Norton, said that he had little interest in going to America because of its devotion to 'the goddess-of-getting-on'. William James was even more outspoken in his contempt for 'the bitch-goddess, Success', whose altars he found spread abroad over the land. Candour compels a reckoning with these idolatries. Are they the real truth of the country and its people?

Finally, any account of our affairs must reckon with the existence of a very large number of persons, unchurched and mildly

[1] The *New York Times*, p. 38. 23 December 1940.

19

anti-clerical, who still take a sympathetic interest in the world of religious ideas. This fringe round about organized religion is much more considerable in America than elsewhere. In the Old World the line between the churched and the unchurched tends to be sharply drawn. If you are religious you belong to some church. It is not so with us. Among intelligent persons there is what the Quakers call a 'concern' for religion, even though that concern is primarily speculative rather than practical. The late Josiah Royce of Harvard has said:

At a very recent time in the history of European discussions, attitudes of critical hostility or of thoughtful indifference towards Christianity were prominent factors in discussion, and occupied a favoured place in the public mind. Such was the case, for instance, in the last century, during the early phases of the controversies regarding evolution. As a philosophical student I myself was trained under the influence of such a general trend of public opinion. These attitudes of critical indifference or of philosophical hostility towards traditional faith, are still prominent in our world of religious discussion; but side by side with them there have recently become prominent tendencies belonging to a third group—tendencies which seem to me to be, in their treatment of Christianity, neither predominantly apologetic, nor predominantly hostile, nor yet at all indifferent....

With the apologists, then, and against the hostile or the thoughtfully indifferent critics of Christianity, a student may stand, as one to whom the philosophy of religion, if there is to be a philosophy of religion at all, must include in its task the office of a positive and a deeply sympathetic interpretation of the spirit of Christianity, and must be just to the fact that the Christian religion is, thus far at least, man's most impressive vision of salvation, and his principal glimpse of the homeland of the human spirit.... Christianity stands before us as the most effective expression of religious longing which the human race, travailing in pain until now, has, in its corporate capacity, as yet, been able to bring before its imagination as a vision, or has endeavoured to translate, by the labour of love into the terms of its own real life.[1]

[1] *The Problem of Christianity* by Josiah Royce, vol. I, pp. 8–11. The Macmillan Company, New York, 1913.

I cite this passage because it is not an isolated exception to the attitude of a large number of Americans, mainly those in our universities and colleges, toward the whole subject of religion. Such persons in the institutions where they serve give academic instruction in the general field. They have been for fifty years, and still are, men of such distinction that their courses command the respect of their colleagues and the interest and confidence of groping minds among undergraduates. Their attitude communicates itself to editors of the more serious magazines of the country. The *de luxe* publication *Fortune*, which is primarily an organ of big business, has been running for months past a series of articles on religious issues, by such men as Maritain and Hocking; the editors themselves also turning aside from the immediate problems of banking and industry to launch out as laymen with papers on the subject. Our sober monthlies all expect, as a matter of course, to carry constant rather than occasional papers on the state of our churches, the prospects for religion, the past failures and the future potentialities of Christianity.

Those who write these articles, and those who in much greater numbers read them, are studiously careful to keep their skirts clear of churches as they now are. They fear, were they to lend their names to any form of organized religion, that they would find themselves in a false position, wrongly labelled. They seldom come to church and they almost never join a church. Yet they are serious lay interpreters of basic religious ideas, though not professional apologists for any single sectarian creed. Any account of the religious life of America to-day will be false to the facts if it ignores the presence of this mid-world of persons, no longer hostile or indifferent to religion, though not as yet ecclesiastically or theologically minded. In due time they will deserve special mention and interpretation.

Again, such persons may represent only a cultural backwardness in American life. A Scotch theologian in Edinburgh has recently said, however, that among his colleagues he is finding a large number of men, previously hostile or indifferent to religion, who have now been compelled to take a more friendly attitude toward Christianity because of their inability to accept the ethical antithesis to Christianity as revealed by the times through which we are passing. If his account of the facts is in any way accurate, the persons of whom he speaks are undergoing an experience which can only be described as a conversion. Here in America we have had no converts of this sort, at least in appreciable numbers. But we have had and still have 'intellectuals' who, since the beginning of the present century, have been moving in the direction taken by Royce's mind. There has been nothing spectacular in this movement. It has never been tabulated by the Census in the form of statistics. It refuses to have its ranks numbered. Yet there it is, one of the most considerable and influential factors in our total religious situation.

Such, then, are the three or four generalizations which will serve as a background before which specific statements of fact may safely be made. They have set the scene for the action thus far. Up until the time of the present war they seemed to enjoy a promise of permanence. But the drastic changes in our life, now in process, are so radical that these premises may require hereafter new and different formulation. Therein lies the significance of the present hour for the future of religion in America.

CHAPTER II. *THE THIRTEEN COLONIES*

The German historian von Ranke says that history is the account of how things came to be as they are.

As a people we Americans are not historically minded. We shrink, perhaps, from Mr Henry Ford's blunt dictum that 'history is the bunk', yet we can understand his preoccupation with each new model of his car.

The truth is that our own history, beside the prior histories of Europe and Asia, is brief. The total record of our now three hundred years bulks small beside the longer centuries, even the millennia, which are remembered in the Old World. This being an area in which we cannot match our many fatherlands, and in which therefore we cannot excel, a hiding instinct prevents our making parade of our relatively brief chronicles. We take the nation's history for granted; locally we often have much pride in it, but we cannot pretend to a longer past than we have.

Quite apart from our natural reserve in the matter there is the further fact that when we came here, whether in the persons of our colonial forbears or in our own more recent person, unconsciously perhaps rather than consciously we broke with the homelands which we left behind. The act of emigration does something to the human mind. Whatever ties may have bound Abraham to Haran, once he obeyed the command, 'Get thee out of thy country, and from thy kindred, and from thy father's house, unto a land that I will shew thee', his mind and heart were thereafter set upon the Land of Promise. It cannot be otherwise with any pioneer. Thus the author of what is, at the moment of writing, the best-seller on American bookstalls tells his story. He is an Armenian, born in Alexandropolis. When Bulgarians and Turks successively raided Greek territory in 1909 his family was despoiled by each marauding army. We lived, he says, refugees in our own home. After many wanderings and much suffering in various Balkan states, the family came to this country. His father promptly put the children in the common schools, saying, 'We have come to a New World, we must learn new ways of living. Forget Europe.' Such deliberate forgetfulness is a commonplace among us.

Not only so, but the more characteristic exemplars of the American mind have encouraged us to compensate for the want of depth in our national self-consciousness by stressing the eternal contemporaneity of the past. Thus Emerson, in a famous essay, says that there is properly no history, only biography which becomes in turn autobiography, and he bids us dare to live all history in our own person. This is a most unscientific account of the past, but it is good Transcendentalism. Emerson's whimsical neighbour, Henry Thoreau, in refusing an invitation to take a trip to Europe, declined on the ground that the Atlantic Ocean was after all only a big Walden Pond. He believed, perversely and provincially, as Emerson said in pronouncing his funeral oration, that all the values of the universe could be found at the point of intersecting latitude and longitude which marked the town of Concord. We have taken much comfort from such arbitrary modes of self-assurance. Meanwhile, if a people is busy, as we were for at least two centuries and a half, in staking out claims in a new world, there being always the receding novelty of the alluring West, the future absorbs and satisfies the mind.

It would be convenient for the purposes of this book if the present religious scene could be described in purely contemporary terms. Alas, that is impossible. The happenings in our original colonies will seem to any English reader matters of minor importance in the longer and wider history of the British Empire. Indeed, it was precisely because they were so construed at the time that the American Revolution was allowed to get out of hand. Even to Americans the story of those little scattered groups up and down the Atlantic coast belongs to the 'day of small things' which the prophet bade us not to despise, but which we find it hard to relate to later days of big things.

There will be, however, no hope of enabling any English reader to understand the state of religion in modern America if he is to be spared some brief introduction to our colonial history. The Constitution, which set the pattern for the new nation, was itself the yield of the experience of the colonists. So far as our religious life is concerned, the present situation in the country was foreshadowed and in some measure actually anticipated by early colonial usage. Moreover, since the several . major religious traditions still in force are European in their origins, and since they furnish at the present time one .of the strongest surviving bonds with you, they become to-day common ground upon which minds otherwise too isolated or too insular may meet. Therefore, for the sake of a better understanding of each other, we can well afford to take a little time to go back to the common 'pit whence we were digged'. The humble beginnings of the religious life of our country are, of course, dear to many of us. We cannot expect you to invest them with the importance we accord them, nor to muster the feelings we have for them. But by telling the story briefly we can help you to understand us a little better, at the points where our ways of life diverge from yours. We can at least tell you why, if you were motoring through our countryside, you might normally expect to find a white wooden Nonconformist meeting house on a New England village green, and a little red-brick Anglican church in the Virginia countryside, both built in the mid-eighteenth century.

Meanwhile, the lay writer, seeking to tell this tale, is dependent upon historians of two distinct types. We were familiar during the nineteenth century with what is now known as the 'filial piety' school of history. Members of this school accepted un-criticized, and at their face value, statements made by the found-ing fathers as to their motives in coming here, and their aims in setting up their institutions. The sources so construed seemed to warrant the conclusion that those motives were predominantly, if not solely, religious. Thus, one of the gates to the Harvard Yard bears a tablet with an account of the founding of the College in 1636, taken from *New England's First Fruits* published in London in 1643.

After God had carried us safe to New England, and wee had builded our houses, provided necessaries for our livelihood, rear'd convenient places for God's worship, and settled the civill government: One of the next things we longed for and looked after was to advance learning and perpetuate it to posterity; dreading to leave an illiterate ministery to the churches, when our present ministers shall lie in the dust.

Whether these moving lines were warranted by the fact, and whether they meant what they seem to mean, is a question which vexes our present-day university. It is with us as with those who would prefer not to believe that the early Christians actually had all things in common—some less literal interpretation of the text is often sought.

The last few years, therefore, have seen a candidly secular rewriting of the record, primarily in the interests of the economic interpretation of history. The unfilial historian points out that the colonies were, and had to be, business ventures commercially sustained, if not commercially inspired. Behind the professed piety of the colonist lay the profit motive which prompted hard-headed men at home to back the project. Whatever his religious professions, the colonist was, therefore, the witting or unwitting agent of sound business. No one can deny the pounds-shillings-and-pence hurdle to be negotiated before a shipload of emigrants could be cleared, or their subsequent indebtedness to those who had financed them.

Some unfilial historians have therefore gone on to 'debunk' the founding fathers of America, as being either hypocritical or pathetically self-deceived. Opinion has vacillated between these two alternatives. It is admitted that obscure and guileless members of a colony may not have been guilty of insincerity, truly believing what they said of themselves. But certain modern writers have taken pleasure in pillorying the more prominent leaders of the colonies as pious frauds. Their reputation has suffered much in consequence, and many of their more drastic acts are, it is true, hard to reconcile with their claim to a pure spirituality and an elevated morality. They were for the most part stern, hard men; we can only say in their defence that if they were hard on others, they were even harder on themselves. One sometimes suspects that this secular, somewhat cynical, rewriting of the story of American beginnings is prompted by the desire of emancipated persons to be rid of all sense of further obligation to the Puritan tradition.

At the present moment, however, there seems to be, if not a willingness to rehabilitate filial history writing, at least an unwillingness to concede the findings of the unfilial school. To what extent was the Massachusetts Bay Colony of 1629 religiously occasioned and inspired? James Truslow Adams has defended the thesis that four out of five of the colonists had no sympathy with the Puritan Church; that they were variously traders, adventurers, and roustabouts. But Professor Samuel Eliot Morison, who for some years held the chair of American History at Oxford, appraising the findings of both schools, concludes that 'religion, not economics or politics, was the centre and focus of the Puritan dissatisfaction with England, and the Puritan migration to New England'. A competent Harvard colleague of Professor Morison's says that the great migration to Massachusetts was largely due to certain men of the seventeenth century, 'who took religion seriously, and often followed spiritual dictates in comparative disregard to all ulterior considerations'. Present history writing in America concedes, therefore, the complexity of motives which lay behind the colonization of the country, and while it can no longer consent to oversimplified interpretations of the event, it is unwilling to deny and delete the religious factor.

The problem is not one which is wholly American. In so far as modern England can understand herself in the terms of her life at the turn of the sixteenth century, she can understand us as of that time, and in so doing can help us to understand ourselves better to-day. It is your problem as much as ours, this of the mixed motives of the men of those days.

English colonization of America begins with the year 1578, when Elizabeth gave to Sir Humphrey Gilbert *Letters Patent* 'for the inhabiting and planting of our people in America'. This grant anticipated a settled colony, and was not a mere charter to a trading company. Sir Walter Raleigh, who was the chief promoter of this plan for colonization, drafted Richard Hakluyt as his publicist.

Hakluyt prefaces his stirring *Discourse* (1584) with the pious confidence that,

this westerne discoverie will be greatly for the inlargement of the gospill of Christe, whereunto the princes of the refourmed relligion are chiefly bounde, amongst whom her majestie ys principall....

Now the Kinges and Queenes of England have the name of Defendours of the Faithe. By which title I think they are not only chardged to Mayneteyne and patronize the faithe of Christ, but also to enlarge and advaunce the same. Neither ought this to be their laste worke, but rather the principall and chefe of all others, according to the commandemente of our Saviour, Christe, Mathewe 6, Firste seeke the kingdome of God and the righteousness thereof, and all other things shall be mynistred unto you.

He then cites the success of the Spanish and Portuguese in Catholic missionary ventures in the Caribbean and to the southward, and urges upon his fellow countrymen the duty of a counter-Protestant mission in the northern hemisphere, prompted by the prospect 'not of filthie lucre nor vain ostentation, but principally the gayninge of the soules of millions of those wretched people' who inhabited these shores, and their possible rescue from 'dumbe idols to the lyving God, from the depe pit of hell to the highest heaven'. Added urgency was given to Hakluyt's exhortations by the presence of the French in Canada. If Protestant England failed to act and to act speedily, Catholics to the south and Catholics to the north might close up their ranks in a joint occupation and colonization of the still vacant territory lying between Florida and Canada.

Hakluyt's appeal to his fellow-countrymen was not confined to the spiritualities; it was fortified by a recognition of the temporalities as well. America would prove a sound investment, the unemployed in England could be used in the trade which would spring up, social discontent at home could be relieved to this extent, criminals from overcrowded prisons could be shipped overseas. Piety therefore would not prove unprofitable, and far-seeing persons at home would thus be able to make the best of both worlds.

The settlement in Virginia in 1607, that at Plymouth in 1620, and that of Massachusetts Bay (the Boston area) in 1629, were duly followed by the colonization of other parts. The motives which prompted and backed these ventures were undoubtedly mixed, as mixed as those of much of our modern life. A selfless religious zeal was shrewdly compounded with a frank self-interest. If the English reader of to-day is prepared to strike some balance between the strain of genuine piety in the England of the late sixteenth or early seventeenth centuries and the sound commercial instinct of the time, he will then know by inference how far America was in the first instance a country religiously conceived.

You, too, are not without your unfilial historians. The pass-key to the truth of the times seems to have been the hatred and fear first of Spain and then of France. That *motif* still lives on in America, as we shall later see, as a stubborn national tendency toward anti-Catholicism. Dread of Catholicism is part of our Protestant heritage, though neither Spain nor France is now its political occasion. Thus a recent writer says, with fidelity to the fact,

The Elizabethan seamen were Protestants of the Protestants when it came to hating Roman Catholicism, but their personal religion was a strange compound of 'fervid patriotism, a varied assortment of hates, a rough code of morals, and an unshaken trust in the providence of God. To the heathen they brought not peace but a sword. To the Pope, whom they named with the Turk and the Devil, they wished destruction. For Queen and country they would go anywhere and attempt anything !'

As for the theory that England had a foreign mission to perform among the natives of America, Sir Walter Raleigh (the Sir Walter of modern Oxford, not he of the old days) says, 'This scheme for the evangelization of the heathen had no history.' It was merely 'a stock weapon in the argumentative armoury of determined explorers', and those who still defend it 'plead for it, like sharp Christian attorneys, without sincerity'. Perhaps you, on the other side, can help us read this riddle of the true origins of our colonies. It was not until the end of the French and Indian War in 1763 that the struggle between Protestantism and Catholicism for hegemony on the North American continent was brought to a military and political conclusion.[1]

Meanwhile, although the motives behind early colonization were mixed, and the truth of them can never be fully known

[1] For the above facts and quotations, cf. *Religion in Colonial America*, by William Warren Sweet, pp. 3 ff. Charles Scribner's Sons, New York, 1942.

until the day when the secrets of all hearts shall be revealed, certain indubitable happenings stand on the record.

The basic fact in American colonial history is that of the radical difference between the two earliest types of settlement here. One was the proprietary province, the other the corporate colony. (The royal colony came later.) The proprietary provinces were, to all intents and purposes, landed estates of a feudal type granted by the crown to favourites or petitioners. More often than otherwise there was an individual proprietor in England. Thus the Lords Baltimore, father and son, were the first proprietors of Maryland. The Dutch colony of New Netherlands, after it came into English hands in 1664, had as its proprietor the Duke of York, and became New York. William Penn was the proprietor of Pennsylvania, and so absolute was his control of his province that in 1708, finding himself in financial straits, he mortgaged it. Other kindred provinces were owned and managed by proprietary boards in England. It was seldom that the proprietors went out to their provinces; they operated them from at home. Penn was an exception, and he eventually returned to England.

The corporate colony, on the other hand, was made up of a group of persons most of whom intended to emigrate. They incurred heavy financial obligations in getting away. The Plymouth Pilgrims, for example, had been financed by a group of Merchant Adventurers in London. They were to look to their backers at home for a steady supply of corn, cheese, small beer and the like. In turn they were to send back lumber and furs in the bottoms which brought out their food. The arrangement broke down from the first. The first winter at Plymouth had taken toll of half the little group. The summer crops had been meagre, and the prospects for a second winter were grim. November was hardly come when the ship *Fortune* was sighted bringing no food, but an additional fifty colonists. She took back a token payment of beaver skins and timber to the value of £500. This initial repayment, alas, never reached England. The *Fortune* was overhauled and plundered by a French cruiser. The disappointed London merchants made no further attempt to send food to their unprofitable servants. Meanwhile the colonists were left to prove their ability to sustain themselves on an unpromising soil. Captain John Smith had brought back to England a few years earlier the report that it was unlikely that any company could sustain itself off the land in New England. Plymouth eventually vindicated its power to do so, but only after seven precarious years, in which the balance might have fallen either way. The Merchant Adventurers finally compounded with the colonists for the sum of £1800, to be paid in nine annual instalments. Thus, the title to the Plymouth venture passed from England to a holding company of eight of the local leaders. Thereafter as far as money was concerned they owed no man in England anything. Plymouth, which began as a semi-proprietary province, became a corporate colony. It was in due time included within the larger and much stronger Bay Colony just to the north of it.

The Massachusetts Bay Colony was the most characteristic and powerful corporate colony in America. Its original members actually brought their charter with them from England. The charter had intended only economic self-sufficiency; it had not anticipated self-government. But from the outset the Bay Colony seems to have thought of itself as being, in some very real sense of the word, an independent political society. Although it lost its original charter in 1684, it never lost its original character.

Unlike the Pilgrims at Plymouth the Puritans of Boston were Anglicans, not Independent dissenters. When they sailed away, they parted from England with genuine nostalgia. Their words betray their feeling:

We will not say as the separatists were wont to say at their leaving England, Farewell, Babylon ! Farewell, Rome ! but we will say, 'Farewell, dear England, Farewell the Church of God in England, and all the Christian friends there !' We do not go to New England as Separatists from the Church of England, though we cannot but separate from the corruptions in it; but we go to practise the positive part of church reformation, and propagate the gospel in America.

Once they were settled down, however, these men of Boston and Salem, and the rising towns round about, did not fail to take advantage of the want of proprietors at home to whom they were responsible, or of the possible political corollaries of their charter. Whether they originally intended to do so or not may be an open question. The plain fact is that they soon took the conduct of their affairs into their own hands. They were from the first potentially seditious. Distances were great, voyages slow, communication delayed. Governmental orders could be ignored when received, since longer rather than shorter times intervened before any disobedience could be reported back to England and punitive measures sent out. The Bay colonists trusted the pre-occupation of England with other affairs to allow them the irregular liberties which from the first they seem to have enjoyed. Sir Edmund Andros, who was sent over in 1686 as the first royal governor, was most unpopular, and after the news reached Boston of the advent of William of Orange, he was deposed and imprisoned. A second charter, granted the colony in 1691, in restoring many of the liberties granted in the first charter, did much more to restore the rather truculent self-reliance of the colonists themselves.

The subsequent New England settlements of Connecticut, New Haven and Narragansett Bay (Rhode Island) were all organized upon the Massachusetts pattern as chartered colonies. The resultant situation, therefore, was that of a group of chartered colonies to the north, and of proprietary provinces in what were called the middle and the southern colonies, from New York to Georgia.

The early religious life of America was accommodated to, indeed predetermined by, these two different types of settlement. It is true that with the end of the seventeenth century the increasing provision for royal colonies wiped out the distinction between chartered colonies and proprietary provinces, but in the meantime the stage had been set for the history which was to come, as well as for that already enacted. The chartered colonies, being in a position to manage their own affairs, were able to decree the type of religion, and thus of church, which should prevail. Massachusetts Bay, which had originally been Puritan-Anglican in its English origins, soon became a community of Congregational (Independent) Churches. Why the theoretical obligation to the Church of England should have worn thin so soon, and finally have given way altogether, is something of a riddle. The Bay people had not intended to become Independents as the Plymouth people were. But at that distance from England it was almost impossible to get anything like efficient ecclesiastical guidance for their affairs, and of itself their isolation did much to encourage the recognition of the Congregational polity as the pattern for the ordering of church life in the Bay. The principle and polity were soon accepted, and the Congregational Churches became the legal establishment in Massachusetts. The precedent set in that colony communicated itself in due time to the rest of New England, Rhode Island of Roger Williams' time being the only exception.

The New England theocracy was modelled on Calvin's plan for Geneva. Church and state were to be its two instruments, but of the two the church was perhaps the more powerful. Suffrage presupposed church membership. The demand of the unregenerate that they be given some share in the conduct of the affairs of state eventually led the New England churches to a compromise known as 'The Half-Way Covenant', by which decent citizens, who were not aware of having been fully regenerated, were given a nominal church membership which enabled them to vote. This bit of ethical bimetallism was one of the most ill-advised steps taken by the Puritans of New England, and was outmoded only when the qualifications for suffrage were no longer defined in terms of church membership. Meanwhile, over all the earlier years, the ministers were persons of inordinate political power. 'It was his father,' says a biographer of Cotton Mather, 'of course with other ministers almost as wise and powerful as he, who actually guided the state. Right here in his father's study the government of the colony was discussed and settled.'

The reign of the New England Puritan ministers was stern and intolerant. We cannot pretend for a moment that it was otherwise. Once they had vindicated their own religious liberties, they failed to accord to others the toleration which they had sought and failed to get in England. Having become a church, they harried the sects. Truculent individual non-conformists were driven out; chief among them a famous and mildly psychopathic lady named Anne Hutchinson, and that much too independent-minded gentleman, Roger Williams. These exiles became the founders of Rhode Island. Baptists in general suffered disabilities, if not expulsion. There was no place for Roman Catholics. In particular the Quakers received the sternest treatment, and it is no comfort to any son of those forbears to remember that four Quakers were duly hanged on Boston Common. Those hangings are, however, the only public executions for religious reasons of which our colonial history has record. The Toleration Act (1689), which was gradually extended to the colonies, while it dis-franchized Catholics and non-Trinitarians, ended outright persecution.

Episcopalians were kept at arm's length in Massachusetts for over fifty years. It was only in 1688, two years after a royal governor had been assigned to the colony, that the first Episcopal Church appeared in New England, King's Chapel in Boston. That church, after many vicissitudes, was duly reorganized at the close of the Revolution on the Congregational polity and in turn became a Unitarian parish over a hundred years ago. During colonial times its rectors cannot have had a happy time of it in the heart of the Puritan stronghold. One rector, writing back to England to ask for a helper, dwells upon his lonely lot, but assures his fellow churchmen at home that he is in the meantime 'main-taining a stout and offensive attitude towards all!' In short, a Congregational establishment, and a consequent distaste for all non-Congregational sectarians, was the order of the day in early Massachusetts. Others than Puritan Congregationalists were either driven out or put under varying disabilities.

It is not a pleasant story to re-read, and to this day the memory of it is accountable for many of the anti-Puritan sentiments of a later time. One can only say in defence of Massachusetts Bay that its rulers were, in their own terms, running true to many elder European forms, and more particularly that their venture was for years precarious, since they laboured under the necessity of having to consolidate the frail group in the terms of a single stable society. Such was the situation in these chartered colonies. They were in the main self-sufficient societies, responsible to themselves, and they handled their affairs accordingly. The present-day fact is that the oldest churches in New England are still Congregational—or Unitarian, following the schism within the Congregational body in the early 1800s. Their white meeting houses in towns and villages—as well as their First Churches in the cities—are like the elms around the village greens; they have been longest rooted in the scene.

In the proprietary provinces it was quite otherwise. The proprietors felt themselves entitled to due development of their estates and proper returns on their investment. The proprietary colonies tended to recognize the Episcopal Church as the established form of religion in their areas, but they were not in a position to make theocratic claims for that church. Salaries of parsons were collected and paid from taxes. After the middle of the seventeenth century, with the end of the Commonwealth and the Restoration, the flood tide of emigration from England had begun to slacken. Meanwhile the proprietors still needed settlers, whatever their religious beliefs. Therefore, they welcomed all comers, and even went out of their way to solicit colonists from persecuted sectarians on the Continent. Hence the influx of German pietists, who came in great numbers to Pennsylvania, of a smaller number of French Huguenots, and of occasional adventurous Scandinavians. Furthermore, the Scotch-Irish from Ulster, suffering from legislation which was wrecking the woollen trade, began to come in great numbers at the end of the seventeenth century. Some of them landing in Massachusetts were shunted on into the hinterlands of what are now Maine, New Hampshire and Vermont. They were not felt to be theologically out of bounds, but their form of church government did not accord with that of the colony centred in Boston, and they were encouraged to stake out their own claims to the west and north. The majority of the Scotch-Irish went, however, to Pennsylvania and colonies to the south, where they settled in the 'Piedmont', the rising ground between the coastal plain and the Appalachian Mountains. They formed the spearhead of the eventual westward movement across the Appalachians.

The province of Maryland had an interesting origin, and, as a state, has had in consequence a distinctive history. It is no accident that one of the first Catholic cardinals in America was James Gibbons of Baltimore, elevated to the Sacred Purple in 1886. The original proprietor of Maryland was Sir George Calvert, created Baron Baltimore by James I in 1629. He made a voyage to survey the prospective site of his settlement for which a royal charter had been promised. He died before the document had been signed and the proprietorship passed to his son, Cecil Calvert. The second Lord Baltimore was a more rigorous man of business than his father had been; nevertheless Maryland became, when settled in 1634, an asylum for Roman Catholics. Cecil Calvert was able to send out Catholic laymen to take up the lands, and Jesuits to minister to their spiritual wants. On the other hand, as immigration from England to the colonies slowed up after the Restoration, he was under the necessity of recruiting colonists freely from non-Catholic sources. The only other colony, up until Revolutionary times, in which Catholics enjoyed anything like toleration, was Pennsylvania. Even in Rhode Island, which boasted its defence of religious liberties, they suffered disabilities. Not even Pennsylvania, with all its tolerance, gave to Catholics the early importance which was theirs in Maryland, simply because of the original Catholic proprietorship in the latter province.

The total picture in most of these proprietary provinces and palatinates—Pennsylvania, New Jersey and Delaware being the exceptions—is that of a single religious body enjoying establishment, or its financial equivalent in payment of the clergy of the original or dominant church. This was, in the main, the Anglican Church. But in all these provinces the presence of dissenters and sectarians had to be conceded for business reasons. Back home it was not possible to allow sentiment to interfere with the just claims of invested capital. Thus in 1691 certain Virginians were seeking in England a charter for the College of William and Mary. It was represented to Edward Seymour, then Lord of the Treasury, that it was necessary to have in Virginia, as Massachusetts had at Harvard, a seminary for the training of ministers, since Virginians as well as New Englanders had souls to be saved. 'Souls!' said Seymour, 'Damn your souls; make tobacco.' This was certainly an overstatement of the case for the investor, yet it suggests the pressure which was brought to bear upon debtors over here. A less truculent, but none the less explicit, notice was served on the Council of Virginia in 1750 by the Lords of Trade in London at a time when the Establishment in Virginia was opposing the recognition of Presbyterians in the colony: 'A free exercise of religion...is essential to the enriching and improving a Trading Nation, it should ever be held sacred in his Majesties Colonies. We must therefore recommend it to your care, that nothing be done which can in the least affect that great point.' There is no mistaking, in words such as these, the motive for toleration in the colonies which had been proprietary in their origin. This note of salutary warning was one which was often sounded from home. It usually carried across the sea and was heeded, though sometimes reluctantly, on this side. We have here one of the reasons why the Anglican Church, even in the colonies where it was nominally established, never achieved anything like an ecclesiastical monopoly, and often failed to command even a majority.

The middle and southern colonies were therefore peopled, as the northern colonies at first were not, by groups very diverse in their religious origins and professions. The Scotch-Irish Presbyterians were avowedly anti-British because of the oppression they had suffered in Ulster, and were, in all places where the Episcopal Church was actually or nominally established, stout dissenters. The Baptists were numerous throughout the south and made much trouble for local establishments. They had no major ancient grudge against England, but by their polity they represented Protestantism in its most extreme, individualistic form, and were early imbued with the idea of the rights of man. They were particularly aggressive in Virginia, and as the Revolution drew on, they joined hands with Anglican rebels in defence of the general principle of liberty. The latter group, it is true, was interested mainly in political liberty, the former primarily in religious liberty. For the moment the sacred cause of freedom threw them into each other's arms, but they had no basic affinities and drifted apart as soon as the cause was won.

As for the Methodists, who with the Baptists were eventually to constitute the two largest Protestant bodies in America, they

came too late on the scene to have had any part in the disciplines
and ardours of the earlier colonial period. They arrived only with
the mid-eighteenth century. George Whitefield had taken an
active part in the Great Awakening of the mid-eighteenth century
and so effective was his preaching that even his pronunciation of
'that blessed word Mesopotamia' was said to have been enough
to throw the faithful into transports of religious ecstasy. John
Wesley did come out to America as chaplain to General Oglethorpe, the founder of Georgia, and small groups of his followers
emigrated thereafter. Wesley himself had no inclination to stay
and soon went back to England. He was from the first a staunch
Tory and a supporter of the policies of George III and his
ministers. He thought that certain of the English measures taken
toward the colonies were on the harsh side, yet throughout the
Revolution he remained loyal, and in so far as he had any influence on Wesleyans in America, he advised them to be neutral.
His influence was such on his followers, and their numbers so
negligible, that they did not figure prominently in Revolutionary
affairs.

Meanwhile settlements such as that in Pennsylvania had been
peopled not only by Quakers, but by continental sectarians,
German pietists for the most part, who, in various ways, shared
the Quaker distrust of the kingdoms of this world and therefore
refrained from full participation in the political, and more
especially the military, duties of citizenship. They were—and
many of them remain to this day—pacifist and quietist. Their
unwillingness to bear arms in Indian wars, involving thus a
willingness to tolerate massacres on the western fringe of Pennsylvania, and later their reluctance to join the Revolutionary
armies, created something of a problem for local patriots. Meanwhile they had settled and brought under cultivation what is said
to be the richest single agricultural area in all the world—the
ample acres a hundred miles west of Philadelphia. Their little
communities were economically a signal success; they were quiet
and for all the common purposes of daily life law-abiding. Their
homely other-worldliness was and is a rebuke to politicians, even
though in a crisis they may seem to fail the statesman.

To one of these Mennonite communities in Pennsylvania there

went, during the first World War, a banker from Philadelphia charged with the duty of trying to sell as many government Liberty Bonds as possible to this rich and prudent people. The elders of the church gathered in the living room of a farmhouse to hear the visitor; dressed in their plain garb, shovel hats, homespun grey—long-bearded, seated in a semicircle. The salesman appealed first, with all his skill, to the sound commercial instincts of his hearers. Finding that this appeal failed of a response, he then turned to what he supposed would be the more powerful moral motive. This was to be the war to end all wars. If for that reason only, in paradoxical defence of their pacifism, they should subscribe to the bond issue. They heard him out, and then there was a long and awkward silence. Finally the senior elder gave voice to the sense of the meeting and dismissed their visitor with a single devastating pronouncement, 'There will be more wars yet.' Whether their verdict was prompted by worldly wisdom or by other-worldly concern is beside the mark: such was their verdict.

During all this period even those religious bodies which still acknowledged the duty of reverence and obedience to a mother church in Europe suffered grievous handicap for the want of properly authorized ecclesiastical superiors, especially bishops, in residence here. Prior to the Revolution America never had a bishop of any kind. Among loyal churchmen on both sides there was much agitation in favour of the appointment of colonial bishops. Both the SPCK and the SPG, which were organized about the year 1700, addressed most of their early efforts to the spread of Anglicanism among English settlers in these parts. The latter of these societies sent over more than three hundred mission clergy. Edmund Gibson, Bishop of London, 1723–48, who enjoyed legal jurisdiction over the colonial church, offered £1000 toward the support of a colonial bishop. Beyond the need for decent control of the churches there was the greater need of provision for ordination of the clergy. As it was, candidates for ordination had to go to England to be ordained. Those voyages were costly in lives as well as money. There is a long list of young men who died of smallpox on the journey.

The situation was, however, complicated. Non-Anglicans did

not welcome the prospect of colonial bishops. The most prominent Congregational ministers in Boston fulminated against the whole project. Business interests in what had been the proprietary provinces feared that the advent of bishops would discourage immigration of others than Anglicans. Furthermore, some of the southern clergy were themselves opposed to the introduction of a local episcopate, seeing in it 'just another agency of British tyranny'. At home the rise to power of the English Whigs acted as a brake upon too zealous agitation. Horace Walpole, writing to the Archbishop of Canterbury in 1750, suggests the wisdom of going slowly in the matter. Altogether, though the proposal was much before the common mind for a half century in both England and the colonies, nothing came of it, and Anglican colonists went bishopless through the whole pre-Revolutionary period of our history.

It is a matter of common knowledge that, even after the Revolution, when an American episcopate became a necessity, the first candidate for such office, Samuel Seabury of Connecticut, was automatically denied English consecration because he would not take the British oath of allegiance and had to get himself consecrated in Scotland. One of the results of that act is the presence in the Prayer Book of the Episcopal Church in the United States of certain distinctive items in the Scottish liturgy, in particular the citation of the 'Word and the Holy Spirit' in the prayer of Invocation in the Communion service. Whether the fortunes of Anglicanism in America might have been different, had the church at home sent out bishops in colonial times, is one of those fascinating and futile questions which, to no purpose, we so often ask of the past.

The Roman Catholic Church proceeded in the same way. Its practising members in America, even up to the time of the Revolution, were not many; perhaps some twenty-five thousand in all, of which the great majority were still in Maryland. But no Catholic bishop came to these parts, properly accredited and assigned for duty here. When in due time, as with the Episcopal Church, our Roman Church needed and plainly was entitled to local bishops, Rome was still reluctant to make the concession, and John Carroll, who was to become the first Roman

Catholic bishop in America, had to serve an equivocal interim term as Prefect-Apostolic without a see.

This failure of episcopally ordered bodies in Europe to assign bishops to the American colonies was also probably prompted in part by a dread of delegating authority which, at that distance, might be improperly, if not wantonly, exercised. Colonists were known to be too independent as it was. It was on the whole wiser not to seem to lend spiritual sanctions to their native truculence. Therefore there grew up even in the more centralized and authoritarian types of the colonial church the habit of relying upon their own resources and of finding sufficient sanction for their acts in their own necessities and convictions.

The bodies which were organized upon something like the Presbyterian polity often acknowledged a nominal obligation to a presbytery or classis in Europe. They seem to have kept in some sort of loyal touch with their communions at home. Jurisdiction, however, became more and more local. Among the Independents, the Congregational polity had never required reference to any central or higher authority, since the single individual church was its own master. This polity accounted not only for the New England churches, it was also in force among other groups, like the Baptists and Quakers. The question of reference and deference to a parent body in England or on the Continent simply could not arise. As for the Puritan Churches of New England, their pulpits became with the passage of time little more than centres of sedition. The sermons of the pre-Revolutionary period in the New England meeting houses resounded with the defence of liberty. The favourite texts were, 'Where the spirit of the Lord is, there is liberty', and 'Ye shall know the truth, and the truth shall make you free'. From the standpoint of present-day America such sermons were bold and prophetic preambles to the Declaration of Independence. From the standpoint of any Englishman they must read as the grossest impropriety and rankest treason. The parsonage of the Reverend Jonas Clark in Lexington was a rendezvous for patriot leaders. On the night of 18 April 1775, John Hancock and Samuel Adams were in hiding there. When Paul Revere arrived to say that the British were coming, his guests asked parson Clark what his people would do—would they fight? He answered, 'I have trained them for this very hour'.[1]

A recent commentator on the period has said that there is probably no group of men in history, living in a particular area at a given time, who have spoken so forcibly on the subject of liberty, as the Congregational ministers of New England from 1750 to 1785. It is only fair to say that their sermons prompted in more than one quarter the reflection of a certain Tory official, William Gordon, who said of his minister, 'I most heartily wish, for the peace of America, that he and many others of his profession would confine themselves to gospel truths', a pious sentiment shared by many a conservative parishioner even in these later days!

As far as the American Revolution is concerned, it is well to realize that, when it came, it was not in any sense of the word something new. Luther's nailing of his *Theses* on the church door at Wittenberg was quite as truly the end of a period and a process, as a beginning. It was the moment when ideas which had been in solution and suspense for at least two hundred years were at last visibly precipitated in history. So with our Revolution. It gave us our independence and thus became for us the dawning of a new day. But the sound of the historic 'shot heard round the world' at Concord bridge really marked a *fait accompli*. When the fighting was over and freedom was won, a loyalist Chief Justice could only say, 'I trace the late revolt...to a remoter cause than that to which it is ordinarily ascribed. The truth is the country had outgrown its government and wanted the true remedy for more than a half century before the rupture appeared.' John Adams added that the Revolution was effected before the war commenced, since it was already in the minds and hearts of the people.

For the various complex and by no means consistent reasons thus enumerated, the scene was already set in America for the

---

[1] The march from Boston was merely a routine minor expedition in search of hidden arms—very much the sort of thing carried out by the Black and Tans in their raids in Ireland during 'the troubles' some twenty years ago. The troops cannot have anticipated the reception they got, or have foreseen at that moment the beginnings of revolution.

separation of church artd state and the subsequent rank growth of denominationalism, which ever since have conditioned and characterized our national religious life.

I cannot resist adding here a little incident which illustrates with perfect clarity the initial difficulties which we often have in understanding each other, in England and America.

In this Boston and Cambridge area it is our custom to take the frequent English visitor for an afternoon motor trip out to the town of Concord. The distance is pleasantly geared to two hours of leisure. There are at least no more unlovely 'hot-dog' stands along the roadside than on any other main artery out of the metropolitan area. Concord itself is still the uncommercialized and quiet village that it was a century ago. There are the homes of Emerson, Thoreau, Hawthorne, and Alcott. There is Walden Pond, still unspoiled, now a state park. There is also, and this is always slightly embarrassing, the 'rude bridge that arched the flood' where the real fighting began, the 'battlefield', with its statue of the Minute Man standing on the far side and looking across the stream, ready for the oncoming British foe.

On one such occasion I had the pleasure of taking on this little tour a gentle and utterly gracious canon of one of the English cathedrals. He was a passionate sightseer and antiquarian. The road to Concord is lined with tablets commemorating sporadic resistance offered the British troops along their line of march. In substance they all read as follows, 'Behind this stone wall Farmer Jones, with his six stalwart sons, and four gallant neighbours, resisted the advance of the invaders, and here ten of the enemy fell.'

My guest copied each inscription with meticulous care into a little note book, and when he had noted down the last, he said, 'What a beautiful and generous thing it is of you to put up these memorials to our fallen English soldiers!'

CHAPTER III. *THE SEPARATION OF CHURCH AND STATE—ITS CAUSES*

Thomas Jefferson's tomb carried as an epitaph an inscription which he had written: 'Here was buried Thomas Jefferson, author of the Declaration of Independence, of the Statute of Virginia for Religious Freedom, and father of the University of Virginia.'

The statute in question was passed by the Virginia Legislature in 1786. At the time Jefferson was in France. The letter of the Act is, perhaps, the work of the Legislature, but the spirit of it, and its substance, derived from prior drafts which Jefferson had already made. His epitaph is unequivocal, and the fact that he eventually included the text of the Act as an appendix to his *Notes on Virginia*—first edition, 1784—would seem to confirm his general claim to its authorship.

Since this Act is said to be 'the first law ever passed by a popular Assembly giving perfect freedom of conscience', it deserves citation at some length.

Well aware that Almighty God hath created the mind free; that all attempts to influence it by temporal punishments or burdens, or by civil incapacitations, tend only to beget habits of hypocrisy and meanness, and are a departure from the plan of the Holy Author of our religion, who being Lord of both body and mind, yet chose not to propagate it by coercions on either, as was in his Almighty power to do; that the impious presumption of legislators and rulers, civil as well as ecclesiastical, who, being themselves but fallible and uninspired men have assumed dominion over the faith of others,... hath established and maintained false religions over the greatest part of the world and through all time; that to compel a man to furnish contributions of money for the propagation of opinions which he disbelieves is sinful and tyrannical;... that our civil rights have no dependence on our religious opinions, more than our opinions in physics or geometry; that therefore the proscribing of a citizen as unworthy the public confidence by laying upon him an incapacity of being called to offices of trust and emolument unless he profess or renounce this or that religious opinion, is depriving him injuriously of those privileges and advantages to which in common with his fellow citizens he has a natural right; that it tends also to corrupt the principles of that very religion it is meant to encourage;...and, finally, that truth is great and will prevail if left to herself, that she is the proper and sufficient antagonist to error....

Be it therefore enacted by the General Assembly, That no man shall be compelled to frequent or support any religious worship, place or ministry whatsoever, nor shall he be enforced, restrained, molested, or burthened in his body or goods, nor shall otherwise suffer on account of his religious opinions or belief; but that all men shall be free to profess, and by argument to maintain, their opinions in matters of religion and that the same shall in no wise diminish, enlarge, or affect their civil capacities.

The precedent set by Virginia was followed by the makers of the Federal Constitution. The VIth Article of the Constitution provides that, 'No religious test shall ever be required as a qualification to any office or public trust under the United States.' Two years after the Constitution had been adopted Madison proposed ten amendments, known as the Federal Bill of Rights, which were in turn accepted and appended to the original document. The first of these amendments says, 'Congress shall make no law respecting an establishment of religion, or pro-hibiting the free exercise thereof.' From these two pronounce-ments the formal separation of church and state in America has followed.

The Constitution provides for national procedure by the United States in their entirety. It does not concern itself with domestic state practices. As a matter of historic fact, local church establishments lingered on in certain instances for some years after the adoption of the Constitution. Thus, Connecticut con-tinued support of its Congregational Churches, by means of taxes applied to clergy stipends, until 1818; New Hampshire made similar appropriations until 1819. The established churches of the colonies passed finally from the scene in Massachusetts in the year 1833, when Orthodox Trinitarian Congregationalists demurred to paying further taxes for the support of such of the original Congregational Churches, with their ministers, as had become Unitarian. Separation of church and state in America was a federal fact from 1789 to 91, and became the fact in every single constituent state of the Union, a little over forty years later. It is inconceivable that the issue should ever be reopened in this country.

Since the precedent set by America has been followed in a number of the modern democracies, and by certain members of the British Commonwealth of Nations, the problems involved deserve due consideration. The formal separation in America of these two historic institutions has, it is true, solved certain difficult administrative problems in our society. But it has not solved the age-old problem of the interrelation of religion and citizenship. All that America has done is to restate a problem which may be theoretically insoluble, and which persists in thrusting itself upon us constantly in spite of such tentative and expedient solutions as we may devise.

In these last years the riddle of church and state has taken on fresh urgency in the western world. The Oxford Conference on Life and Work, 1937, made the subject its central theme. Has America achieved anything important by her separation of church and state? Has she anything to contribute on the matter to the still imperfect wisdom of Christendom? What has been the effect of the separation upon the moral and spiritual life of a people? Few questions which Americans are asking themselves about their religion, or which may properly be asked of them, are more pertinent or harder to answer. To understand what is implied by such questions, it is necessary to consider briefly their antecedents and their occasion.

Our American situation, which we now accept as a matter of course, represents a radical departure from what had been the usage of Christendom for nearly fifteen hundred years prior to the framing of our Constitution.

During the first three centuries of its life Christianity was a more or less illicit religion, constantly under suspicion and always liable to persecution. In the year 313 Constantine, reversing the policy of his predecessors, published the Edict of Milan, often known as the Edict of Toleration. Just how far Constantine thought of himself as a Christian is an open question. Whether the church was not to be thereafter more effectually killed by kindness than by previous persecution is a still further question. Church historians are not agreed as to the measure of service or disservice done our religion by Constantine's famous Edict and its consequences. In tacitly giving the Christian Church the power to rule, the emperor entirely altered her relation to society and her part in the making of history. One cannot read many of the details in the subsequent record of the dominant and reigning church of the next millennium without finding sober warrant for Dean Inge's remark, made over thirty years ago in a series of lectures on *The Church and the Age*, which incidentally won him his reputation for gloominess, 'Like certain ministers of state, the Church has always done well in opposition, and badly in office.'

For twelve hundred years after the promulgation of the Edict of Toleration the church was in office in the Western world. The pattern of life, in which the two arms, the sacred and the secular, united to support and administer the affairs of society as a whole, is a matter of familiar record. For the sake of having some point of departure, a recent description of this classical conception of the Christian society will serve as well as any other:

We begin with the concept of a Christian society, in which spiritual and temporal authorities, both divinely commissioned, were to cooperate in realizing here on earth the City of God. It was primarily the business of civil rulers to maintain public order and promote the welfare of their subjects in this present world; in this temporal sphere it was the duty of every Christian to yield willing obedience.... On the other hand, the church, acting through its priesthood, its bishops, and its visible head in Peter's successor, the Bishop of Rome, was concerned with the spiritual and eternal welfare of man. In this higher sphere the church was entitled to the unquestioning allegiance of all Christians from the humblest serf to the most exalted temporal rulers—magistrates, princes, kings, and the emperor himself. Clergy and laity agreed on this general principle of the two spheres. The good citizen and the good Christian must, in the words of the Gospel text, 'Render unto Caesar the things which are Caesar's; and unto God the things which are God's'.[1]

It is a matter of common knowledge, as Professor Greene goes on to point out, that agreement as to the precise application of the principle was not always easy to reach. Much of the history of the period is that of the rival efforts of emperors on the one hand and popes on the other hand, to gain the ascendancy. Nevertheless, the principle was clearly defined and agreed upon in theory.

The advent of nationalism and Protestantism in the sixteenth century brought to an end the life of the single undivided and nominally Christian society of the prior centuries. Thereafter there were to be many states and many churches. Yet, in so far as Protestantism and nationalism took over much of the apparatus of Catholicism and of the Catholic world of pre-Reformation times, it kept the classic church-state pattern for society, the difference being that the pattern was reproduced in many instances rather than stated in a single instance, and in miniature rather than in the large. The Reformers could not avoid the problem, nor could the new princes rising to power. So long as there is a political society in existence, and so long as religion within that society is institutionally organized, some working solution must be found for the problem of the interrelation of church and state. In general one may safely say that over most of Europe the solution proposed at the Peace of Augsburg, 1555, was to obtain for many years thereafter—*cujus regio, ejus religio*—the religion of any given state shall be that of its ruling prince, or by inference, of the majority of its people.

Thus, throughout Europe there sprang up those local Protestant partnerships between church and state, many of which are still operative to-day. In the Scandinavian countries, perhaps more than in any others at this late date, citizenship and churchmanship are two aspects of a single life. Save for negligible sectarian minorities, Swedes and Norwegians are Lutherans as a matter of course. As for England, this idea of the single society

[1] *Religion and the State*, by Evarts B. Greene, pp. 4, 5. New York University Press, New York, 1941.

with its two aspects or functions was one which Richard Hooker took for granted, 'There is not any member of the Church of England but the same man is also a member of the Commonwealth; nor any member of the Commonwealth, which is not also of the Church of England.' The church and the commonwealth make 'personally one society'.

This theory of an established church for each of the nations of Europe might have gone on serving Christendom well in accordance with the elder pattern, even under changed conditions, had its local establishment remained the only Christian society within a given nation. But there was from the first a promise, if not a principle, of proliferation in the Reformation, which seems to have made it hard for Protestantism to be content with any single given point of ecclesiastical arrival. In particular the major Protestant Churches, which crystallized early, were apparently regarded by their more ardent members as spiritual compromises and moral half-way houses. Hence there began to appear all over Europe movements which proposed, often in terms which were as imprudent as they were impatient, to 'finish the work of the Reformation'. These movements took shape as heresies and schisms. From the middle of the sixteenth century we meet them in Germany under the blanket name of Anabaptism: by the end of the century there were at least forty such different groups on the continent, each with its distinctive form of faith and practice. This situation gave rise to what Troeltsch calls the familiar 'church-sect' pattern of religious life in Europe since the sixteenth century.

During the latter part of the sixteenth century and over much of the seventeenth century the lot of the sects in Europe was an unhappy one. They were minority movements, enjoying no protection under the law. They were penalized for their faith in countless ways; they were driven about, often imprisoned and martyred. Holland was one of their places of refuge. From Holland or through Holland, as in the case of the Pilgrim Fathers, many of them came to the New World.

It is true that during colonial times the idea, and, to a greater or less degree, the actual fact of an establishment came as a matter of course to America. The establishment in Puritan New England was a formidable reality, conceding nothing in the way of pre-eminences and powers to the Established Church at home. The non-theocratic type of life in the proprietary provinces made the Episcopal establishments open to the presence and therefore the active opposition of the sects. Each of the middle and southern colonies had its own local church-sect situation to deal with, the sects in question having been determined by the cosmopolitan type of colonization sought by the proprietors. The Episcopal Establishment had to reckon with the nonconformity of more than one sect, usually with that of a number of sects making common cause against it. On this basis it was often outnumbered, and politically was fighting a rearguard action.

Why was it, then, when the colonies had perpetuated here, each in the terms of its own life and earliest citizenry, the tradition of an established church, that this idea, and with it the fact itself, vanished off the scene when the national independence was won?

Surely, the first and most obvious answer to the question is this—it would have been impossible for the colonies to have agreed upon any single church as that which should become a national church. New England had been as aggressive in fighting the Revolution as it had previously been active in forwarding it. The only church which New England would have accepted as a national church would have been that of the Congregational order. She would never have accepted the Episcopal establish-ments which had been in nominal force from New York southward.[1]

Apart from New England the one other colony most to the front in the making of Revolution and in the subsequent framing of a Constitution was Virginia. Many Virginians would un-doubtedly have welcomed a nationally established Episcopal Church. They were not, however, in a position to press any such proposal. They knew that New England would never conform,

[1] In 1775 there were formally established churches in three of the New England colonies; these were Congregational. The Anglican Church was established in four counties of New York and in five of the southern colonies. It should be added, however, that these Anglican establish-ments were technically imperfect, since they had neither bishops nor ecclesiastical courts.

and were reconciled to that fact. Moreover they were themselves despoiled of many of their stronger religious leaders. Indeed, it is an open question how strong those leaders had been. There are many references to the Virginian clergy of pre-Revolutionary years which seem to suggest that an appreciable number of them had become, if not sporting parsons, at least easy-going churchmen of the Woodford type. In any case, by the time the Revolution was over, three-quarters of the Episcopal clergy in Virginia had gone back to England, and the church was left shorn of its leadership.

One would have supposed, given the strong Church of England tradition in Virginia and the relatively close connection of its churches with the mother country, that the laity of the colony would not have been so seditious. Much Virginian life at that time was, in a necessarily restricted form, that of the modest country estate in England. To this day every visitor to Mount Vernon, a few miles down the river from the city of Washington, is expected to say how like the English countryside the place was—and still is—and that George Washington was, *au fond*, a late eighteenth-century English country squire. There is no small measure of truth in these reassuring platitudes.

However, the strong Tory or Loyalist element in the colonies was as a whole made up of merchants, traders, and large landowners. It was for the most part the moneyed people who deplored the Revolution and tried to stave it off. Virginia had no sizable cities, and therefore no considerable commercial class. As for its landed proprietors, not a few had drifted into debt to backers in England. The old and ever renewed struggle between the planter-debtor and his creditor inclined many harassed Virginians to welcome revolution as an easy way of dodging their obligations. And as for the Anglican Church in Virginia, the fact that it had been able to live for over a hundred and fifty years without a single bishop in residence had satisfied it that, if need be, it could carry on its own life independent of England. Local vestries had run the church, and their procedure was to all intents and purposes congregational in its methods. Furthermore, with the success of the Revolution, the Episcopal Church was under the shadow of the defeat suffered by the mother country.

Episcopalians in Virginia were not in a position to suggest that their church should be an establishment for the emerging nation.

The two oldest churches in the colonies, therefore, the Congregational in New England and the Episcopal in Virginia, which might conceivably have pressed in theory for an American establishment, cancelled each other out. Neither would have agreed to accord the other national recognition, and neither was strong enough to override the other before a Congress and in the making of a Constitution.

If for political and military reasons the Congregational Churches of New England were left, when the Revolution ended, in a stronger and more strategic position, they were by no means as strong as they may appear to have been. Massachusetts had lost her original charter in 1688, and though she was granted a new charter in 1691, this second charter required religious toleration for all except Roman Catholics and non-Trinitarians. The excesses of the earlier theocracy became impossible thereafter. With the coming of the eighteenth century liberal ideas began to invade the Puritan stronghold of the Calvinistic theology. This movement, which was to become explicit Unitarianism at the beginning of the nineteenth century, was implicit in much of the preaching and writing being done by pre-Revolutionary ministers. The laymen of Massachusetts who went to the second Continental Congress and the Constitutional Convention, first to declare American Independence and then to fashion the Constitution, were of the liberal rather than the conservative party, theologically. They would have had no interest in trying to foist the passing theocracy of an earlier time upon the country as a whole. If the Episcopal Church in Virginia was weakened by the exodus of its loyal clergy, the Puritan Church in New England was weakened by theological controversies within its own borders. Neither was in as strong a position in the 1780s as it had been in earlier times.

As for other religious bodies in the country: none of them aspired to become establishments, and most of them repudiated the very idea of an establishment. In this respect they were frankly sects; they asked, not to be accommodated to the order of this present world, but merely to be quit of the hostile attitudes and acts of that order as addressed to themselves. All they wanted was to be let alone and allowed to go their own way.

The Quakers, who had been numerous and influential in colonial times, centred in Pennsylvania, had withdrawn from open participation in the politics of that province by about the middle of the eighteenth century, acting under an impression that their political activities up to that time had injured their integrity as a spiritual society. What was true of them was true of all the scattered pietist groups in the middle and southern colonies. They had no aspirations to sit on worldly thrones beside temporal rulers. They were separatists by a conviction which had been matured out of bitter experience in the Old World.

The Baptists were undoubtedly the most aggressive and also the most effective single religious body in the colonies, so far as the demand for religious liberty was concerned. Roger Williams in Rhode Island had conditioned the thinking of Baptists on these problems and had long before prepared their minds for the separation of church and state. He lived only some forty miles from Boston; but between Providence and Boston a great gulf was fixed, theologically and ecclesiastically. Williams believed that the sources of the state should be sought and found in the secular rather than in the spiritual order. The right of magistrates is natural, human, civil, not religious. The officer of the state gains nothing and loses nothing by being a Christian, or by not being. Likewise, the Christian merchant, physician, lawyer, pilot, father, master are not better equipped for fulfilling their social function than are the members of any other religion. There can be no such thing as a Christian business, or a Christian profession of law or medicine. These vocations stand in their own right. No state may claim superiority over any other state by virtue of being, or professing to be, Christian. The state is not irreligious; it is simply non-religious. As for the church, Williams said it was like a college of physicians, a company of East India merchants, or any other society in London, which may convene themselves and dissolve themselves at pleasure. Roger Williams's ideas in these matters were and still are overstatements and over simplifications of the problem. Indeed, he followed the logic of his own thinking so far that he outgrew the visible organized church, even of his own independent kind, and finally parted company with all institutional religion. Yet his overstatements were so true to Baptist convictions that one can readily see how this strongest single sect in the colonies, advocating religious liberty for all, was in entire good conscience prohibited by its own faith from any slightest interest in a union of church and state.

Given a situation as complex as that which we have briefly described, it is difficult to see how the makers of the American Constitution could have done otherwise than they actually did in providing for the separation of church and state. The men who framed the Constitution were all laymen; no priest, clergyman, minister, or rabbi had any part in it. James Madison voiced what must have been the common sense opinion of the meeting when he said, 'In a free government the security for religious rights consists in a multiplicity of sects.' One can only add that, if multiplication of sects beyond the numbers already on the ground in the 1780s is a further guarantee of religious rights, such rights are even more secure to-day than they were a hundred and fifty years ago !

Meanwhile it is difficult not to read out of the records of the time the layman's familiar impatience with theological controversy, and his readiness to invoke a plague on all their houses. For these laymen who cut the tangled knot were the rather emancipated, if not sophisticated, type of person who was much to the front, the world over, in the latter half of the eighteenth century. For the want of any more accurate term it is the custom of our historians to describe them as 'Deists'. The term presupposes belief in a divine creator to whom reverence is due, but disallows many, if not most, of the orthodox beliefs of the Christian Church. In particular the God of the Deists was, so far as the course of man's affairs was concerned, a non-interventionist. He left his servants largely to their own devices. They were upright, conscientious, moral men. There was among them no cult of atheism or connivance in lowered moral standards. They built no altars to the goddess of reason in their capitols, but they were not theological zealots, since the virtue of tolerance which they praised and practised forbade excesses of religious zeal. Washington was a formally devout Episcopalian, but it is said that there is no record of his ever having taken the Sacrament. Thomas Jefferson belonged to no Christian body, though he attended church regularly and thought highly of the ethical teachings of Jesus. Benjamin Franklin said that religion is a private affair which right-thinking men do not care much to discuss. John Adams of Massachusetts belonged to the liberal wing of New England Congregationalism, and had parted company with his Calvinist forbears. There seems to have been abroad, among such men, a weariness with the sophistications of theology and an unwillingness to invite further ecclesiastical rivalries. In the attempt to understand them one is reminded of Professor Whitehead's remark about the Wisdom literature of Israel, that it is religion, but 'religion at a very low temperature'.

More than one of our historians admits, therefore, that our federal government took form at a time when men of affairs were determined to avoid the earlier excesses of religious zeal, and were honestly persuaded of the merits of toleration. If so, their frame of mind was clearly reflected in their pronouncements. The absence in their documents of any references to the Bible is most marked. The name of God does not appear in the Constitution. More than one pious group has attempted over subsequent years to get the name written into the text, but to no effect. It may well be an overstatement to say, as one writer says, that 'the new republic was born in as secular a spirit as the later French republic', but there is a measure of truth in the words. A more guarded statement is, perhaps, nearer the fact:

At no period of our history, probably, were organized religion and social idealism so divided as at the time of the formation of the Federal Government.

The whole atmosphere of the entire literature is secular. When one remembers that the Puritan principle, so far as it was Calvinistic, recognized the Jewish theocracy as a model for all time for all governments, the fact that the Old Testament is never alluded to as an authority by the principal authors of the Constitution should give some pulpit rhetoric pause.... The republic's ablest group of statesmen, in defending the proposed constitution in appeals to the widest public, and using skilfully every argument that would make the new document palatable to the greatest number of people, saw fit to ignore the whole subject of religion. It is not that it is attacked, or made little of, but the fact that it is entirely ignored, that marks the disappearance of the Puritan theocratic idea.... The purely negative character of this attitude appears on the face of the instrument.[1]

The liberal Deism of the Constitution makers, with its honest concern for religious liberties, was primarily English in its origin. The writings and utterances of the time, whether political or theological, constantly cite John Locke and acknowledge their indebtedness to principles he had pronounced. The French Encyclopaedists were not wholly unknown, but prior to the Revolution our colonists were far more closely in touch with liberal thinkers in England than with those in France. English books, rather than French, were the literary stock in trade.

With the 1790s there was, it is true, a brief theatrical outburst of popular enthusiasm for France. Civic feasts were held in celebration of the success of the French Revolution; many a house showed the liberty cap; many a hat carried the cockade. Formal titles, such as Sir and Mr, Dr and Rev., were discarded as survivals from an effete English culture. They were replaced by the 'social and soul-warming term Citizen'. The Citizen's wife was greeted as Citess, though there was some doubt as to the accuracy of this designation and certain purists preferred Civess.

For fifteen or twenty years following the Revolution the country was patently at a moral and religious low water. This state of affairs was in part merely a matter of normal post-war

[1] *The Religious Background of American Culture*, by Thomas Cuming Hall, pp. 184–6. Little, Brown, and Company, Boston, 1930.

Our American ten-cent piece, the smallest silver coin in circulation, is a suggestive symbol. It carries on its face the fasces in which the thirteen original colonies are gathered in the federal bundle. This device is, perhaps, rather infelicitous at the present moment. The reverse side of the coin shows a woman's head, with a winged headdress topped by what seems to be the French liberty cap. The single word LIBERTY encircles this head. At the lower left, in a text so small that only the sharp-eyed can read it without a magnifying glass, is the pious statement, IN GOD WE TRUST. The idea of God is wholly subordinate and subservient to that of Liberty. The design does not go back to the end of the eighteenth century, but it represents faithfully the mentality of that time. The men who fought the Revolution and wrote the Constitution cared primarily for the ideal of liberty. Religion was significant, not as a major independent concern, but as a fortification of the whole conception of freedom and a means of furthering that end.

reaction. Even while the Revolution was in process, Thomas Jefferson had been preparing for friends in France his *Notes on Virginia*, in which he said, 'The spirit of the times will alter. Our rulers will become corrupt, our people careless. From the conclusion of this war we shall be going downhill.' These were sober words from our most distinguished apologist for the inherent excellence of human nature and the virtues of the average man, but they were amply fulfilled at the time as, alas, they were to be fulfilled again in 1865 and 1918.

The decline in public morality was matched by a brief popular cult of rationalism, as against all orthodoxies. Allusions to Greek and Latin authors tended to supersede the old conventional citations from the Bible. Classical place-names—Rome and Athens, Syracuse and Utica—were sown over the countryside without the slightest concern for their relevance to the scene. Deistical societies were founded in the larger cities, addressed by lecturers who were prepared to prove that the Deluge was physically impossible, that the dimensions of the ark precluded its carrying its alleged cargo, and that such stories have an adverse effect on the Moral Temperament of Man. A journal known as the *Temple of Reason* was launched, but was from the first embarrassed by subscribers who did not even 'pay the Postage of their Letters, when they order the Paper', let alone paying for the paper itself. Proposals were afoot for building a Temple of Nature in New York City, to be used 'for the worship of One God Supreme and Benevolent Creator of the world; and for other purposes of a literary kind'. Persons of talent who wished to celebrate the moral and civilized character of mankind were invited to join an Ancient Society of Druids.

What is more to the point, the colleges of the country were passing through a period of extreme religious indifference. Channing, who was to become the great spokesman for New England Unitarianism, said that Harvard was never in a worse state than when he entered it in 1794, that the French Revolution had diseased the imagination of students and encouraged a general scepticism. Dartmouth reported its students as unruly, lawless, and without the fear of God. At Princeton there were only three or four students who made any profession of piety.

The College of William and Mary was said to be a hotbed of infidelity. Timothy Dwight, the president of Yale, complained of the profaneness, drunkenness, gambling and lewdness of his charges, as well as their contemptuous indifference to every moral and religious subject. These comments have a familiar post-war ring, but for the last decade of the eighteenth century the cult of irreligion was undoubtedly accentuated by an adulation of republican France. The cultural prestige of France was, however, soon ended by the self-defeating course of affairs in that country, and by a general reassertion of the traditional concern of Americans for religion. The forces of moral decency, if not of formal faith, rallied to the defence of the cause, and by 1810 the country was beginning to be once more on an even keel.[1]

It is impossible, however, to resist the conclusion that in its date the framing of the Constitution of the United States coincided with the late eighteenth-century cult of rationalism, and that the prevalence of enlightened deistic ideas among educated classes was in part responsible for the studied silences of the document as to the existence of God, and its unwillingness to commit itself, even in the most general terms, to any Christian ideas. One can only say that, given the prior history of colonial times and the subsequent record, the framers of the Constitution must be credited with religious understatement, rather than with over-statement. There had been and there was to be more religion in American life than the Constitution would seem to suggest. But it is probably true that the deliberate silences of the document upon the whole matter, and its understatements, were the price which had then to be paid for a vindication of the principles of toleration and liberty in matters religious. Indeed the word toleration was already in process of being outmoded, since tolerance implies the existence of some authoritative body which exercises that virtue. The refusal of the federal government to assume and to exercise any religious authority whatsoever precluded all opportunity for toleration on its part, and cleared the ground for religious liberty in the broadest conceivable terms of that ideal.

[1] On this whole period, cf. *Republican Religion* (The American Revolution and the Cult of Reason), by G. Adolph Koch. Henry Holt and Company, New York, 1938.

CHAPTER IV. *THE SEPARATION OF CHURCH AND STATE—ITS CONSEQUENCES*

The separation of church and state had deprived American churches of subsidies from government. This loss has not been, however, the most serious consequence of the formal divorce. It is in the field of education that we have suffered most. State-supported schools, colleges and universities are prohibited from giving anything like formal religious instruction to the young. Your situation in England has been difficult and perhaps equivocal since the days of Dr Clifford and the time of the Campbell-Bannerman government. You are apparently now trying to reintroduce some sort of religious instruction into rate-supported schools. If you succeed, you will have done something which there is no slightest prospect of our being able to do. Religion, save for occasional minimal Bible reading, is academically and legally out of bounds in schools supported from the public funds. We are not easy or happy over our present lot. One of our most incisive American educators has recently reviewed and reappraised our situation.

Three hundred years ago Anglo-Saxon teaching was done chiefly by the church. In early days English and American education was, in the main, created and sustained, inspired and controlled by religious groups. But, to-day, in the greater part of the Protestant world, at least, education is secular. It is the state which is replacing the church.

From church to state! In three centuries we Protestants have transferred from one of these institutions to the other the task of shaping the minds and characters of our youth. Do we realize what we have done? This is revolution. It is the most fundamental aspect of the social transformation which has brought us from the mediaeval into the modern world. I doubt if any other change is as significant as the substitution of *political* for *religious* teaching. We have changed our procedure for determining what kind of beings human beings shall be.

In an earlier Europe it was generally recognized that the

churches were the guardians of our 'way of life'. They had convictions about the nature of the world and of man. And from this it followed that they knew how men should live. They had beliefs and values which could be used for the concrete guidance and control of human behaviour. That was their social function.

If then political governments are taking the place of the churches we must ask what are the beliefs and values which those governments express and represent. Does New York City believe anything? Has it any convictions out of which a scheme of teaching may be made? Here is the most terrifying question with which present-day education is faced. We are no longer certain what a nation or state or county or town or village believes, if indeed it believes anything.[1]

Nevertheless the legal separation of church and state in America should not be misconstrued. The country has never been committed to irreligion. Washington is quoted as having said that America could not be formally called a Christian country, but the letter of the law did not prevent him from providing his army with chaplains. For many years now American presidents have issued stated or occasional proclamations, calling for the observance of special days of prayer and thanksgiving on which acknowledgment is to be duly made of the blessings which God has vouchsafed the land, and divine guidance is to be invoked for the future. These pronouncements are couched in general terms which cannot invite the criticism of any religious body and should, in theory, command the consent of all: Protestant, Catholic and Jew alike. The specific term 'Christian' seldom or never appears in such documents. Again, the two houses of the United States Congress, like the state legislatures, have their chaplains, chosen impartially from the major religious communions, and their sessions are formally opened by prayer.

The most important governmental recognition of religion made in America is the exemption of church property from taxation—at least so much of it as is used for purposes of worship and religious education. This is, of course, a matter of the local rates. The easement thus given to churches is a tacit vote of con-

[1] *Education Between Two Worlds*, by Alexander Meiklejohn, pp. 3–6, abridged. Harper and Brothers, New York, 1942.

fidence in their contribution to the life of a people. If we add to the tax-free property of churches the similarly exempt properties owned by private schools and colleges, hospitals and the like, many American city governments find themselves in straitened circumstances. It is said, for example, that in the City of Cambridge—where Harvard is housed, where we have the Massachusetts Institute of Technology and countless other smaller institutions, where churches, hospitals and parochial schools abound—47 per cent of the real property is tax-exempt. Municipal bills must be paid by the remaining 53 per cent of the property. From time to time state legislatures threaten to come to the aid of the hard-pressed cities by allowing the assessment and taxation of church property. Thus far, however, such projects remain stillborn. At this point the inflexibility and the influence of the Catholic Church are perhaps the main bulwark of the existing status in our larger cities. Meanwhile, it seems to be agreed that the traditional exemption of churches from taxation is warranted by the fact; communities need churches, and should encourage rather than discourage them.

The principle of religious liberty has made room within the United States, as with you, for the conscientious objector to war, whose refusal to bear arms rests upon religious convictions. In a country as diverse in its European origins as is ours, the privileges granted the conscientious objector are liable to abuse by persons of enemy sympathies, and the problem of exemption from military service is a far more complicated one than it is in Britain. Furthermore, popular passions are with us always hasty and often cruel. Emotionally we are an intemperate people; we have not yet achieved the mature British jealousy for the rights of minorities. At this point we are politically well in arrears of your people. From time to time, therefore, our public officials seem to bow to the gales of hysterical patriotism. Nevertheless, in the present emergency the federal government has refused to be stampeded and has attempted to deal as fairly as possible with those whose religious convictions, if universalized, might lay the country open to invasion and conquest by the enemy. One can only say that at the moment the rights of the religious conscience are receiving fuller recognition and more generous treatment than at any time in our past history. The example of England in the present war has set us a happy precedent, and the wanton disregard of religious scruples in the Axis countries has prompted a wholesome reaction here.

For the most part detailed jurisdiction in religious affairs is a matter for the states rather than the federal government. All our states concur in the formal separation of church and state. It is true that in many quarters, if not in most, now one church and now another enjoys whatever prestige is given by its longer history. A denomination which has been on the ground for two or three hundred years is accorded tacit deference and respect not given to a later arrival. This is, however, merely a matter of social convention, and in the eyes of the law the latest, smallest, most eccentric religious body is entitled to all the recognition accorded to the older and more conventional communions.

State laws concerning religion are mainly matters of police power. They aim to protect the right of the citizen to worship freely and without let or hindrance, in accordance with his convictions. Sunday laws are still nominally in force in all states, providing that day of rest which human nature apparently requires. These laws assure quiet and protection during the hours of church services. Public worship may not be disturbed by interruption within, or noisy confusion outside the building. Nuisances are not tolerated within certain distances of religious edifices. In all these respects the law is rigorously administered, and any church with a grievance is sure of redress in court.

As for the rest of our Sunday legislation, it varies greatly from state to state and is often more honoured in neglect than in observance. The presence of great numbers of Catholics in the larger cities has inclined America away from the British Sabbath toward continental customs. Professional sports, with paid attendance, are becoming a commonplace. The legitimate theatre is still inclined to give its players their day of rest, but performances on Sunday are multiplying. The movie houses are more often open than closed from Sunday noon on through the evening. It is only fair to say that in view of the indoor life of most of the population, much modernist Protestant opinion favours a relaxation of the older blue laws as to Sabbath observance, though the Lord's Day League continues to fight a rear-guard action against what it regards as a breakdown of morals and a departure from ancestral piety.

State statutes uniformly carry laws against blasphemy. Six states nominally exclude a religious unbeliever from the witness box, and in these states the dying evidence of an atheist is inadmissible in evidence. The laws of seventeen states require of children in school a ritual salute of the flag. These laws have latterly occasioned involved and interesting litigation. The members of Jehovah's Witnesses regard the required salute as an idolatrous act, and forbid their children to conform. The children have been deprived of school privileges and the parents haled into court. Local courts and state supreme courts have disagreed in their decisions, and the whole issue has been sent up to the Supreme Court of the United States, which first declared these requirements legal, but now in a recent decision has declared them illegal and has authorized the return of the non-saluting children to their schools.

In all these matters the religious affiliation of the majority of the voters in any given states does much to influence legislation and the administration of the law. The distinction between Catholic and Protestant is well recognized and in the general area of 'morals', rather than of ethics in the strict sense of that word, the differing usages are reflected on the statute books. In predominantly Catholic states it has been difficult, if not impossible, to write into the laws permissive legislation enabling properly qualified persons to give information as to methods of birth control. With the Roman Church this is a matter of principle, and at this point she is unyielding. If a Protestant minority feels that it has rights in the matter those rights are over-ridden at the polls, and legally there seem to be no means of redress.

Among the Protestant groups of longer standing there is a certain apprehension at the mounting political power of the Catholic Church It is, however, only fair to say that, in states where Protestants are in the majority, the writing of their will into the laws is accepted as a matter of course and creates no occasion for comment. The Catholic minority accept this situation without protest, biding the time when they shall outpopulate and thus outvote their Protestant neighbours. From the impartial premises of the law no criticism can be passed on either group for voting as it does, and the minority in either instance has no constitutional ground for complaint.

All these transactions take place in the terms of individual suffrage. Churches often exercise themselves openly in instructing their members as to public issues, and their pronouncements are occasionally spread on the pages of the papers, though the secular press is disinclined to allow its columns to become an arena for denominational quarrels. No church, however, so far as such issues are concerned, is in a position to try to exercise direct corporate influence upon either state legislatures or the national Congress. It is often rumoured that the larger religious bodies maintain unofficial lobbies in Washington, which attempt to bring pressure to bear upon individual senators or representatives. It is further true that churches are constantly prompting their members to write letters or send telegrams to their representatives urging them to vote rightly on some disputed issue. This is the only legitimate approach which the ranks of religion can make to government. Congressmen who receive these communications must discern in them at any given moment certain verbal identities which suggest an absence of spontaneity and the presence of pressure groups, but it is said that they do not disregard them altogether, tending rather to regard them as political barometers indicating the state of the political weather in their constituencies.

Church bodies meeting in convention often pass resolutions on many, if not most, of the controversial social problems of the time. A sceptical old minister among us has described this type of transaction as 'the most harmless form of amusement which the human mind has ever devised'. The resolutions are usually sent to governmental high places. It is, however, a recognized fact that their content is as a rule well ahead of the social philosophy of a denomination as a whole, and these pronouncements are probably to be interpreted as outposts held by more advanced persons rather than as an expression of the opinion of the majority. They have an educational value for the body as a whole; they probably have little direct effect upon legislation or public policy.

The late Archbishop of Canterbury is quoted as having said recently that it is the office of Lambeth to remind Westminster of its duty to God. So long as the Church of England is by law established, his statement is incontrovertible. There is, however, no parallel person or church in America officially charged with any such task. The assumption of any such right would be regarded by all concerned as a grave impropriety and would defeat itself automatically. The single voter at the polls makes and unmakes national policy in areas where religious ideas and moral standards impinge upon politics and statecraft.

A candid and accurate description of the American situation may be found in a 1944 Lenten Message sent by the Moderator of one of our larger denominations to all its clergy. His words indicate the only way in which the Christian Church in this land may hope to influence affairs of state:

> Now as the hope of victory grows strong, our minds turn to the peace which is to emerge. Speaking with utmost realism, this is not going to be fashioned by ministers of the Christian Church but by those who officially represent the Allied governments. Nor will the Church dictate the peace by its pronouncements. And yet the Church can profoundly affect the peace. There are 50,000,000 professed Christians in the United States. If any large part of them are determined on a settlement based on a Christian spirit, and one which shall include agencies and methods that involve Christian responsibilities, they can have it. Pious wishes do not assure sane and righteous results. Ponderous resolutions shape no treaties. But Christian votes do.
>
> After the first World War we moved blindly on narrow party lines. Our high purposes sank in a political morass. It must not happen again. We must support the leaders who believe what a Christian man ought to believe, and only those who so believe. This will be the sure test of whether our Christian faith can function. We shall act as individuals but our united action can prove the efficient power of Christ's presence in the Council room of the nations. If we ought to disregard old party allegiances to find men who respond to Christian ideals, let us resolutely do so. The Church must be felt on this great issue in the ballot booth.

The American separation of church and state has not solved, therefore, and in the very nature of the case cannot solve, the age-old problem of religion and citizenship. The claims of Caesar and God by no means always coincide, and when they fail to coincide the religious man must make his choice and proceed accordingly.

We may have saved ourselves, it is true, from the public and often unedifying conflicts between church and state which have so often marked the history of the Old World. Being denied the opportunity to play politics in the open, our churches have been delivered from much of the unhappy compromise which inevitably attends that process. But the reference of all such matters back from the religious body to the individual believer denies to our churches as a whole anything like effective corporate influence upon the course of national events.

Meanwhile, the formal separation of church and state breeds on the part of each a certain caution in its approach to the other, lest some too-forward action be construed as the tacit admission of an illegal liaison. Each is cautious about trespassing on the preserves of the other. Two minor incidents may serve to illustrate this prudence.

In preparation of its decennial Census the United States Government gathers statistics as to the various religious bodies in the country. The necessary questionnaires are not sent to denominational headquarters; they are sent to each individual church or synagogue in the country. It is a matter of common knowledge that the latest Census of religious bodies, that of 1936, was conspicuously incomplete. That Census was incomplete for two reasons: first, the appropriation made to the responsible bureau was inadequate; secondly, the ministers of many denominations were in a recalcitrant mood. The 1936 questionnaire carried a statement that it was the duty of the clergy to reply, and that failure to do so would involve either fine or imprisonment, or both. This statement, which was not restricted to requests for information as to churches but was appended to questionnaires in all other fields, seemed to many ministers to be a violation of the principle of separation of church and state, and perhaps to portend a possible insidious invasion of the area of religion by the state. Leaders of some of the more intransigent denominations urged non-cooperation with the census bureau, and the church presses of these bodies advised ministers not to return the facts and figures, lest the camel get his head too far into the tent. Some 40,000 churches failed to respond.

The acknowledged incompleteness of the 1936 Census is mainly due, therefore, to the sensitiveness of the more extreme sectarians in America to disturbing signs of the times in Europe, and a determination to resist from the outset the slightest move on the part of our government, which might be interpreted as a withdrawal of liberties once accorded the churches, and a portent of some form of American Erastianism, if not outright totalitarianism.[1]

Conversely the government is careful not to seem to identify itself with any single denomination. If I may be forgiven a personal reference, I can indicate the nature of this reticence. Last spring I was asked to join with our university choir here at Harvard in recording two brief services for Good Friday and Easter which were to be broadcast, under the auspices of the OWI (Office of War Information), to Europe in general and to England in particular. The original invitation, coming from a minor official, stated that the broadcast should not be 'religious', but might be 'inspirational', and then went on to add that it was doubtful whether the Lord's Prayer could be used in the service.

It is fair to say that a direct appeal to headquarters in Washington mitigated these restrictions and gave us an open field, since the higher-ups did not share the prudential timidity of their local representative. Washington agreed that it would be difficult, if not impossible, for a Christian minister to prepare services and brief addresses for these two historic holy days without some reference to the Christian religion. As to the Lord's Prayer, I was empowered to follow my own preference. Meanwhile, the initial reservation as to the saying of that prayer was prompted by the difference in usage as between the liturgical and the non-liturgical churches in America. The liturgical churches say 'trespasses'; the non-liturgical churches say 'debts'. Each is punctilious in observing its own tradition. Whenever we meet for

[1] Cf. *Yearbook of American Churches*, ed. by Benson Y. Landis, pp. 140–41. Year-Book of American Church Press, Jackson Heights, N.Y., 1941.

interchurch gatherings, there is always a moment of indecision and confusion as the prayer is said. In the ordinary Sunday broadcasts over commercial stations each church abides by its own usage. But when it comes to a government-sponsored broadcast, inferences are sure to be drawn from the form which is followed. If the government authorizes or sanctions 'trespasses', there is the suspicion that officialdom is tacitly pro-Episcopalian; if it approves 'debts', the inference may be that it is pro-Baptist. It should be said, again, that generous and wise heads in Washington will usually come to one's rescue in these dilemmas, but the incident, in its first form, suggests the reluctance of minor public officials to run the risk of seeming to identify the government in any way with one or another of our many denominations.

Is America a Christian country? By history, heredity, culture and dominant practice—Yes. Countless court decisions can be cited to confirm this fact. The religiously indifferent and unchurched half of our population cannot deny the fact and indeed make no concerted attempt to do so. The marked absence among us of anything like organized anti-clericalism is in striking contrast to the situation in many an Old World land. Anti-clericalism is ineffectual, if not impossible, here, because there is no one church which may be made its obvious target. The anti-clerical agitator must fire his philippics from a shotgun rather than a rifle, and his shot scatters so widely that much of it fails to find a mark. In the main he can merely complain of what he regards as the bourgeois complacency and conservatism of middle-class Protestantism. He cannot single out any one religious body as being more culpable than another. It is useless for him to rant from his soap-box in the park against the 'Old-Two-Seed-in-the-Spirit-Predestinarians'.

If any single instance of the cultural acquiescence of America as a whole in traditional religious observances might be cited, it would be the fact that practically all our wedding ceremonies are conducted by ministers of religion in a church, in the home of the bride, or in a parsonage. Civil marriage by a justice of the peace or any other officer of the law satisfies all the legal requirements, but only the most emancipated persons, with a definite antipathy to religion, turn in that direction. Civil marriages are much less common with us than with you.

Furthermore, visiting or refugee scholars from Europe have often made puzzled comment on the fact that most of our formal academic assemblies are opened with prayer and concluded with a benediction. It is so at the time of the high school graduation exercises in any village or town. It was so when Harvard observed a special convocation to confer an honorary degree upon Mr Churchill, and to hear his vigorous address. Even in the tax-supported state universities baccalaureate sermons are often preached to graduating classes at special Sunday services. Such public recognition of religion is accepted as traditional and wholly proper.

As to the achieved fact—we are still very imperfectly Christian. No one suggests for a moment that Times Square in New York at midnight is a patent 'earnest' of the Kingdom of Heaven. After the last war the chaplains and YMCA workers who had been serving with our armed forces published a joint report in which they declared that America is at best only a needy mission field; that knowledge of the Christian religion, its beliefs and its moral ideals, is in pathetic default among our men. This all but universal ignorance of religious truth they regarded as the plainest finding drawn from their experience with a cross-section of total American manhood. It indicated to them a widespread breakdown of adequate religious instruction on the part of the churches with which many of the men were nominally identified, and boded ill for the religious future of the country. Their opportunity for appraising the situation was unusual; their conclusions sobering.

One of the most marked cultural differences between our two countries is your English preference for understatement and our American habit of overstatement. Lest these pages fall too easily into the local vice of overstatement, our right to call ourselves a Christian country may be defended in a few measured words written not long since by a man who knows both countries well, and who, in this instance indeed, may be said to speak for both countries. He is writing about the interrelation of church and state:

We can abstract three positive historical points: that at which Christians are a new minority in a society of positive pagan traditions—a position which cannot recur within any future with which we are concerned; the point at which the whole society can be called Christian, whether in one body or in a prior or subsequent stage of division into sects; and finally the point at which practising Christians must be recognised as a minority in a society which has ceased to be Christian. Have we reached the third point? Different observers will give different reports; but I would remark that...a society has not ceased to be Christian until it has become positively something else. It is my contention that we have to-day a culture which is mainly negative, but which, so far as it is positive, is still Christian.[1]

If those words are true of England, they are equally true of America. We are not as yet self-exiled from that vast, vague, yet historically identifiable and precious reality known as Christendom.

[1] *The Idea of a Christian Society*, by T. S. Eliot, pp. 12, 13. Faber and Faber, London, 1939.

CHAPTER V. *THE DENOMINATIONS*

George Tyrrell once wrote an historic essay on the *Divine Fecundity*. He says that the universe, so far from being aimless and meaningless, teems with aims and meanings. Our own Professor Hocking goes on to say that religion in history manifests a principle of fertility rather than of utility; 'the work of religion is a perpetual parentage'.

The religious history of the United States is that of an ecclesiastical fecundity and fertility carried to a point which must distress any theologically minded Malthus. We are badly over-populated with denominations. The unpalatable fact is so well and so widely known that there is no use our attempting to conceal that which we cannot deny. This is a land, perhaps the only land in Christendom, which can spawn an Aimée McPherson and a Father Divine with wanton disregard of all the sober Christian conventions. In this respect we are made, as Saint Paul says, a *theatron*, a public spectacle, unto the world.[1]

Since there is no evading the total, preposterous, puzzling situation, it had best be conceded at once. The Federal Census for 1936 reports 256 religious denominations in the continental United States. James Madison may sleep quiet in his grave; we have not failed to breed that multiplicity of sects to which he looked for the vindication and preservation of our religious liberties.

The three stout volumes of the Census report, recording and classifying the facts, are fascinating reading. No formally organized church, with recognized officials and a headquarters, is too modest or too bizarre to be excluded from these pages. The census taker is no Pharisee, giving thanks that he is not as the strange peoples whose statistics he gathers and enters on the record. He is as passionless as the man from Mars.

---

[1] Thus, Dr Hensley Henson, in his account of the Lambeth Conference, 1930, says 'The American Bishops are evidently dominated by the crazy sectarianism of their country.' Not that we do not know our Henson!

Thus, on page 651 of vol. I of the 1936 edition, you will find information regarding the 'Church of Daniel's Band', organized and incorporated at Marine City, St Clair County, Mich., in 1893. This denomination has five parishes, two in the cities and three in rural districts. Its pastors' salaries average $332. Its two city churches spent $6 in 1936 for improvements on their 'edifices', while the more zealous rural parishes spent $45. If these facts seem too meagre to deserve serious citation, you may turn to p. 693, which will introduce you to a more considerable communion, 'The Fire Baptized Holiness Church of God in the Americas', with fifty-nine parishes, organized at a general council held at Anderson, South Carolina, in 1898. In 1926 this body took unto itself in union the 'Mount Moriah Fire Baptized Holiness Church of Knoxville, Tenn.' The resultant 'merger' is patently a more substantial body than Daniel's Band: it paid its pastors an average salary of $500, and is amortizing debts on its buildings at the rate of $1867 a year. A still larger body is the 'Church of God and Saints of Christ' which dates from the year 1896, when, as the Census states, 'William S. Crowdy, a Negro employed on the Santa Fé Railroad as cook, claimed to have a vision from God, calling him to lead his people to the true religion and giving him prophetic endowment. He immediately gave up his employment, leaving his home in Guthrie, Okla., and went into Kansas, and organized the Church in November, 1896, at Lawrence, Kans.'

An entry such as this is typical of the accounts given of the origin of many of the smaller American sects. It is as far removed as possible from all 'fine old ecclesiastical arrogance'. The words may prompt an initial mood of mild amusement, but the amusement soon gives way to sober second thoughts. There is something almost biblical in the simple and direct account of the vision vouchsafed to William Crowdy, and his subsequent vocation. Save for the fact that William Crowdy was a cook on a Santa Fé diner, rather than a herdman and gatherer of sycamore fruit, the story of his calling runs true to classical form, as in the prophecy of Amos. If it seems presumptuous to number William Crowdy among the minor prophets, it is well to remember the humble lot of many of the founders of Protestant sects. Some one has commented recently on the prominence of cobblers in this connection. If a cobbler in the seventeenth century, why not a dining-car cook in the nineteenth century? Did not Brother Lawrence irradiate a kitchen with the Presence of God?

If it be said that it is only by their fruits we may test the validity of men's visions and vocations, distinguishing thus between the deluded fanatic and the true prophet, we must reckon with the fact that nearly fifty years after his calling, William Crowdy's work survives in some 200 churches with 35,000 members. The man must have been sincere, and there must be a measure of objective truthfulness in his movement; otherwise it would have lapsed because of insincerity and unreality. The original incident and the resultant denomination are in their own way wholly characteristic of America. John Ruskin has a line about 'this any place where God lets down the ladder'. When William Crowdy found the ladder let down in Guthrie, Oklahoma, he did not question it, because of the unlikely locale. And if, as Francis Thompson goes on to say, the ladder may well be 'pitched betwixt Heaven and Charing Cross', there is no cosmic reason why it may not also be pitched between Heaven and Lawrence, Kansas. In short, the prodigality of our American denominations is itself the sign of a widespread confidence among us in the religious possibilities of the 'everlasting here and now', as against 'the preposterous then and there'. We have a naïve belief in immediacy rather than antiquarianism. If it be admitted, as it must be admitted, that such a faith is peculiarly liable to the perils of self-deception and the excesses of fanaticism, with the sad tragedies and the moral scandals which so often ensue, it still remains true that the principle is valid. Our profuse denominationalism is itself a mark of religious contemporaneity and vitality. We shall have occasion to return later to the whole problem of the small sect in America.

Meanwhile the total body of facts requires interpretation, for it is by no means as grotesque as it may at first seem to be. Knowing the rather blatant American habit of parading large figures —dollars, miles, cars, telephones—I have convenanted with myself to keep figures off these pages as far as possible, relegating them to Appendices. But we come, at this point, to a moment when it is impossible to give any idea of the truth of our religious denominations in want of the actual figures. I shall try to make them as few and brief as possible. Instead of giving precise numbers in each instance, I shall use, for ·the purposes of comparison, round numbers of 100,000 or more.[1]

The present population of the continental United States is approximately 134,000,000. Of these persons 67,300,000 are listed in an 'inclusive church membership'. This figure presupposes on the part of adults formal, voluntary membership in a religious body or identification with some local church. It also includes the children in their families. No one knows better than the conscientious churchman how much dead wood church rolls carry. The number of devout and active church members is always less, perhaps much less, than the total figure in a yearbook. Nevertheless, half of the population of America has a nominal connection with a church. Furthermore, the gains in church membership over recent years have been proportionally greater than the gain in population. Thus, from 1930 to 1942 our population increased 9·1 per cent, while church membership increased 12·9 per cent.

The inclusive church membership is divided, as has already been said, into 256 distinct denominations or sub-denominations. Of the 67,300,000 persons included in the rolls 23,000,000 are Roman Catholics, 4,600,000 are Jewish, and 1,200,000 are Eastern Orthodox. These three denominations account for 28,800,000 of our church members.

This leaves a nominal Protestant Church membership of some 38,500,000. The Roman Catholic Church and the Jewish synagogues, cited above, count each as a single denomination. The total figure for Eastern Orthodoxy includes some eleven different bodies, representing the many countries of their origin in Europe. There remain, therefore, some 243 denominations to compass the Protestant constituency.

[1] Since the U.S. Census of Religious Bodies, taken in 1936, was for reasons indicated in the last chapter incomplete, I am making supplementary use of statistics found in the 1943 edition of the *Yearbook of American Churches*, ed. by Benson Y. Landis, under the auspices of the Federal Council of the Churches of Christ in America.

Our Protestant Churches may be classified, and in the census and yearbook are classified, by families. For example, the Baptist Churches because of their individualistic polity, are peculiarly liable to interior schism—yet each new resultant denomination falls within the total circle drawn by the term 'Baptist'. If we take the major Protestant types they are divided as follows:

Baptist (nineteen denominations)	11,400,000
Methodist (nineteen denominations)	8,400,000
Lutheran (twenty denominations)	4,000,000
Presbyterian (ten denominations)	2,800,000
Protestant Episcopal (a single denomination)	2,100,000
Disciples of Christ (a single denomination)	1,700,000
Congregational Christian (a single denomination)	1,100,000
Total	31,500,000

These seven family types account for by far the greater part of our Protestant Church membership. It should be understood that each of the first four types includes a number of small sects as well as the major denomination bearing the family name. Thus 'The Methodist Church' has a membership of 7,400,000; leaving eighteen smaller bodies, also Methodist in origin or polity, to divide between them the remaining 1,000,000 members.

Limits of space forbid anything like a detailed history of each of the major denominations. But two or three preliminary observations may be made to indicate the difference between the English pattern of church life and that in America. As you will have seen, the Roman Catholic Church is much stronger with us than with you. It is a later rather than an earlier fact, since its considerable growth did not begin until the middle of the last century. Nor is it, as with you, a survival of the pre-Reformation Church in the Anglo-Saxon tradition.

You should note next the very considerable number of Lutherans. To this should be added other forms of Protestantism from the continent. The Dutch Reformed Church is still strong in New York. The Evangelical and Reformed Church, a union of two prior bodies, with some 700,000 members, is a vigorous daughter of two non-Lutheran German bodies. Our predominantly English type of Protestantism is supplemented by German and Scandinavian churches to which you have no considerable parallel.

As for the denominations more familiar to you, they are with us much what they are with you, and save as they have been ·subtly Americanized, they need no description. You will have noted, however, the very large number of Baptist and Methodist Churches. These two constitute well over half our American Protestantism. Their numerical strength is due largely to the fact that, as they marched westward with the Frontier, the polity of the former fitted the manners of the frontiersmen, and the piety of the latter met their moral and spiritual needs. It has been much the academic fashion lately to credit the present pattern of American life to the Frontier, not merely in its occupation of the middle and farther West, but also in its reaction upon the Atlantic seaboard. The case for the Frontier as the final and determining factor in the making of modern America was perhaps overstated by its first academic proponents, but there is in the whole theory far more truth than falsehood.

Practically all of our smaller denominations represent would-be reformations within older and larger bodies, Puritan movements looking to simpler forms of church life, supposedly patterned on the New Testament. For example, the Mennonite bodies, all of which derive from a single pietistic German sect that came to this country in colonial times, are now divided into eighteen churches, each of which is duly listed as a 'denomination'. Thus we have under the Mennonite aegis a church of the Hutterian Brethren with seven congregations, the Kleine Gemeinde with two congregations, and the Stauffer Church with another two. The entire family of Mennonite Churches, divided into these eighteen sects, numbers hardly over 100,000 members. It is in the bodies which inherit the Reformation passion for a church purged of worldliness and purified after the primitive pattern that we find in America these schisms and sub-schisms of the more evangelical types of Protestantism. Here is the truth of most of our excessive denominationalism. Thus, we inherited from you, in due time, our share in the Plymouth Brethren. The original movement as it came to us is now represented by eight

THE DENOMINATIONS

distinct denominations, separated by theological or ecclesiastical subtleties which seem to most of us almost meaningless.

Church history is familiar with movements of this sort originating within the parent institution and leading on to schism. Perhaps the striking and puzzling fact about the American situation is the power which these small sub-sects have to take root in this soil and to survive. More often than otherwise, over the centuries and elsewhere, such movements, if originally schismatic, have been suppressed by persecution, have died out from their own oversimplification of the religious life, or have been reabsorbed into the parent body. There has been little reabsorption here of small sects by the larger, parent churches. One can only conclude that the formal separation of church and state with its correlative vote of confidence in the private conscience has given our small schismatic reforming sects a vitality which they have by no means always enjoyed in other lands.

Meanwhile, the general liberal movement in religious thinking which was much to the front in the late eighteenth and early nineteenth centuries led to the division of two or three of the historic denominations which had carried over from colonial times. Thus in the first decade of the 1800s Unitarianism crystallized as a denomination distinct from the orthodox Congregationalism within which it originated and from which it parted. In 1827-8 a number of Quakers, following the preaching of a certain Elias Hicks, withdrew from the Orthodox Society of Friends to become a Hicksite (Unitarian) Society. In 1837 a liberal movement within Presbyterianism divided that body into Old School and New School. In this instance the issue of slavery was prophetically felt as a contributory factor, since the Old School was predominantly southern in its constituency, while the New School was northern.

When we come to more recent schisms involving large numbers of believers, our history is interesting. After 1840 we had no major religious schism primarily due to theological or ecclesiastical disagreements, to disputed matters of faith and order. Such schisms of this dimension as we have had were occasioned by economic and political differences, though it is true that these differences were given on ethical interpretation. Negro slavery a century ago became the rock on which three of the larger American churches were to split. As cotton became king in the south, and as the line was more sharply drawn between the agricultural south and the industrial north, our churches found themselves torn in two by the economic and political antipathies of the time. Earlier in the century all churches had reprobated slavery, and though many Christians in the southern states continued to deplore it, their identification with the life of the south finally compelled them to condone it. The actual split in the denominations which were divided over the issue was in some instances occasioned by a direct vote on the moral validity of slavery; in other instances—as with the outbreak of the Civil War—the point in dispute was the right of a state to secede from the Union. Even though secession may have been the nominal occasion of division, the underlying fact of slavery was its cause.

The three largest religious bodies in America to be divided by slavery were the Baptist, the Methodist, and the Presbyterian. In the two former instances the schisms came in the 1840s; in the latter instance only after the Civil War had begun, in December, 1861.

In the Baptist body the matter came to a crisis in 1844, when the Georgia Baptist Convention recommended for appointment as a missionary a man who was an acknowledged slave-holder. The southerners intended to make their recommendation a test case. The northern churches refused to accept the nomination, and the southern Baptists then withdrew from the national body, forming their own Board of Domestic Missions. In the following year the southern churches as a whole met to form the Southern Baptist Convention.

Officially the Methodist Church tried during the '30s to prevent the subject of slavery coming to the fore, deploring the excesses of the abolitionists and urging moderation on both sections of the country. By 1840 the more ardent anti-slavery clergy in the north were threatening to withdraw altogether from the church if open discussion of the matter were to be killed in the General Conference by gag rule. Meanwhile a bishop in Georgia had become, by a second marriage, a slave-holder, and the Conference of 1844 was confronted with the fact. Northerners suggested that he either give up his slaves or resign. Southerners said he had not violated any rule of the church. Compromise was no longer possible, and being outvoted by their northern brethren, the southerners proposed a Plan of Separation which led in 1845 to the formation of the Methodist Episcopal Church, South.

Anti-slavery sentiment in the Presbyterian General Assembly (New School) was stronger than in some other bodies. The Assembly of 1846 condemned slavery unequivocally, and that of 1853 ordered a census which should show the number of slave-holders among Presbyterians the country over. Kentucky reported that many of its members held slaves on principle, believing the institution to be right. This pronouncement, repudiated by the body as a whole, led in 1858 to a minor schism which became a major fact in 1861 with the formation of the General Assembly of the Presbyterian Church in the Confederate States of America, now 'The Presbyterian Church in the U.S.' The northern body is known as 'The Presbyterian Church in the U.S.A.', a sophistication, or distinction without a difference, which has nothing to do with theology or polity.

To the credit of the Protestant Episcopal Church it can be said that this body refused to allow the slavery issue to divide it. 'Although there were ardent patriots on both sides among the bishops, yet there was an absence of bitterness which speaks well for their Christianity.' It is true that the southern churches organized themselves during the war as of the Confederate States, but the northern body refused to concede that the southerners had withdrawn. At the General Convention of 1862 the names of southern delegates were called in their absence. With the end of the war southern bishops were welcomed back to their place in the national body, and the church resumed its undivided life. As Professor Sweet says, this exception to what was the course of events in other denominations cannot be easily dismissed on the ground that the Episcopal Church had never been violently partisan on the slavery issue and therefore had no bitterness to overcome. The incident reflects the genius of Anglicanism for tolerating differences of opinion and conviction within the framework of its corporate life.[1]

[1] On this matter of the northern-southern schisms, cf. *The Story of Religion in America*, by William Warren Sweet, pp. 448 and ff. Harper and Brothers, New York, 1939.

This sobering period in American church history is thought-provoking. The fact that we have had no other schisms of the same dimensions can be construed in two quite opposite ways. It may suggest an unashamed secularity in American church life; a Christianity too closely identified with the political and economic life of the people, too much coloured by the clay with which it works, not far enough above the battle to achieve dispassionateness and catholicity. Conversely it may suggest that in many of the divisions and subdivisions of Protestantism over the past four hundred years political and cultural factors have been prominent as a contributory cause of schism, if not the major cause. For better or for worse the whole matter stands out in American church history in its naked clarity. There was no question of creeds or orders at stake; the only question was, ' Is slavery a sin?' The northern churches, in spite of much vacillation during the middle of the century, inclined to that conclusion; the southern churches dissented, affirming that slavery had biblical sanction and was therefore permissible.

Of these denominations the Baptist and the Presbyterian still remain divided, north and south. The Methodist Churches, on the other hand, were formally reunited as a single denomination in 1939. The problems of slavery and secession are now ancient history in the United States. But any one who knows this country well understands how strong the old sentiments of the Confederacy still are in the south, how the memory and the memorials of **its armies** are still treasured, and how ill the cause of the Union was served by northern carpet-baggers during the evil days of 'Reconstruction'. It is said that late in the autumn of 1914 a northerner, who had gone to Virginia, asked a southerner what people down that way thought of the war, and got the instant response, 'There's not a man here who doesn't think that Lee was wrong to surrender!' The Christian religion ought, in theory, to be able to heal these hurts, but proud, loyal, stubborn human nature being what it is, the final reunion of denominations divided by our Civil War still calls for much patience and grace.

What, now, are we in America chargeable for, or what are we to be credited with, in the way of actual denominational innovation? There is one considerable body in the United States, already cited which you in England will not identify and to which you have no precise parallel, although it is known in Canada—the Disciples of Christ. This denomination was founded over a century ago by a certain Reverend Thomas Campbell, a member of the Secessionist branch of Ulster Presbyterians, and was first known as the 'Campbellites'. He settled in western Pennsylvania and began a ministry there. He was censured by his synod for administering the Sacrament to those outside its boundaries. Impatient at the limits of sectarianism, and anxious to serve the needy people of the Frontier society, he withdrew from his own church and launched out in behalf of the essential unity of the Church of Christ, in which, he said, there should be 'no schisms or uncharitable divisions'. As for a creed, he proposed that nothing should be required 'as articles of faith or terms of communion but what is expressly taught and enjoined...in the Word of God'. This note has been one which has been constantly sounded by our denominations. There is nothing novel here, since all churches seek biblical warrant for their faith and orders, and all lay hopeful claim to catholicity. But American Protestantism, in particular, has always been markedly biblical in its emphasis.

Meanwhile the Disciples flourished where many another similar movement has languished. They were organized in 1810 as 'The First Church of the Christian Association of Washington, meeting at Cross Roads and Brook Run, Pennsylvania'. The founding fathers were men of piety and purpose. Their denomination took root in a society where pioneers had lost their connection with churches in the East, and where a simple form of faith and practice fitted the primitive life of the community. Indeed, one of its latest chroniclers attributes its remarkable growth to the fact that it had no awareness of a parent body in the Old World and therefore no sense of sentimental or organizational debt to that world. As was said of Lincoln, so it might be said of the Disciples, 'Nothing is here of Europe'. The movement had something of 'the freshness of the early world'. As vigorous life gave the Church of the Disciples an impulse to expand, it made no attempt to turn back across the mountains to the seaboard, but moved westward with the times, and has now become in the Middle Western States one of the half-dozen strongest Protestant bodies in the country. The Disciples do not represent, however, any radical theological innovation and may fairly be regarded as a modification of a prior Presbyterianism, with the addition of certain practices and recruits from Baptist circles.

Aside from the multitude of small sects, which for the want of any other classification must 'fall in behind', American Christianity has made only two novel additions to the diversity of Protestant denominations: the Church of the Latter Day Saints (Mormons), and the Church of Christ, Scientist (Christian Science). Both these bodies are now assured of permanent life, in so far as history allows permanence to institutions, and both are active missionary groups, spreading their gospel in many lands.

In the common mind Mormonism is still identified with the theory and practice of polygamy. Brigham Young, appealing to a revelation said to have been vouchsafed to his predecessor Joseph Smith, promulgated the doctrine of plural marriage in Utah. His pronouncement occasioned widespread criticism elsewhere and resulted in various acts of Congress forbidding polygamy. In 1890 the church issued a manifesto calling on the saints to refrain from contracting marriages forbidden by the law of the land. Polygamy among the Mormons has been ancient history for fifty years, though some of the polygamous marriages antedating the '90s were allowed to live out their time.[1]

Meanwhile the history of the Latter Day Saints has become one of the more romantic and perhaps characteristic chapters of American life. Joseph Smith, who founded the movement in 1830, professed to have had heavenly visitations commissioning him to restore the Church of Christ. He claimed also 'to have received historical records on golden plates of the ancient inhabitants of this western continent', which he translated as the Book of Mormon. Apparently the modern Mormon is not

[1] Since the above passage was written, the New York papers of 8 March 1944, report that some twenty members of a small schismatic group of Mormon Fundamentalists in Utah have been indicted for the practice of polygamy.

inclined to place too much importance on the naïve legends of the earlier record. From the first the Mormons aroused antagonism and soon migrated from their birthplace in western New York to northern Ohio and thence to southern Illinois. As they moved westward, hostility increased. Joseph Smith, the president of the Church, and Hyrum Smith, the patriarch, were murdered by a mob in Carthage, Illinois. Persecution did in this instance what it always does; it consolidated the group and strengthened its will-to-live. The story of the migration of the major part of the body from the Mississippi valley to Utah is one of the epics of America. The sufferings endured were surpassed only by the courage and steadfastness which brought them in due time to the Salt Lake Valley in Utah. There they settled and there they have survived. This trek of the Mormons across the plains and the mountains and the desert remains one of the most gallant and successful ventures in the whole pioneering movement westward during the '40s. Much of the aura of those times was captured and preserved in Conan Doyle's *Study in Scarlet*.

As for its faith, Mormonism has an eclectic creed. It professes belief in the three persons of the Trinity; in the prospect that men will be punished for their own sins rather than for the sin of Adam; in the possibility of universal salvation through Christ's atoning death; in repentance and baptism by immersion for the remission of sins; in the laying on of hands, and charismatic gifts of tongues, prophecy, visions, healing and the like. The Bible and the Book of Mormon are regarded as the dual word of God, supplemented by later revelation. The church is Adventist in its faith, looking to Christ's return to reign on earth, to a recovery of the lost glories of the first paradise, and a gathering of Israel through the restoration of the Ten Tribes. It is assumed that Salt Lake City will be the site and scene for these happenings, which will mark the end of the present world order.

In practice the Church of the Latter Day Saints might well set an example to many a more loosely organized denomination. Its government is rigid and effective. In particular, its conception of religion is intended to cover the whole of life and not some sequestered area of interest. 'A characteristic feature of this church is the extent to which it enters into, moulds, and influences every department of the life of the people. It aids them when sick or in poverty, looks after their education, provides their amusements, and ministers to their social needs. It is also closely identified with the economic life of the people through its connection, as investor, with numerous industrial and commercial ventures. In the organization and management of establishments the principle of cooperation enters to a greater or less extent. The close association existing among the people, through the unifying influence of the church, has made these cooperative enterprises, in almost every line of economic endeavour, numerous and successful.' These words, together with the foregoing paraphrased account of Mormon theology, come, it is true, from the official statement furnished the Census Bureau by the church itself, but it is only fair to say that disinterested visitors to Utah find the text faithful to the fact.

Around Salt Lake City, as its centre, the Church of the Latter Day Saints has built up, under geographically adverse conditions, a unified and self-reliant society. During the bad period of depression which followed 1929, when millions of Americans were forced on to the federal relief rolls, the Mormon Church refused for years to delegate its responsibility to the government and undertook to care for its own poor and needy. The legend of the golden plates presents an interesting problem to the critical historian. The letter of what is still the faith of the church will seem to many a modernist incredible. Yet the Mormons have a record of heroism, industry, and pious common sense which cannot be deleted from the annals of American religion. The body now has about 1600 churches, the majority of them in rural communities, with a membership of nearly 900,000. Most of these people are in the state of Utah and the abutting state of Idaho. In so far as they have spread, they have moved westward toward the Pacific coast rather than eastward to the world that exiled them a century ago.

A single phase of their practice deserves final mention. It is assumed that every youth, at about the time he comes into his majority shall give a year or so to the church as a foreign missionary. These youths go out, after the pattern of the gospels, by two and two. I have met them in 'digs' around the British Museum.

Perhaps they have called at your door. They go not merely to English-speaking countries and to the continent; they go to the Orient and to islands of the sea. It is a little hard to understand how young and professionally untrained lads, ignorant of the cultures to which they go and innocent of the languages, can hope in their short visits to make many converts to the faith. I once hazarded this perplexity to a high official in Mormon circles. He admitted the grounds for my doubt as to the efficacy of missions so conducted, but wisely added that whatever the missioners might accomplish or fail to accomplish in terms of conversions, their experience confirmed them in their loyalty to their church, so that after their return they were never lost to the church. Many another church might take a leaf out of that book.

The other denomination which may be credited to us as an American contribution to the denominationalism of Christendom is the Church of Christ, Scientist. This story is more familiar to you and needs less elaboration, since the Christian Science movement is well known in England. Indeed, a colleague of mine was once asked in England whether all Americans were Christian Scientists, presumably because that church is the only one of ours which conducts a considerable mission to your island. Mary Baker Eddy founded her church in Boston in 1879. She has become an almost legendary figure, inviting not only the loyalty of her disciples, but the patient inquiry of psychologists and the cynical condemnation of sceptics. She has been variously revered, psychoanalysed, and dismissed from serious consideration as a pathological and highly neurotic female. She is not the first person in the history of religion to have been accorded such diverse appreciation and appraisal, nor will she be the last. Meanwhile her movement has survived, and though its present growth is no longer as rapid as in earlier days, Christian Science keeps well abreast of the gains made by other denominations. Unlike Mormonism the Christian Science Churches are much more frequent in the cities than in the country districts. The proportion of women members, as against men, is larger with Christian Scientists than with most other bodies, the ratio being about three to one. As American denominations go, its churches are relatively wealthy.

The group passed through one stormy period some years ago when the officers of Mother Church were apparently vying with the officers of the Publishing Society for control of the entire denomination. Despite Saint Paul's warning to the members of the church in Corinth against going to law before the unjust, the case was carried to the courts to become one of the historic bits of litigation in the more recent annals of Massachusetts. Neither gained a total victory; to-day the Church and the Publishing Society, which is the major means of spreading the gospel, while working amicably together, have each an independent legal status. The *Christian Science Monitor* must be one of the most widely circulated newspapers in the Western world. One expects to find it in the reading room of any large European hotel. Here in America it sets a high standard for sober, non-sensational journalism.

As for the influence of Christian Science upon American religious life; its example has done much to reawaken in a few church circles an interest in faith healing. The medical profession, while still unable to accept the premises of Christian Science, takes a more tolerant attitude than once it took toward the probable influence of mind on matter, and is perhaps less hostile to the movement than it was fifty years ago. William James, trained first as a physician and a psychologist before he turned philosopher, says, 'The method of averting one's attention from evil, and living simply in the good, is splendid as long as it will work. It will work with many persons; it will work far more generally than most of us are ready to suppose; and within the sphere of its successful operation there is nothing to be said against it as a religious solution.' It is true that James is unable to concede the finality of either the doctrine or the practice, but his words represent what may be called the tolerant lay opinion of the country to-day. When the church reports to the Census that 'the most distinctive feature of Christian Science is its absolute distinction between what is real and what is apparent', the words are reminiscent of a volume which was a *vade mecum* for 'Greats' men in Oxford a generation ago, Bradley's *Appearance and Reality*. Quite apart from all theological sophistications, the strength of the movement and its inherent liabilities are those of any form and all forms of absolute idealism. One sometimes wonders why Christian Scientists do not append to *Science and Health* the twelfth chapter of the seventh book of Saint Augustine's *Confessions*—his answer to his own experience with Manichaean dualism—in which he says, 'All things which are corrupted are thereby deprived of some good. But if they are deprived of all good they must altogether cease to exist.... Evil, then, the origin of which I had been searching out, has no being of its own, for had it a being it would be good.

Two other relatively small denominations deserve special mention, although they are not peculiar to America or indeed especially characteristic of it: the Unitarians and the Society of Friends. The former body has some 300 churches with 60,000 members; the latter (Orthodox and Hicksite together) about 900 meetings with 100,000 members.

English Unitarianism originated as a liberal movement within Presbyterianism; American Unitarianism as a similar movement in orthodox Congregationalism. Neither body, however, regards itself as a recent theological and ecclesiastical fact; both look back to precursors in earlier times—to men such as Servetus and Socinus, to the Arians of the fourth century, if not to the writers of the Synoptic Gospels. American Unitarianism was in process from the middle of the eighteenth century in the persons of forward-looking ministers who were breaking away from the traditional Calvinism of New England. The first parish formally to avow Unitarian beliefs was King's Chapel in Boston, previously Episcopalian, but left to its own devices after the Revolution. The earliest church to take what is now the denominational name was the First Church in Philadelphia, founded in 1796. The election in 1805 of Henry Ware, a theological liberal, to the Hollis Professorship of Divinity at Harvard furthered the cleavage with the orthodox in Massachusetts. The classical statement of Unitarian belief is still held to be an ordination sermon preached by William Ellery Channing at Baltimore in 1819. The American Unitarian Association was organized in 1825.

American Unitarianism originated within the older Congregational Churches of Massachusetts, and was the theological expression of the more advanced thinking of the last half of the eighteenth century. Unitarians are to-day usually labelled and then dismissed by all orthodox churches as persons who deny the divinity of Christ. It is true that from the first they repudiated and still repudiate the doctrine of the Trinity, but there have been few men in Christian history who have given the historical Jesus a more simple and devout loyalty than was accorded him by James Martineau with you and by such men as Channing and Francis Greenwood Peabody with us.

Unitarianism will be grossly misunderstood, however, if it is judged solely, or even primarily, in the terms of its anti-Trinitarianism. It was a revolt against the whole grim doctrine of human nature and the mechanical means for man's salvation which had become the convention in American Calvinism by the .middle of the eighteenth century. Unitarianism, with its more cheerful view of human nature, and its confidence in man's power to help himself spiritually and morally, was the theological parallel to the political perfectionism presupposed by the American Republic. The parsons who preached revolution from 1750 to 1775 were the theological liberals of New England, pre-Unitarians.

According to Congregational polity the majority of the members of a given church, or its 'society', are the owners of the property. When the schism between the Trinitarians and the Unitarians became imminent in Massachusetts, the Unitarians often outnumbered and thus eventually outvoted their orthodox brethren. With the resultant right to determine the faith and practice of a single church, as well as to hold the church building, they virtually forced the orthodox minority out. The seceders from a 'First' church usually organized a 'Second' church. Thus it is that, in many a New England city and village to-day, the old colonial meeting house is that of 'The First Congregational Church (Unitarian)', while the more recent and usually less graceful church across the way is 'The Second Congregational Church (Trinitarian)'. Of the 300 Unitarian Churches in America to-day nearly half are in Massachusetts alone.

In the East, American Unitarianism is still culturally a part of the national heritage from colonial Congregationalism.

Whether it represents the true and direct succession or divergence from past tradition is as yet an unsettled problem. Suffice to say that possession of the name of a 'First' church, and with it the records of the parish and in many instances title to the original building, serves to keep the older Unitarian Churches in the East in conscious connection with the earlier history of American Christianity. In other parts of the country, however, Unitarians have been inclined to proffer themselves and their faith as a more direct transcript of contemporary life. A Unitarian Church in a mid-western city is often recruited from thoroughly disaffected members of conservative bodies and tends to emphasize its break with the past and its professed concern for modern thought and life.

Many of the more advanced Unitarian Churches, particularly in the middle and farther West, have candidly parted company with any theistic belief. They do not feel called upon to deny, but they are unable to affirm; thus, so far as faith in God is concerned, they are agnostic rather than atheistic. The resultant religion is properly and accurately described as 'humanism'. During the past decade a lively controversy has been going on between the older theistic and newer humanistic wings of American Unitarianism. In some quarters it is an open question whether Unitarians care to continue the use of the term 'Christian' as a form of self-designation. In such instances, the word 'Liberal' does duty instead, and not inappropriately. The gospel which such a church preaches is more often than otherwise spoken of as 'liberal religion'.

Unitarianism has never bulked large in numbers, but it has had an influence on American religious thought out of all proportion to its numbers, partly because of the distinguished names it has carried on its rolls—such men as Channing, Emerson, Theodore Parker, Charles Eliot, the distinguished President of Harvard, Francis G. Peabody, William Howard Taft, President of the United States and Chief Justice of the Supreme Court, but in equal part also because it has boldly faced theological issues which other denominations have preferred to shirk and has pioneered in areas of religious thought where the opportunity for theological adventure and experiment is inviting, if not imperative. Much of the substantial achievement of earlier

Unitarianism, in freeing man from the iron grip of Calvinism, has now become the common property of orthodox denominations. To this extent the history of American Unitarianism is that of a vicarious struggle for freedom of thought, the gains of which have been communicated to less liberal communions rather than restricted to the single denomination.

Meanwhile, if you are familiar with the place which English Unitarianism has in the social, economic, and cultural life of such cities as Birmingham and Liverpool, you will have an exact counterpart to the situation in a city like Boston. The London *Times* carried some years ago a letter from a prominent Anglo-Catholic, written at a time when there was grave question as to the propriety of allowing a Unitarian minister to preach in Liverpool Cathedral. The letter conceded the preacher's admirable personal qualities, but with characteristic British understatement, regretted that he could not be numbered among 'the closer friends of Jesus'. You would find the same prudent reservation among orthodox Christians here: nevertheless, as in Liverpool and Birmingham, so in any New England city, many of the more serious and serviceable activities of the community are in the hands of persons who apparently can be numbered only among the more remote friends of Jesus. Unitarianism to-day stands in America at that border line where traditional religion passes over into the newer forms of humanistic thinking with which we are familiar in our universities and in many of the professions. There may be a want of dogmatic certitude; there is much ethical earnestness and a deep sense of social responsibility.

The other relatively small body which deserves mention is the Society of Friends. The great Quaker migration to America began in 1681, when William Penn received a grant of the vast province of Pennsylvania. This was in payment of a debt of £16,000 which the British government owed Penn's father. But the coming of the Pennsylvania company had been preceded by the arrival of many Quaker missionaries in all the colonies. Their zeal was exceeded only by their indomitable courage. They started meetings all along the coast from Massachusetts Bay to the Carolinas. Most of the colonies gave them scant welcome, and many persecuted them. Massachusetts enjoys the sad distinction of having been the most cruel of all. Two Friends were hanged on Boston Common in 1658; a third, Mary Dyer, was reprieved at that time and sent out of the colony, but she bravely returned two years later to meet her death on the gallows; a fourth was hanged in 1661.

Rhode Island, which should have been in theory a city of refuge for all harried souls, gave the Friends scant welcome. There was a limit even to Roger Williams's patience. Williams ran foul of George Fox in consequence of large public meetings which the latter held in Providence and Newport. The controversy yielded a famous tract by Williams, *George Fox Digg'd out of his Burrowes*, and a spirited answer by Fox, *A New England Fire-brand Quenched, Being Something in Answer unto a Lying, Slanderous Book, Entitled George Fox Digged out of his Burrowes, etc.* This unedifying debate was conducted on both sides with scant courtesy and much mutual vilification. To the honour of Maryland be it said that the Catholic proprietor granted Quakers a tolerance denied them in many another colony and province, a gracious act duly returned in the welcome which Pennsylvania subsequently gave Catholic settlers there. Meanwhile Pennsylvania was to become with the end of the seventeenth century what it has continued to be ever since, the centre of Quaker life in America. It should be noted, however, that the voluntary withdrawal of the Society of Friends from active conduct of the political affairs of the province in the middle of the eighteenth century was to mean thereafter an inwardness of corporate life, and in some measure an aloofness from affairs of state. Hence American Quakerism would seem to have had during the latter half of the seventeenth century and the first half of the eighteenth century a prominence in the religious life of the land which, at least until most recent times, it was not to enjoy thereafter.

Quakers are widely scattered in the United States. The largest single group, in classification by states, is that in Indiana (20,000). Ohio follows (8500), North Carolina has about the same number; then comes Iowa, Kansas and California with about 5000 each. Pennsylvania, the original centre of the movement, now numbers some 11,000, the Hicksite group being in the majority (7500 to 3500).

Though the Society has been much before the public in recent years through the work of the Friends' Relief, which has been generously supported by many non-Quakers, the denomination as a whole has been losing in numbers rather than gaining. The loss has been greatest in states like Indiana (10,000 in the last thirty or forty years) where, by processes of convergence and borrowing which involve imitation of the ways of other denominations, the silent meeting has given place to regular services of worship conducted by 'hireling priests'. Apparently, once the worship in Quaker meeting loses its historic differentia, it sacrifices also something of the secret of its appeal and often suffers in comparison with the settled usage of the traditional churches. Conversely the Society is slowly gaining in numbers in the seaboard cities on both coasts, where mature persons, wearied with what seem to them the rhetoric and the compromises of most churches, turn to the Quaker meeting for the sake of its quiet and its unequivocal sincerity. It should be added that the Society has no desire to become merely a city of refuge for persons otherwise disillusioned, nor has it any wish or purposes to become numerically a major denomination. It conceives of itself as leaven in the lump, not the lump itself.

As with you in England, so with us in America, the constancy of Quakers, their fidelity to their historic faith which has been tried and vindicated in many sufferings, is now a cherished fact in the religious life of the country. It is fair to say that many meetings have been divided by the present war and that many Friends are in combat service. The Society has not censured those of its members who have taken up arms, and has jealously preserved its historic confidence in the conscience of the individual. As for those who have remained true to the hereditary principles of pacifism and non-resistance, there is no question as to their status. The community at large may not be able to understand them and for the most part disagrees with them, but it respects them. We have seen in this country—as against the hysteria of the first World War—much less witch-hunting than was previously the fashion.

Quakers have restated their doctrine of non-resistance, so that it can no longer be dismissed as pure quietism or inert passivity.

If they are unable to kill, they do not ask for safety or exemption from suffering. They are willing to take any risks, even that of death itself, in fulfilling their ministries of healing and reconciliation. Their only gravamen at the moment arises from the fact that the gathering of their numbers in camps for conscientious objectors denies them the opportunity to go far afield in ambulance units or as relief workers among half-starved peoples. In the meantime many of them are serving as 'guinea-pigs' in our great hospitals where they are infected with some disease virus and then given experimental inoculations. One group has been vicariously testing the limits of the safe consumption of salt water, in behalf of castaways at sea. In this respect America has not been, in the present emergency, as generous or as wise in dealing with its Quakers as has England. The American Quaker, willing and anxious to go about his mission in remote and dangerous places, has felt frustrated by being kept at home, chopping down trees and clearing national forests. He has no awareness of grave injustice or grievous hardship meted out to him; rather he finds himself thwarted by a calculated kindness, which may or may not be a shrewd policy decreed in high places. The Society has advised its members to report for the draft and take the consequences. This means assignment to one or another of the civilian camps. The only pacifists, Quakers or otherwise, who have received prison sentences are those who failed to report in the first instance.

The country at large looks to the Society of Friends to bring to the post-war years and the tasks of reconstruction, its now wide experience in relief work. Without forfeiting its idealism, the Society has matured, from its history over the last twenty-five years, much sound wisdom and many techniques which we shall need in the near future. An American Friend coming to you by plane from New York to Lisbon, and from Lisbon to England, to consult with his fellows about matters of 'common concern' found himself waiting at the landing-field while your immigration officers looked over his passport and his papers. He overheard one of them say, 'Well, he's a Quaker, and if you can't trust them, whom can you trust?' We join with your officials in that spontaneous vote of confidence in the Society of Friends.

CHAPTER VI. *THE DENOMINATIONS* (*cont.*)

When William James published, a generation ago, his now famous Gifford Lectures on *The Varieties of Religious Experience*—to which we shall have occasion to refer again—they were greeted in many quarters with amusement, if not derision. Just at that time a popular American naturalist had written a book called *Wild Animals I Have Known*. It was suggested that the proper title for James's work should be 'Wild Religions I have Known'. James was always attracted to cranks and geniuses and un-classified waifs, none of whom were impounded with the con-ventional ninety-and-nine, safely walled in by historic creeds and codes. This trait is usually attributed to an ineradicable Scotch-Irish strain in his blood. Nevertheless, he and his work are characteristically American.

The church historian in search of wild religions has in the United States a happy hunting ground. There is no other land in Christendom where the fauna is as diverse and as grotesque. We have already said that of the 256 denominations listed in the Census, a relatively small group accounts for by far the greater number of our church members. The larger members of these family groups make up over 95 per cent of the church member-ship of the nation. As for the rest, some 200 denominations compass only 3 per cent of our church membership, a matter of 2,000,000 out of the 65,000,000 total.

These small sects, often including only two or three parishes and a pathetically meagre handful of members, are therefore a relatively negligible minority. Most of them are as unknown to us as they are to you. They have little or no commerce with other churches. They take no part in interdenominational ventures or ecumenical conferences. How can they, when most of them regard themselves as already being, each in its own manner, the achieved Church Universal? To concede the existence of other churches, to say nothing of their validity, would be in itself an act of heresy.

Yet here in America is a laboratory where the processes which

94

yield sects may be studied with interest, and perhaps with profit. If the student in the field will approach our small sects with sympathy, he may learn something from them. There has been no place, other than Germany in the late sixteenth century during the days of Anabaptism, where the soil has been as congenial for the seeds of sectarianism. The fact may be to our discredit rather than to our credit, yet such is the fact.

These small sects are found in the dingy side streets of the great cities, in lonely pockets in the mountains of Kentucky and Tennessee, in the still semi-isolated areas of agricultural states, at the heart of a group of Negro shacks in the deep south. From time to time some such movement comes out of its hiding into the bright neon lights of a Broadway or an Atlantic City board-walk, to attract the idle and aimless crowd strolling past in its unending quest for 'some new thing'. Southern California is one of the favourite locales for these groups. In the main, how-ever, the small sect is the creation and the solace of those whom the great world has passed by.

The story of Jesus—(says Mark Rutherford)—is the story of the poor and the forgotten. He is not the Saviour of the rich and prosperous, for they want no Saviour. The healthy, active, and well-to-do need Him not, and require nothing more than is given by their own health and prosperity. But every one who has walked in sadness because his destiny has not fitted his aspira-tions; every one who, having no opportunity to lift himself out of his little narrow town or village circle of acquaintances, has thirsted for something beyond what they could give him; every-body who, with nothing but a dull, daily round of mechanical routine before him, would welcome death, if it were martyrdom for a cause; every humblest creature, in the obscurity of great cities or remote hamlets, who silently does his or her duty without recognition—all these turn to Jesus, and find themselves in him.[1]

This has by no means been the whole story of Jesus down the centuries, yet if it were ever to cease to be part of the story, some-thing would have been lost from the record which was true at the first and which has remained true ever since. 'Not many

[1] *Autobiography of Mark Rutherford*, pp. 47–8. T. Fisher Unwin, London.

wise men after the flesh, not many mighty, not many noble, are called.' All of the more sober small sects in America might be accounted for, and thus catalogued and dismissed, in those words from the First Epistle to the Corinthians.

Nor does a more critical and dispassionate account of the facts alter our judgment of them. It is a commonplace with church historians that reform movements within the Christian religion have usually begun near the bottom of the social scale. The Methodism of John Wesley is the classical example of this thesis. We are more indebted to Troeltsch than to any other modern scholar for a study of the initial event and the resultant development.

The really creative, church-forming, religious movements are the work of the lower strata. Here only can one find that union of unimpaired imagination, simplicity in emotional life, unreflective character of thought, spontaneity of energy and vehement force of need, out of which an unconditioned faith in a divine revelation, the naïveté of complete surrender, and the intransigence of certitude can rise.[1]

Troeltsch's analysis has recently been restated with direct reference to our own 'queer religions' in a study of *The Small Sect in America*, which gives local chapter and verse for the general truth. Thus its author says:

These groups originate mainly among the religiously neglected poor, who find the conventional religion of their day unsuited to their social and psychological needs.... Finding themselves ill at ease in the presence of an effete and prosperous bourgeoisie, their emotional nature unsatisfied by a middle-class complacency, their economic problems disregarded by those who have no such problems to meet, and their naïve faith smiled upon by their more cultured fellows, the poor and ignorant revolt and draw apart into groups which are more congenial. They elevate the necessities of their class—frugality, humility, and industry—into moral virtues and regard as sins the practices they are debarred from embracing.... Their standards of conduct are invented from the simple lives they are at all events compelled to lead and

[1] Quoted in *The Social Sources of Denominationalism*, by Richard Niebuhr. Henry Holt, New York, 1929.

which are congenial to their simplicity. They give free rein to
their emotions and attribute the pleasant thrills thereof to a
divine agency. They look for their escape from their hard lot into
a heaven of bliss and comfort which is foreign to their workaday
existence, and usually picture a coming time when the judgment
of society shall be reversed and they shall change places with the
prosperous and comfortable....The sect is born out of a com-
bination of spiritual need and economic forces.[1]

Some of these sects are survivals, in original form, of post-Reformation Anabaptist and Pietist movements in Germany. Thus
the Dunkers ('Baptizers') came to this country in 1728 and
have perpetuated their own original ways for over two hundred
years. They have various subdivisions, which together now
number 200,000 communicants. So also the Mennonites, whom
William Penn welcomed to his province at the end of the seventeenth century. A two hundred-year-old colony of Schwenkfelders still lingers on in Pennsylvania. The list might be extended
at much greater length. As with survivals of spoken Elizabethan
English in the Kentucky mountains, so with these elder forms of
Reformation piety, many a usage has lived on here in America
long after it has passed away in the land of its birth. Harnack
speaks somewhere of 'the sanctifying power of blind custom' in
the life of the church. That power is signally manifest in the
stubborn life of the small religious bodies transplanted in America
from Europe. These sectarians are mainly agricultural. Their
communities are more or less closed against 'the world'. Their
people live an industrious and economically successful life, but
remain for the most part uninfluenced by the environing culture.
Theologically they are arrested groups; socially, self-sufficient
societies.

The minor Lutheran bodies—apart from the large German,
Swedish and Norwegian churches—must also be numbered here:
the Slovak Lutheran Synod, the Danish Lutheran Church, the
Icelandic Synod, the Finnish Suomi Synod. Here also we must
cite and classify the less numerous members of the Eastern
Orthodox communion: the churches of Albania, Bulgaria,

[1] *The Small Sects in America*, by Elmer T. Clark, pp. 18 ff. Cokesbury
Press, Nashville, 1937.

Roumania, Serbia, Syria and the Ukraine. It will be seen, then, that we owe to Europe no small portion of our lesser sects.

European bodies are not, however, as characteristic of us as the sects which have grown up on this soil. Let us take a few local examples. At the close of the Civil War, and as an attempt to combat the lax morality and irreligion of the post-war years, a 'Holiness' movement sprang up, taking at first the form of camp meetings within Methodist circles. As a matter of record, some forty of our smaller sects represent would-be reform movements which began within Methodism, as renewed attempts to recover or to achieve the perfectionism which Methodism originally professed and has never ceased to seek. These occasional and patiently renewed camp meetings finally crystallized in the First Church of the Nazarene, organized at Los Angeles in 1895 by the Rev. Phineas F. Bresee—a name that Mr Sinclair Lewis might have been happy to coin! The body now numbers some 2800 parishes, with 180,000 communicants. The initial aim of the Nazarenes was to advance perfectionism, which is vouchsafed by the direct action of the Holy Ghost. The 'perfect heart' is given in an instantaneous 'second blessing'. Or consider again, for example, the 'Duck River and Kindred Associations of Baptists', now found in the hill country of Tennessee and Alabama. We are not much helped in understanding them to learn that they represent a schism from the Calvinistic Elk River Baptist Association over the question of the universality of the atonement, occupying on this matter 'a middle position'.

The 'camp meeting' has been mentioned. It was a gathering of folk in country districts, often numbering many thousands, for a series of revival meetings held in the open air or in some rough central tabernacle, and lasting many days. Booths and tents or covered wagons, surrounding the meeting place, furnished sufficient lodging. The proceedings were uniformly ecstatic. As late as 1893 one visitor watched such transactions at Cane River in the Chilhowee Mountains. Some of the attendants were granted the 'holy laugh'; others received the 'barks', yelping like dogs at the foot of a tree—this act was called 'treeing the devil'. Still others were given 'holy jerks', paroxysms and convulsions. Ladies of fashion visiting the meeting were not immune to these ecstasies. At an earlier time the famous Peter Cartwright grappled with a victim of the jerks who was trying to pull a bottle of moonshine whiskey from his pocket 'to drink the damned jerks to death'. Of such was the Kingdom of Heaven in many a Frontier community a hundred years ago, or in many a pocket in the hills a half century ago. The camp meeting still survives in a denatured and genteel form at popular seaside or mountain resorts, shorn of its primitive pathology, but keeping still something of its gregarious and holiday character.

Many of our small sects are communistic. One of the most famous was the mid-nineteenth century Oneida Community in New York. This group ran foul of the law, because its doctrines of 'spiritual liberty' and 'spiritual affinity' allowed its members to ignore the irksome bonds of monogamous marriage. The founder himself seems to have been conspicuously successful in adding works to his erotic faith, to say nothing of tippling to excess. He explained that his habits were necessary to free him from the 'law'. Public criticism, backed by police measures, ended this historic venture where all things, women included, were had in common. The community now survives in a secular form, making excellent plated silverware, widely used as wedding presents for dull monogamous marriages by those who cannot afford to buy 'sterling', solid silver.

Others of the communistic sects have gone to an opposite extreme and require absolute continence and celibacy. Thus there still linger on among us little, pathetic, and yet strangely lovely Shaker villages, where what was a vigorous society a century ago now makes its last-ditch stand.[1] Their buildings are bare and their dress plain. The fact that they are unable to perpetuate their own society in a new generation gives them no concern. They are recruited, in so far as may be, by converts from the world who turn away in weariness from common life, or are welcomed in poverty and illness. They are already 'children of the resurrection' for whom this present world order has passed away. Their

[1] The Society of 'Shaking Quakers' was formed in England in 1747. Ann Lee led an exodus to America in 1774. The Shakers in America numbered 1000 in 1800, 6000 in 1850–60, and then declined to 1000 in 1900.

nun-like women may be seen in the foyers of the big summer hotels along the coast of Maine, spreading out for sale exquisite needlework done in the seclusion of their back-country communities during the tedious depths of a long winter.

It would be worth your while, were you ever crossing the American continent, to stop for a day at the Amana Society in Iowa, a communistic sect originally, though now reorganized on another basis. They are neither antinomian nor celibate. They farm the ample acres around their six small villages, and run a woollen mill. They had much searching of heart in the last war as to whether conscience would allow them to sell their blankets for use by soldiers. Their dress is still that of the German peasantry from which they sprang. Perhaps the most moving sight in the community is their burying ground, where they lay their dead away as they die, row after row. The simple markers at the heads of the graves are uniform; there is no attempt to preserve the integrity or the affections of any single home in the presence of the 'universalizing touch of death'. God's neutral acre is a final earthly seal on the commonalty of their life.

Countless of these small sects are found among the Negroes. The organization of such groups and membership in them give to the Negroes concerned a sense of solidarity and importance denied them by the racial discrimination meted out to them by the white world round about. The Negro's love of long words and high-sounding phrases comes out in the names they give their countless denominations. Thus we have 'The Apostolic Overcoming Holy Church of God' with its 'cathedral' in Mobile, Alabama, where an orchestra of horns, tambourines and cymbals brings the old negro spiritual abreast the times in jazz rhythms. While the preacher expounds the gospel fortified by ejaculations from the floor, 'Ain't it so?', 'Amen', 'Yes, Lord', stray members of the congregation moved by the spirit may also be prophesying in unknown tongues, as a sister waltzes up and down the aisles.

Time would fail to tell of them all: 'Christ's Sanctified Holy Church Colored', 'The Church of the Living God and Pillar and Ground of Truth', 'The House of God, the Holy Church of the Living God, the Pillar and Ground of Truth, the House of

Prayer for All People', 'The National David Spiritual Temple of Christ Church Union', 'The Latter House of the Lord, Apostolic Faith', 'Triumph the Church and Kingdom of God in Christ', 'The Pentecostal Fire-Baptized Holiness Church'. They are all here, all on the Census record, all recognized and protected by law.

Small sects get into difficulties only when their practices take them outside the accepted limits of common decency, or when some leader is found guilty of financial sharp practice. Otherwise, so far as the conduct of their affairs is concerned, they enjoy the tolerance and the freedom accorded the oldest and most decorous communion in the country. The Jehovah's Witnesses are constantly running foul of their communities and thus are haled into the courts. They are violently anti-Catholic, and their lay missioners go from door to door carrying portable phonographs and records. No sooner have they gained entrance to some French or Irish home than they wind up the Victrola and put on an anti-Catholic record for the edification of their listeners. This practice does not commend itself to the community as a whole, and often invites police interference as a violation of the rules governing canvassing.

The Witnesses are a litigious body, and appeal every adverse court decision to a higher tribunal. They have reached the United States Supreme Court on three or four occasions within recent years. The latest decision of the Court forbids their ordering their ten- and twelve-year-old children on to the streets to hawk their literature. They are stubbornly pacifist, taking their unequivocal stand upon the letter of the sixth commandment. They have no ordained clergy but, asserting their faith in the priesthood of all believers, they hold that all their members are ministers, and on this ground have asked that the entire body be relieved of liability to military service. The courts have not conceded this contention and many Witnesses are now in prison, or in camps for conscientious objectors where, apparently, they are as intractable and as non-cooperative as they are in the outside world.[1] Their present name is recent. They were formerly

[1] A Quaker friend tells me that, when Quakers in the camps for conscientious objectors gather for silent meeting, a Jehovah's Witness stations himself outside an open window and turns on his omnipresent Victrola.

known as 'Russellites', and later as 'The International Bible Students' Association'. They are spread widely over Europe, as well as America, and to their credit be it said that many of them have been gathered into German concentration camps. If a recent report is to be trusted, a large number of them were martyred for the faith in one of these camps, probably that at Dachau. They are, at the moment, one of the most interesting and problematical religious bodies in America. They have many affinities, culturally, with primitive Christianity in pre-Constantine times. As pacifists they get far more notice than the Quakers or the Mennonites. They do not, however, regard themselves as a church or a denomination and are thoroughgoing anti-clericals. Their intolerant attitude toward all nominal and would-be Christian bodies; the Roman Church in particular, seems to some of us to betray a want of Christian charity.

From time to time some sect is financially victimized by its leader, who allocates to his own use moneys—often the entire capital of a follower—which have been contributed to the cause. How far such a leader is self-deceived, and how far he is a common crook, is by no means easy to say. Religious fanaticism is a heady wine. Browning addressed himself to this problem in the person of Mr Sludge, the Medium. He doubted if his subject could have understood himself—how far he was sincere and how far a fraud —therefore he made no attempt at a moral appraisal of the man. The most notorious incident of this kind in recent American history is that of 'The House of David', founded near Chicago in 1903 by 'King Benjamin' Purnell. He announced that he was the 'seventh messenger' of Revelation x. 7. He was commissioned to foretell the imminent end of the world, and in the meantime to gather the 'Israelites' into a communistic forecourt of heaven. His followers surrendered all their property to him. After twenty years of hope deferred, some of his disillusioned disciples decided to return to the world. They brought suit for recovery of their property and for wages covering the years in which they had worked without pay in the community. Meanwhile unpleasant stories began to get abroad about the luxurious life which King Benjamin was living in 'Shiloh Palace', solaced by the society of not unattractive concubines. The police and the courts wound up the affairs of this dubious sect. King Benjamin was an ethical leftist, and the fate of his movement has had a wholesome effect upon other promoters of like mind, who would equate their religious liberties with moral license.

Mr Clark, in his review of the small sects, has attempted their classification. He lists them as follows: (1) the pessimistic sects which despair of social progress and look for a catastrophic ending of the present world order; (2) the perfectionist sects, which seek to realize the elusive ideal of holiness through freedom from the desires of the flesh; (3) the charismatic sects, which rest their case upon spiritual gifts such as tongues, trances, visions, and 'jerks' in general; (4) the communistic sects, which require the renunciation of all personal property, and occasionally hazard the secret practice of free love; (5) the legalistic sects, which stress observance of rules and distinctive manners, such as the substitution of hooks and eyes for buttons, foot-washing, or an antipathy to musical instruments in church (there are said to be some 400,000 persons in America who have a religious objection to church organs—given some of the organs one does hear, their scruples may be said to have at least an aesthetic, if not a theological, warrant!); (6) the egocentric sects with whom religion is a device for escaping pain and disease, and a means of promoting physical comfort; (7) the esoteric sects, which guard a mystery known only to the initiated. These last are mainly Oriental in origin, with only the remnants of Christian reference: Theosophists, Vedantists, Baha'is. The classification is of necessity arbitrary and at points imperfect, but serves to identify the various motives which prompt the organization of these minor movements and to indicate the human needs they profess to serve.

As for the class as a whole, it has few contacts with the rest of the religious life of the country. Each body tends to affirm its own catholicity and religious finality. The smaller such a church, the more stoutly it insists upon its universal character. Obviously some kind of psychological compensation is at work here. There is among these people a settled scepticism as to the possibility of any improvement of this world's affairs in their present terms, with an unshaken confidence in the speedy end of the world and the advent of a new order from on high. Most of these bodies have, therefore, Adventist leanings. Such churches stand quite apart, therefore, from all remedial forms of social service. Their other-worldliness is not genteel; it is vivid and revolutionary.

The Book of the Revelation is the heart of the sectarians' Bible; they are constantly occupied with its prophetic arithmetic, and just as constantly called upon to revise their figures, when the end of the world does not happen on schedule and must be subject to recalculation. Such persons never question their major biblical premises; they merely review in genuine humility their own skill as mathematicians. They concede the human frailty which we all admit at addition and subtraction, multiplication and division, and set doggedly to work to find a corrected date for Armageddon and the millennium. Let it be said, in defence of these people, that contemporary history seems to be on their side rather than on the side of those of us who are the heirs of an old-fashioned, up-grade, omnibus liberalism. Some of the sects hold views of nature even more bizarre than their views of history. That the world is flat is a commonplace with certain of them; others have a theory that we live on the inside of a concave earth's surface. None, of course, accepts any slightest approximation to the doctrine of evolution.

It is difficult to see how many of these beliefs can remain tenable in face of the teaching of the common schools. But it must be remembered that in the 'Bible Belt' States, such as Tennessee, a Fundamentalist majority at the polls can rule a doctrine of evolution out of a curriculum. Some of the sects maintain their own lower schools, and, if they decently impart the minimal requirements of the three R's, they may satisfy a lax local board of education, which does not profess to plumb the mysteries of time and space or to read the riddle of the universe. In all these matters the human mind, backed by the human heart, has a curious ability to live a departmentalized life, making fullest use of all the latest forms of applied science at the same time that it harbours the grossest cosmic superstitions. One must suppose that the slow spread of decent education will finally discredit many of these faiths. Meanwhile the patent failure of modern learning, with its technical skills, to vindicate itself in an achieved

Utopia gives to such movements the world over not only new life, but apparently new warrant.

Furthermore, so long as there remain in our America at the bottom of the economic and industrial scale, or in devastated dust-bowls, men and women forgotten and unhelped by the present world order, there is no known device which can prevent their finding solace in their escapist faiths. Until there are no longer any pitiful poor in our slums or on our thankless farms, we shall have in America these strange cities of spiritual refuge devised by such persons for their own emotional and moral shelter. The small sect in America, while it makes little contribution to the religious culture of the country as a whole, and has no connection with its normal church life, is an adverse comment on the imperfections and injustices of our society. As long as illiteracy and poverty survive among us, just so long will their victims be emotionally dependent upon the powerful artificial stimulus of their strange creeds and ways. I have given, perhaps, undue space to these small sects, at the cost of space which might have been more properly assigned to the larger denominations. But I have done so because these movements are, within their meagre limits, characteristic of us and less familiar to you than are our major bodies, which parallel those already known to you at home.

A word should perhaps be said of the egocentric and esoteric sects, the sixth and seventh in Mr Clark's classification. These movements differ from those just described in that they recruit their following from the more privileged rather than the less privileged classes in the community. Their members are on the sunny side of want and often are well-to-do. They are in general seekers after 'New Thought', an eclectic compound of Greek philosophy, Indian mysticism, Confucian ethics, with a mild admixture of traditional Christian doctrine. The result is a synthetic would-be 'world religion' which sums up the wisdom of the ages. A 'Bible of the Race' is always more or less in process of compilation.

There is in America a recognized type of person who derives great satisfaction from this stratospheric view of things. Such persons are usually imperfectly educated, and their rather lax mental processes allow sweeping generalizations about the riddle of the universe and the mystery that is man. As in the prior instances of the small sects, a process of compensation is plainly at work here, but the compensation is intellectual rather than emotional or moral. The larger vision proffered by such faiths is supposed to represent an advance on the near-sightedness of the humdrum denominations. The aura which surrounds such movements is that of a modern 'gnosticism', a semi-secret and higher truth known only to the initiated. Popular leaders of these cults gather their followers by the hundreds and even the thousands in the cities. The sense of having attained to the higher knowledge gives to these followers intellectual reassurance and undoubtedly much help for personal living. Their only serious vice is that of over-simplification. These cults are in the main personal followings. The type is constant, but its concrete instances are always changing. The group as a whole is unorganized and therefore unmentioned in the Census.

The denominational picture, then, begins to yield some semblance of order out of its initial chaos. For the great majority of our denominations we are indebted to Europe, and this means Europe in its totality, not England alone. All your English churches are here. In addition we have churches of which you know nothing, save by rumour and report. The Slovak Evangelical Lutheran Synod, which can be at the most a name to you, is a living fact with us. Our prodigal denominationalism is the price we have paid for our greedy cosmopolitanism. Should we have been better advised to have restricted our immigration long ago? Should we have remained culturally true to our Anglo-Saxon beginnings? Is the secret of the small sect to be found in the cheap labour imported years ago and never yet elevated to a decent economic level? Should we be saved the wanton fecundity of the Negro sects if only we could solve the Negro problem? Some of these problems are academic in that they are already ancient history; others are contemporary and therefore still valid.

Given the totality of our denominations you will be struck by certain facts which mark us off as religiously unlike yourselves. Some of these facts were briefly mentioned in the previous chapter. The most conspicuous instance is, of course, the primacy of the Roman Catholic Church, so far as the numbers for any single communion are concerned. Its main racial strains are Irish, French Canadian, Italian, Portuguese and Eastern European. You will notice, next, the prominence of the Baptist and Methodist Churches, which are much the largest Protestant groups. The strength of these churches, as has been indicated, is primarily due to a factor upon which American historians lay great emphasis, the determining part which the Frontier played in the making of the nation. Not only did frontiersmen carve out their own destinies after they crossed the Appalachian mountains and began their century-long westward trek which ended only with the Pacific, but the Frontier reacted upon the Atlantic seaboard, compelling its banks and industries and arts to accommodate themselves to ever mounting demands from the West.

At that time the polity of the Baptist Church and the footloose, circuit-riding ministry of the Methodist Church served the needs of a new and mobile society better than they could ever have been served by the older and more immobile churches in the East. Great use was made of lay ministries, and that fact has to this day a survival value. The individualistic polity of the Baptist Church fitted at once any immediate and local occasion. There was no need to wait upon supervision from the East. The free play of religious feeling encouraged by traditional Methodism matched the instinctive demand of frontiersmen for an emotional outlet. The vices of a Frontier—drunkenness, profanity, gambling and immorality—were a challenge to the moral zeal of Methodism, and gave to its circuit-riding ministry a never failing theme for stirring sermons. The undogmatic and biblical faith of the Baptist body, like the experiential religion of Methodism, suited a society unversed in dogma, chronically suspicious of the formalities that go with a liturgy, and wedded on Sundays as on week days to the familiar informalities of an unsophisticated life.

You will then have to make a place for those bodies which are continental in origin; not only German Lutheranism, but the Lutheranism of all the Scandinavian countries as well; and aside from these the substantial non-Lutheran bodies, some of them negligible survivals from early Anabaptism; and others, like the

Evangelical and Reformed Church, a sober and substantial body centred in Pennsylvania and Ohio, or the Dutch Reformed Church still vigorously active in New York, and the Christian Reformed Church, a Dutch Calvinist body centred in western Michigan. These transplanted Reformation churches from the continent account for five or six millions of our church members. Historically they have no connection with England; their theology presupposes the theological confessions of the sixteenth century, and their usages as well as their church government look back to Germany, Holland, Switzerland, France, Norway or Sweden. These groups are particularly strong in Pennsylvania, in the Middle West and the nearer north-west. They have become a welcome, stable, and substantial part of American life. The Lutheran farmer in Minnesota concedes nothing, and need not make any concessions, to the elder American types. His place among us has been won and his worth proven.

Of the Jewish synagogue it is not so easy to speak. The Jews are, in the presence of the census taker, at either an advantage or a disadvantage. Jewry holds that all members of the race are by nature and spiritual necessity members also of the synagogue. Therefore the statistics for our Jewish congregations are merely a transcript of those for the Jewish population as a whole, a matter of some 4,500,000. The American Jew, like the European Jew, is a city dweller. In America he is relatively more prominent in New York than elsewhere, though he is scattered up and down the eastern coast and in the larger cities across the country. It is said that every third person living on Manhattan Island, the geographical heart of New York City, is a Jew. The theoretical equation of the race with the synagogue makes it difficult, if not impossible, to estimate the actual degree of religious practice. Apparently Jewish religious leaders are reluctant to gather and then to publish figures, lest the result seem to concede a distinction between the people and its religion, which their tradition disallows. Israel in its entirety is the congregation.

As for the classification and membership of Jewish congregations: their religious officials not only return no detailed figures to the Census, they are disinclined to concede the interior division of Jewry into orthodox, conservative, and reformed

bodies. The distinction does, however, exist in fact. An unofficial pamphlet claims that there are 2500 orthodox congregations in the United States with a technical membership of
400,000 and a constituency of 1,200,000; 500 conservative congregations with 250,000 members and 1,000,000 constituents;
300 liberal congregations with 60,000 members and 250,000
constituents. There would seem to be, therefore, 2,000,000 Jews
who do not belong to synagogues. The ratio of churched and
unchurched Jews is, therefore, approximately that of the country
as a whole. Plainly orthodox and conservative congregations are
in the majority. These preserve, in the New World, many of the
traditions of the Old World, and the orthodox rabbi from
Eastern Europe, with his constituency, represents among us one
of the most inflexible survivals of an ancient culture. The proportion of theological liberals is far higher among Protestants
than among Jews. Apparently the restraints and sanctions of
orthodox Judaism are such that, once they are relaxed, irreligion
and secularism seem to be the obvious alternative. Hence the
prominence of a well-known type among us, the radical leftist
Jew, who has parted company with all religion.

It is difficult at the present moment to appraise the amount of
anti-Semitism abroad in America. The reputed ability of the
Jewish merchant to drive a shrewd bargain and the coherence of
the race in the practice of the professions are matters of common
gossip. Various types of black-shirt agitation are deliberately
fanning the never extinguished embers of anti-Semitism. Here
and there certain religious leaders are suspected of lending themselves to such propaganda. Father Coughlin's crusade against
'the international bankers' has been generally so construed.
Many persons feel the situation to be dangerous, and prophesy
American pogroms. Occasional sporadic outbursts of direct
physical assault take place, usually between gangs of boys, at
points where residentially there is friction between Jews and
Gentiles in our cities. None of us are happy over the Jewish
problem, and many are apprehensive. Meanwhile the tragic
sufferings of the race in Europe have been such that men of good
will have no slightest wish to add to the sorrows of Israel by too
candid criticism of local situations. Liberal members of both

races are making resolute efforts to interpret each to the other and
to defend our common citizenship, if not indeed the total religious tradition of the two peoples. There can be little commerce, indeed there is no commerce, between Orthodox
Judaism and Fundamentalist Protestantism at the two extremes.
Such liaison work as we have goes on between theological
liberals in both groups. Our total world needs many more men
like your Claude Montefiore and our own George Foot Moore
here at Harvard, each of whom did the cause of the ongoing
religion of the two traditions inestimable service in scholarly
interpretation. Montefiore's *Synoptic Gospels* and Moore's
Judaism are works of great learning and even greater charity.

Given the strength of the establishment in England, you will
be struck by the relatively small membership of the Protestant
Episcopal Church in the United States. As we have already seen,
this church suffered sadly from the Revolution, and began its
renewed life in the Republic without the whole-hearted support
of the Mother Church in the old country. To-day, however, it
is one of the most influential of our denominations—no one
questions the fact—and is for many of the total purposes of our
common Christianity a strategically placed body. Its appeal is
perhaps greatest in the cities, and thus it is more urban than rural.
The Prayer Book, with its implicit pledge that in services of
worship the offices shall be read decently and in order, is probably
the greatest single source of attraction to non-Episcopalians. In
the worship of the non-liturgical churches far too many of our
transactions are accomplished in disorder, and occasionally
approach aesthetic indecency. Popular taste in America has
improved appreciably in recent years, due in large part to better
music over the air, better architecture both public and domestic,
and better books—structurally better, if often less Puritan in
pattern. This improved taste penalizes churches, particularly in
the great cities, which persist in the cults of ugliness, untidiness
and sentimentalism.

The Episcopal Church in America still carries the designation
'Protestant'. Your Anglo-Catholic movement has its counterpart here, but the first half of that term is meaningless in this
country, if not irrelevant. The high-churchman-in-general

accepts the designation 'Catholic', but the word does not have in America the precise relevance and appeal that it has in England, because of the massive fact of our local Roman Catholicism. We know no 'Americo-Catholicism', of Episcopalian status. Conversions from the Episcopal Church to Roman Catholicism are relatively not as frequent with us as with you, for the simple reason that making one's submission to Rome is in this country an act which more or less automatically carries with it acceptance of a predominantly Irish hierarchy and priesthood. Theological issues quite apart, the readjustment of racial and cultural affiliations, when one leaves Protestantism and 'goes over to Rome', is more radical here than in England. Nor is the conception of Catholicism minus the Pope likely to seem plausible in a country where the popular idea of Catholicism implies the Papacy. The word 'Catholic' undoubtedly has for such members of the Episcopal Church as use it of themselves its valid meanings. But it is not, in general, serviceable for propaganada and is likely to be misunderstood by that arbiter of such matters, the man in the street, who is a possible recruit and for whom 'Catholic' means one thing only—'Roman'.

The more far-seeing clergy of the Episcopal Church are deeply concerned to keep the church open to all sorts and conditions of men, whatever their place in the social scale or their economic lot. This endeavour expresses itself in two ways; first through self-sacrificing service in the poorest parts of our cities—matching the mission work in the East End of London; and next in the reconditioning of down-town parish churches to serve as pro-cathedrals, or in the building of new and magnificent cathedrals, which shall appeal to all classes and types in the community. English precedents, such as that at Liverpool, have set an admirable example to American Episcopalianism. There is, therefore, probably no single American denomination in the cities better qualified to serve the whole community in its everyday devotional practices. The Episcopal Church knows better than most other Protestant Churches how to greet and to meet the crowds on the city streets, at a midday service in Lent.

It remains true, however, if such theoretically unpalatable distinctions are to be conceded, that the Episcopal Church is not primarily constituted of those whom Mark Rutherford described. In New York the parishioners of Episcopal and Presbyterian Churches, with the Dutch Reformed as an old aristocratic minority, number on their parish rolls the persons whose names will be most often met in the social, financial, and business columns of the daily paper. In Boston it will be the Episcopalians and the Unitarians. The strength of the Episcopal Church is found in the great cities, particularly in the East. The preponderance of urban over rural churches is duly noted in the Census, the historic churches of the Virginia countryside furnishing the one signal exception. In the cities Episcopalians, as parishioners, are more often than otherwise persons of substance, standing and influence. Other churches, ministering to socially less prominent groups, think of the Episcopal Church as 'worldly', and give thanks that they are not as the 'Piskys', a term of mildly affectionate dispraise often heard in up-state villages. Meanwhile good strategy, simple liturgical services, an open door, where far too many other church doors are closed and locked, the encouragement of private devotions at any and all hours of the day, useful manuals for such devotions, the patent lack of all class distinctions and the presence of a sincerely intended catholicity in the services of cathedrals and pro-cathedrals—all these are marks of vitality, sincerity and imagination.

American Presbyterianism was, as we have seen, Scotch-Irish in its origins, but it has lost its identification with the early Ulster *émigrés*. It is now in some ways the theological stronghold of Orthodox Protestantism. At the beginning of the last century the Presbyterian and Congregational Churches of the East seem to have tacitly agreed that they would avoid geographical overlapping, and would divide the land between them, as far as their two constituencies were concerned. Whatever the theory, Congregationalism cared for New England; Presbyterianism for New York, Pennsylvania and the like. A formal plan of union, intended to give effect to this agreement was in force in the West for some years. Although this agreement was eventually rescinded, it lasted long enough so that the geographical lines between these denominations became clearly marked; they remain visible and even operative to-day. In the City of Boston, for example, there are practically no Presbyterian churches; the few that are there serve for the most part recent immigrants who have come to New England from the Maritime Provinces of Canada. Conversely, there is to-day only one considerable Congregational church on Manhattan Island in New York, while the number of Presbyterian churches in the city is almost legion. Each in its own locale continues to do duty for both, though there is no longer any formal ecclesiastical connection between them. A Boston Congregationalist, moving to New York, would join a Presbyterian Church as a matter of course; the New Yorker coming to Boston would 'bring his letter' to a Congregational Church.

Presbyterianism cannot enjoy, of course, the peculiar distinctions and privileges which are its historic right in Scotland, or the reflected glories which it still has in England. There is no border north of which the President of the United States, as he travels about, automatically becomes a Presbyterian. But the Scotch strain in our people, which has by no means always been mediated to us by way of Ulster, tends as a matter of course to be Presbyterian, and the ties of American Presbyterianism with present-day churches and theological schools in Scotland are close and strong. There is much visiting and moving back and forth; more so probably than in the case of any other American denomination and its parent or kindred body in Europe. Distinguished Scottish preachers have long been familiar and popular figures in our city pulpits. Often they have stayed for a period of years. The resolute piety, the 'legitimate rhetoric' (to use a phrase of Cardinal Newman's), the sober concern for a theology which has a decently articulated framework—all these familiar traits of church life in Scotland have been perpetuated here in American Presbyterianism or, if temporarily lost, are in constant process of being recovered.

Of other bodies there is not space, or perhaps need, to speak in detail. If any has been overpassed, the omission is deliberate and implies no adverse judgment or wilful neglect. A proper pride might prompt me to say something of American Congregationalism; its identification in 6000 parishes with a great upper-middle class constituency of nearly a million persons, rather than the people at the two extremes of the social scale; its historic concern for foreign missions, and its zeal for higher education perpetuated in a chain of church colleges stretching clean across the continent. But the tale is already too long.

Let it be said in conclusion that, in want of the background of an established church which might serve as a point of constant reference for all dissenting bodies, so that what such bodies do or leave undone is predetermined by the faith and practice of an establishment, we in America are without any such single religious body to serve as the norm. We have by virtue of our citizenship no one church to belong to, or to dissent from. In any single instance our church membership may be determined by the dominant usage of a given locality; but no usage is so nation-wide as to serve our citizens as a whole in anything like representative fashion. There is then little awareness of having broken away from any parent church and therefore no occasion to consider the wisdom of returning to that church. We cast no wistful backward glances. There is, even in matters of church union, little remembrance of old hurts to be healed or precipitate schisms to be repudiated. Religiously we are, because of the law of the land and the culture which has been fostered by the law, a society of equals and contemporaries. Each may have his strong affection for his own communion, and his faith in its merits, but he knows that he cannot hope to press his case too publicly. The sheer mass of our equalitarianism will always defeat him. Even the most theoretically exclusive of the churches—the Roman Catholic—has made, at least for the time being, its peace with this fact.

Religion has here, as it has seldom had before, a free field and an open field for institutional trial and error. Our ventures are often made in too contemporary terms and are judged too pragmatically. They are, therefore, often crudely conceived, without due consideration of precedent and proven premises. They are, also, just as crudely appraised, and the praise or blame accorded them may be a most inaccurate measure of their actual worth. Our situation has its dangers; it has also its opportunities. We are a society in which religious experiment may be made without let or hindrance and without too calculating an eye turned toward the state. We should all be perhaps more definitely oriented, had we an establishment. The absence of some such single historic centre of reference leaves us at loose ends, wholly unpatterned in our total church life. Yet no one of us would have an establishment recovered from colonial days or set up in the terms of some later day. We are content to carry on and to continue our experiment of the separation of church and state, to see what a prolonged experience of this nature may prove.

CHAPTER VII. *THE PARISH CHURCH*

In the primary meaning of the word, we have no 'parishes' in America. The only possible exception is that found in the state of Louisiana, where the 'parish' is the civil division corresponding to the county in our other states. But even in Louisiana the word carries no ecclesiastical connotation. In short we have no geographical unit in which residents are committed to the care of one pastor and in which there is normally a church building of an establishment. Nor has the state ever made the slightest attempt to divide the surface of the land between the denominations. Any denomination may build its church anywhere, provided it has the money to do so, and does not violate the building laws. Therefore, we can use the term 'parish church' only in a secondary sense.

The identification of any given American with a church is not, therefore, primarily conditioned by his residence in a country township or a municipal ward. He goes to the church of his liking and his choice, wherever it may happen to be. In peace time, when he has all the 'gas' he needs, he goes to church in his car; hence his range is wide. The resultant group should probably be described as a congregation rather than a parish. This is particularly true in the larger cities, where churches draw their members from wide areas. The single church is, with us, probably more particularized or specialized in its usages than is the case in the normal Anglican parish church. Each tends to be a flocking together of birds of a feather. Here again the separation of church and state, which precludes any formal parochial life, breeds that individualism of which we have spoken more than once.

As to our church buildings, we were born too late to have had any part in Gothic architecture as it matured as a living thing, from the twelfth through the sixteenth centuries. Therefore we have no authentic buildings to match the glorious succession from Iffley Church in Oxford to King's College Chapel in Cambridge. The Gothic style was revived here about the middle of the last century and for forty years thereafter 'Early English' was the norm. With the 1890s the Perpendicular style began to supplant the earlier pattern and is now the accepted convention, if a church is to be built in this tradition. This style is also widely used in our universities—so much so that it is now generally known as 'college Gothic'.

We have countless elaborate churches already built within this pattern, and some great cathedrals in process of prolonged construction. The Episcopal cathedrals in Washington and New York are instances of the latter fact. The chapel at Williams College, built some fifty years ago, was the first of the more recent type. The chapels at Princeton and the University of Chicago are among the noblest new Gothic churches in either of our countries. The Church of St Vincent Ferrers, St Thomas' Church and the Riverside Church in New York are all notable.

In so far as we have an indigenous type of church architecture, it is that which is variously known as Classical, Palladian, Georgian; here we call it 'Colonial'. This became in the mid-eighteenth century the common design both for Episcopal churches in Virginia and for Congregational churches in New England. Again, however, this style copies a past tradition. As against the Gothic, which did not begin to appear until a century later, these colonial churches have an added hundred years of history, and therefore whatever local sentiment attaches to their longer life. Many of them date around the 1740s.

The rival claims of the Georgian and the Gothic styles can never be settled. Each has its own inherent excellence. The latter is intended for the celebration of the Sacrament. The former, as we knew it in the older New England meeting houses, was meant for the preaching of the Word. The pulpit, rather than the altar, was the central fact in the interior design. Many of the free, non-liturgical churches are now putting up Georgian buildings with the conventional east end. It is doubtful how far this arrangement, which sets the pulpit over against the lectern and the prayer desk at the front of an apse and places the communion table in the centre and at the deep end of the apse, is warranted by the usage of the non-sacramentarian churches. When the Sacrament is celebrated only occasionally, the communion table seems to have, during the long intervals when it lacks the bread and the wine, an architectural centrality not required by the faith and practice of the church.

In these modern Gothic and Georgian churches there is much good craftsmanship both in design and in construction. We have now passed on from the period of unashamed mediocrity, which, in the last half of the last century, gave us in the terms of *Main Street* countless edifices that represented no religious tradition and deleted all religious symbolism. They were often built to yield a semicircular auditorium on a sloping floor, pews and aisles converging as in a theatre upon a wide platform with a central desk, the platform backed in turn by a choir loft and a battery of gilded organ pipes. They were listening posts pure and simple where the congregation might sit in passive silence to hear the choir and the minister. There are a deplorably large number of these tasteless buildings still in use, and it will be some years before they wear out, or before congregations can afford to replace them.

Therefore the recent Gothic and Georgian revivals are an architectural improvement upon that undistinguished past. But one is left in two minds about these more recent churches in the elder styles. At one moment they seem lifeless. Santayana once said even of King's College Chapel that in want of the Mass it seemed little more than a chrysalis of stone from which the living creature had fled. That impression is doubly true in this country, in case of churches which have had to be candid copies rather than new creations. What is more, the copies, in the majority of the cases, have usually had to be made in rather meagre dimensions. So, Henry James, back in America after an absence of twenty-five years, looked out from his window on Beacon Hill at the spire of the Park Street Church, a landmark in down-town Boston, and could only say of it that it was 'a mild recall of Wren's bold London examples, the comparatively thin echo of a far-away song'. One often sees these copies and hears these echoes in even the best of our modern buildings.

In such moments one feels a kind of holy impatience that the dead hand should lie so heavily upon all the apparatus of religion. This mood is deepened by the daring glory and beauty of much of our secular architecture. The modern designer concedes the

structural facts of steel and concrete and proceeds honestly thereafter. With these media he is able to put up an Empire State
Building or a Chrysler Building, to achieve a Hell Gate Viaduct
or a Boulder Dam. The vitality and the contemporaneity of these
works are instantly felt. This most recent architecture has often
been given on the continent, and less often with you, candid
recognition in an occasional church building, which is a transcript
of our own time. It is rather surprising that here in America,
which is a country given to innovation, we have seen little of this
trend. One would have supposed that we would have experi-
mented freely with these newest designs. But in our churches,
as in our homes, we are a curiously conservative people.

At another moment and in another mood, one is inclined to
think that we do well to continue to build our churches in the
older styles. If American history is relatively brief, the American
memory is short. One of the cultural contributions which religion should make to our life is that of an intimation of the
further backgrounds of our life, and thus of the Christian tradition in something like its entirety. We are too easily weaned in
liturgical usage from a King James' Bible to some modern
translation. We might likewise be lured away too soon from
classical styles of church architecture to newer styles which, in
reflecting the energetic vitality of contemporary American life,
would become merely ephemeral. As with our office buildings,
so with our churches, we might lapse into the cycle of Chicago,
where as Carl Sandburg has it, we 'build the city, tear it down,
and build it again'. Perhaps the absence of contemporaneity in
much of our church architecture marks a wise instinct as to the
relation of religion to life. In a world of perpetual change—and
in America of change which long antedates decay—it is well to
have some buildings which in their very form suggest that which
ought to abide.

What goes on in these buildings? As for Roman Catholicism
the question is rhetorical, carrying with it its own answer: the
celebration of the Mass, Benediction, preaching missions,
baptisms, weddings, funerals; and for the rest the private devotions of the faithful.

In Protestantism the usages vary. Liturgical and sacramentarian churches have an early communion service on Sundays; in 'Catholic' parishes there is usually a daily Eucharist. All Protestant parishes have an eleven o'clock Sunday morning service, and even though there be a second service still later in the day, the morning service is the major act of the day and gathers the larger congregation. In the non-sacramentarian churches, celebration of the Lord's Supper takes place infrequently, once a month or once in three months, at the close of a shortened Sunday morning service. Invitation to communicate is given generously, and the number of churches with 'closed communion' and 'the fenced table' is on the decline.

A second service on Sunday may be a musical vespers, or it may be a popular preaching service in the evening. Musical vespers, which were the vogue a generation ago, have now been generally outclassed by excellent Sunday afternoon concerts in the larger cities and by nation-wide broadcasts of the ranking symphony orchestras. Given these attractions, the church organist and his choir no longer claim the hearing which they once received.

The Sunday School is still in force, for the most part substantially so. Its sessions for older children are held either immediately before or after the morning church service. In many city parishes the little children are brought by their parents to the morning service, sitting through the 'opening exercises' and leaving at the time of the hymn before the sermon for their own proper instruction in some other part of the building. Young people's organizations, a Christian Endeavour Society or an Epworth League, usually hold gatherings of their own in the late afternoon, variously composed of a social half hour, a light supper, a brief devotional meeting or an address on some matter of current interest.

The week-day activities of our parish churches do not vary appreciably from yours. The old 'prayer meeting' which was a survival of the 'mid-week lecture' of the colonial churches has generally lapsed. In the larger cities its place is taken by twenty-minute midday services in Lent, or special evening services. The women's organizations are well kept up, meeting often for Red Cross activities or for a review of the women's missionary activities in the denomination. Most churches attempt to have men's clubs, but they are an indifferent success.

In our older church buildings the main floor was well above ground-level, reached by staircases in the vestibules. This left an unconsecrated area beneath, which was used on Sundays for the church school and the young people's meetings, and by other organizations for their mid-week gatherings. It usually was— and still is, in so far as it survives—a rather grim place, without beauty that one should desire it. Large chromos hanging on the walls showing biblical characters and scenes did little to relieve the bleakness. The newer churches usually have an adjacent parish house, where more detailed and adequate provision is made for classes in the Sunday School, for women's parlours, for church offices and a library, and, above all else, church suppers.

The social life of the average American parish still centres about this church supper. In towns and villages this gathering is an occasion of first importance. It gives parishioners their one best non-Sunday opportunity to meet and affirm their solidarity as a 'beloved community'. Its culinary good repute is a matter of concern to the ministering women on any given evening. It prides itself on its home cooking and has an aristocratic contempt for bought food. Its menu is classic: baked beans, cold ham, chicken salad, scalloped oysters, doughnuts, coffee ('with the meal'), pumpkin pie, mince pie, ice cream, layer cake. The ingredients might well have been sold and given to the poor, since the cost of the supper is always well above the charge. This latter fact, with the quality of the food guaranteed, is sufficient to make the church supper one of the better bargains in the town, and usually draws in many of the peripheral unregenerate, as well as the saved. It is all rather far removed from the primitive Christian *Agape*, but even if it does not remain faithful to the intention of that first far-off supper, neither is it subject to the abuses which Saint Paul unhappily had to rebuke in his First Epistle to the Corinthians. It is a strictly temperance transaction, though one has often been left at its conclusion mindful of Saint Augustine's plaint in the *Confessions*, 'Drunkenness is far from me, but surfeiting has sometimes stolen upon Thy servant.' Even our city churches do not count themselves so genteel as to have outgrown this custom, though the hurried life of a city and the claims of a crowded calandar deny it the monopoly which it enjoys in smaller places. Henry James, in a passage previously quoted, called this institution a 'sociable'—the old-fashioned country term. It is precisely that: harmless, happy and wholly gregarious. We have cited Saint Augustine in possible dispraise; we may cite him also in praise; this simple and homely (in the American meaning of that word) institution is an instance of what he calls 'that precious habit of living together'.

A word may well be said about purely private services: baptisms, weddings, funerals. At this point there is a sharp difference between what the Census calls urban and rural habits. In the country districts and smaller towns these services are usually held in the home. In its living room a table is spread with a white cloth and thereon a silver bowl for baptism; in the same room the young people stand before the minister to be married; in the same room again the dead lie, while the funeral service is read. This restriction of private services to the home harks back, at least in New England, to colonial times, when the wedding was purely a civil rite—presumably in an attempt to deny it any residual Roman claim to be a sacrament, and when a funeral dispensed with the consolations of religion. Prior to 1686 New England ministers were prohibited by law from performing marriage ceremonies. In that year the governor proclaimed that they should thereafter share in what had been until that time the exclusive duty of a civil magistrate. In 1685 a New England minister offered prayer at a funeral, reportedly the first instance of its kind in Massachusetts Bay. The studied avoidance prior to that time of any religious ceremony in connection with the burial of the dead is presumably to be interpreted as an extreme Protestant reluctance to lay oneself open to the charge of offering prayers for the dead—again a popish practice. At this point the country church in America, by self-denying ordinances of long standing, is not as closely identified with the life of its people as is your village church. On the other hand, the home has the added ceremonial associations of joy and sorrow which ongoing life brings to every family.

In the large cities it is otherwise. If the home is a flat, it is patently unsuited for these offices. What was once the prerogative of the home becomes therefore the duty and, to some degree, the opportunity of the church to identify itself at such times with the whole life of its people. In larger towns and smaller cities the usage is equivocal, the drift being on the whole away from the home toward the church.

In the conduct of public worship we are also, to put it mildly, an undistinguished people. The Roman Mass is of course said without deviation in all Catholic churches, though many prayers in English for special occasions are creeping into the service. The Episcopal and Lutheran Churches have their prayer books to which they are in theory pledged. In the Episcopal Church there is with us, as with you, an uneasy suspicion that the Orders of Morning and Evening Prayer may either pall on those who know them too well or fail to attract those who do not know them at all. Hence there is much free and presumably illicit tampering with the Prayer Book, though there are few Episcopal services in this country which depart as far from the letter of the text as does the eleven o'clock service at St Martin's in the Field. At the ecclesiastical right it is doubtful whether there is as much suggestion of the Roman Missal in the American Episcopal Communion service as in the unashamed Anglo-Catholic churches on your side of the Atlantic.

As for the rest, practically all of our Protestant Churches are non-liturgical. This does not mean that each—and 'each' means the single parish rather than the denomination—does not have a stated order of worship which it habitually uses, but rather that the pattern is simple in the extreme. An order for Sunday morning will run somewhat as follows: Opening sentences (sometimes consisting of responses between minister and choir), a short invocation followed by the Lord's Prayer, a hymn, a responsive reading from the Psalms, an anthem, the Scripture lesson, a second anthem, the 'long' free pastoral prayer, the collection, a hymn, the sermon and brief closing prayer, a hymn and the benediction.

There is at least so much pattern in our non-liturgical usage, but despite the formality of the transaction it retains something of the informality and simplicity of our whole life in earlier days.

Traditionally the American distrusts ceremony and all its accoutrements. There is in Walter Hines Page's letters an amusing account, sent back from London to one of the family, of a reception at Buckingham Palace in which he describes the gorgeous uniforms, the regalia, the decorations, the gold braid and the ribbons, and then concludes with mention of his undistinguished self in his 'neat suit of waiter black'. This note has often been sounded, with no little secret pride, in such of our American classics as deal with 'The Connecticut Yankee in King Arthur's Court'. The Yankee, particularly when he became a frontiersman, lacked the wherewithal for elaborate ceremonials and therefore made a virtue of his necessity. Hence every American child looks at the faithfully coloured pictures of the Horse Guards or the Beef Eaters as at something amazingly gorgeous but wholly alien. Nor does the grown American understand these things much better. One of your most distinguished bishops, visiting us not long ago, ventured into the hinterland and found himself waiting for a train on the platform station in an Iowa city. He was dressed as becomes his office in cockaded hat, a clerical coat, apron and gaiters. A puzzled native circled about him for some time trying to read this sartorial riddle and finally plucked up courage to ask the bishop, 'What's the big idea?' The question was prompted not by any intentional rudeness, but by an honest perplexity.

I once asked a Lord Mayor of Liverpool, himself a forthright and unaffected Nonconformist, why it is that robes and fur and gold chains linger on so long for official dress in a country which is for the most part so patently democratic, in some ways more democratic than America. He said that England is so overcast and dull that it needs artificial colour; while the bright sunlight of this country makes scarlet robes and gilded jewelry unnecessary. Quite apart from your proper jealousy for tradition there may be this other factor in your usage.

Be these matters as they may, the primitive American passion for shirt sleeves is something more than an accommodation to the climate; it is also part of an hereditary passion for informality. With the best will in the world, this informality still survives in the cults of our simpler Protestant Churches. Whatever the order of worship may be, the minister is always tempted to break through its neutral and impersonal pattern with intimate approaches to a congregation which are off the record, urging the people to sing heartily, commenting freely on the transactions as they pass. Behind his temptation to do so and the response which he seldom fails to get, there lies not merely an affectation of simplicity, but a witness to one of the characteristics of American religion, its place and part as a woof woven into the warp of unceremonious everyday life.

In recent years, however, there has been in all churches a desire to 'enrich the worship'. Popular taste, as we have already said, has been improving slowly in the States, and a time is approaching when flagrant breaches of taste are more likely to offend than to appeal. There is a general desire, when we go to church, to have things done decently and in order. The traditional non-liturgical service has resolved itself far too much into an action involving only the minister and the choir. Apart from singing the hymns, a congregation does little save sit and listen. The problem is 'how to give the congregation something to do', a problem which is more or less insoluble apart from a liturgy, the text of which is in all hands.

For the most part the 'enrichment' of worship in our non-liturgical churches is at the moment a matter of adventitious decoration. The minister now wears a black Geneva gown, though this unoffending and unpretentious garment has made its way only slowly and in the face of a residual Puritan fear of popery. Thus, Dr Lyman Abbott, a famous preacher of a generation ago, when confronted for the first time in the vestry of the Harvard College chapel with a Geneva gown awaiting him, said, 'Have I got to wear that? Because, if I've got to, I won't!' The choir is next gowned, often in colours, blue being an accepted fashion. The choir then processes and recesses. This dual procedure is seldom necessitated by the geographical relation of the vestry to the chancel or choir loft. More often than otherwise it demands a preliminary pilgrimage through some subterranean area to get to the church vestibule. How many choirs, in our newest Gothic churches, have I followed from their point of initial assembly, down a flight of stairs, through a cellar where steam pipes and ventilating ducts are a menace to the head, dodging about past furnaces and coal bins, and up another flight of stairs, to be ready to enter the church and come decorously down the main aisle. There is no element of necessity in this journey, and its connotations are those of a parade rather than a religious procession. The resultant impression is that of incongruity, if not of insincerity. But there is no doubt that processionals and recessionals are now highly thought of among us.

As for the text of the service, it is enriched mainly by raids on classical prayer books. It must probably be said that any Roman Catholic will feel that the prayers in an Episcopal liturgy, taken in no small part from the Missal and the Breviary, are rather like the Elgin Marbles, fragmentary and far from home. So any Episcopalian will likewise feel about the increasing number of services in the non-liturgical churches, which betray forays on his liturgy. For the non-liturgical minister there is no easy escape from this charge and this dilemma. At the moment we lack, in all English-speaking countries, the inerrant literary sense which gave us the Prayer Book Collects, often quite as beautiful in translation as in the original Latin. It is hard to improve on 'Almighty God, unto whom all hearts be open, all desires known, and from whom no secrets are hid', and studied periphrasis yields only an unconvincing substitute.

For the moment, such is the process which is going on in most of our American churches—scholars call it 'convergence and borrowing', a kindlier term than 'stealing'. We are being delivered from the traditional infelicities of a too vividly individualistic conduct of public worship by the minister, and are being provided with well tried forms for a common act. In defence of this whole matter of give and take—the liturgical churches seeking more and more occasion for informality and spontaneity, and non-liturgical churches turning back to the elder forms of Christian worship—we have what is probably the best single preparation for church unity. If Christians can be persuaded to say their prayers together, they may eventually be able to square their theologies. It is now a matter of common knowledge that at our ecumenical conferences the services of worship are well in advance of the discussions and debates as to faith and order. Whatever the infelicities, even to the point of ethical impropriety, of this cross-breeding of liturgical and non-liturgical orders of worship, they bode well rather than ill for the final commonalty of all sorts and conditions of Christians.

As for America in particular, one has only a single reservation. Our non-liturgical worship is outgrowing its cult of informality, but in the attempt to do so it is in danger at the moment of becoming merely decorative and 'arty'. One of our sober church historians in this country has said that every religious movement passes through three stages: it begins as a moral reformation; it then devotes itself to a reflective formulation of its faith; and finally it turns to aesthetic elaboration of its ritual. This third phase, he says, marks the beginning of its decadence and will become in due time the occasion for a fresh moral revolt. One cannot help wondering whether the whole aesthetic elaboration of the apparatus for worship, both in your Anglo-Catholic circles and in our free-church circles, is merely a sign that our Christianity is passing into this third stage. Your practitioners and ours will instantly repudiate the suggestion, yet there it is. You must settle those matters for yourselves. With us, and at the present time, the 'enrichment of our worship' is far too much a matter of external decoration and far too little a matter of moral passion or sober theological reflection. The bits and scraps with which we in America are enriching our worship are too much like the frills and furbelows superadded to the dress of yesterday, too little like the lines which a modern designer regards as required by the fabric itself. In the conduct of our worship, as in our church architecture, we are making little use of the thought of the twentieth century. This thought is by no means always mistaken, nor does it necessarily preclude religious restatement in liturgical form. Martineau says, somewhere, that there may be those who reach their God best by painful antiquarianism, but that there are other souls of 'more direct and impatient affection' who must reach God in the familiar and accepted terms of their daily thinking. The problem of a liturgy for these times is as yet only imperfectly solved.

To turn, now to another aspect of our church life. Our parish church, old or new, is in most instances wholly unendowed, and must be supported by 'live money'. Here and there an old city church has appreciable endowments, sometimes holding lands and properties which yield a substantial income. The uses to which such properties are put occasionally raise awkward moral problems. For the most part, however, our parishes, whatever their denomination, must pay their way as they go along. An occasional small gift of $1000 or $5000, is sometimes left a village church by one of its devoted ministering women, but even this is the exception. In the average American parish a mortgage is a far more familiar entry on the books than an endowment, and for one parish which can cut coupons at the bank, there are three which are trying to pay their interest to the bank and to reduce the principal of a debt. A ceremonial 'burning the mortgage', which at long last has been recovered from the bank, is a happy occasion.

The American church member expects, therefore, to contribute to the support of his church, and, as his means go, to contribute generously. My impression is that, in proportion to his income, he probably gives more to his church than most church members in the other lands of Christendom. This very fact, the necessity of supporting an entirely unendowed church, is probably responsible for his greater apparent interest in his church. His head and his heart follow his gift. The mortality among our churches during the depression which followed 1929 was much lower than that of other institutions.

Theoretically an endowed church sets its clergy free from too great deference to contributors in the pews, enabling them to speak dispassionately and courageously on controversial matters. The theory may be occasionally true in fact, and if so would seem to doom the American clergy to a timid subservience to the political and economic opinions of parishioners. Such a clergyman is, indeed, part of the stock in trade of a certain type of novelist and dramatist and cartoonist. Lord Bryce, in writing his *American Commonwealth*, considered the possibility and the prospect of some such basic ethical weakness in the structure of our American churches, but could find little proof of it, and dismissed it. There may be unheroic exceptions, yet the American clergy as a whole, even though they must depend for their bread and butter upon those to whom they immediately minister, are not, as members of a profession, timid or servile.

On the other hand, the fact that the average American parish has to pay its way as it goes along does create for it certain problems of which it is not always aware. The mere mechanical business of raising the necessary money for a year's expenditures, which are devoted primarily to keeping the institution alive and going, absorbs far too much of the time and energy of all concerned. There is said to have been a paddle-wheel steamer on one of our western rivers which could make only so much steam in her boilers; when she blew her whistle the paddles stopped going round. Many American parishes are in something of the same desperate state. The most they can do is to call attention to themselves.

As a whole the country is badly over-churched. The average Protestant church has hardly two hundred parishioners, and though this would be a decent and sufficient group in the country districts or in small villages, it is an uneconomic unit in the cities. Much progress is being made in the direction of local federations, but in most communities churches are driven into a relation which can hardly be described as other than that of competition. The word is an unlovely one in this connection, yet there is no alternative. The minister may not be expected to take his cue from his congregation, and become a pious echo of their opinions, but he is expected to fill the pews and thus enable his church to pay its bills. A conspicuous failure to do so is tacitly interpreted as an intimation that he had best consider a call to some other part of the vineyard.

Hence the sensationalism of many an American pulpit, which, in the blunt language of commercialism, must compete with neighbouring churches as well as with the various forms of amusement, entertainment, instruction, and edification round about. This competitive relationship into which our churches are driven is subtly betrayed by the announcements of Sunday services found in any Saturday newspaper. Ideally each announcement should be modest and all should be restricted to the barest statement of hours of services and preachers at the services. The space given to each church should be uniform. Alas, no such situation prevails: the larger churches buy more space for the display of their wares; the would-be popular churches affect the advertising methods of the movies and the theatre. Sermon topics are couched in the form of alluring rhetorical questions. The hook is baited at its tip with reference to some recent happening which is at the fore of the common mind or by a promised pronouncement about some highly controversial issue on which the preacher has presumably received divine revelation. The American pulpit lives, far too much, a hand to mouth existence off the daily paper, not being able to allow itself wide margins for the patient instruction of the people in the fundamentals of Christian faith and practice. Our decent sensitiveness as a people is dulled in this whole matter, and, save when we force ourselves to acts of sober self-criticism, we do not realize how far the dominant commercialism of the country has driven us into unchristian competition and how gravely we are prejudicing the longer life and usefulness of our churches. Robert Browning says:

> Oh, if we draw a circle premature,
> Heedless of far gain,
> Greedy for quick returns of profit, sure
> Bad is our bargain.

The average American church is tempted to make short-term bargains with history and with the public at the cost of its far gain. The occasion for these bad bargains is not always the vulgarity of the minister and his people, but the over-churched condition of our cities, and the anxious concern of a vestry or a parish committee that the bills be paid.

This situation, partly cultural and partly economic, breeds in the minds and hearts of parishioners a stubborn loyalty to the single parish, at the cost of a generous concern for the whole fellowship of churches. Not, however, that this necessity does violence to the hereditary traits of the national temperament. On the contrary it serves those traits only too well. Our culture, until most recent times, has been individualistic. Our history has required that individualism as the best device with which to face the Frontier. And remember that the Frontier has only recently come to an end. There is in one of Emerson's *Essays* a phrase about the 'iron string of self-reliance'. This string has been twanged in American life almost to the breaking point. Indeed, it is precisely because it has been asked to bear more strain than it can stand that countless persons are now lapsing into the arms of any movement which is willing to take over for them the charge of their lives. But until most recently it has been true to say that:

In no other author can we get as close to the whole American spirit as in Emerson. In him we sense the abounding vitality and goodness of life, the brushing aside of the possibilities of failure, evil, or sin, the importance ascribed to every act of you and me. ... Without any thought-through system, a fact which perhaps endeared him all the more to Americans, Emerson was imbued with the new spirit of American optimism and with the religion of the infinite possibilities in the individual common man.[1]

It is difficult to conceive of any society more radically individual-istic than the little group which made up the Concord intellectuals of Emerson's day. Beyond the point which they reached, organ-ized society becomes impossible; only anarchy remains.

These tempers are now in slow process of becoming ancient history. Many mourn their passing, as marking the loss of what has hitherto been a distinctive characteristic of American life. They represent, in the meantime, the classic American tradition. It would be a caricature of the truth to say that American Pro-testantism had degenerated into what has been called the 'swag-gering individualism' of the Frontier, yet the noun without the adjective, or with some less blatant qualification, still has a residual warrant. This fact is particularly true of the American's attitude toward his church and his feeling for it. His church is primarily the group of persons whom he meets on Sunday mornings, with the fabric which environs them, or at one and another of the clubs and 'socials' which his church offers him. For these, if he is loyal, he has a fellow-feeling and a genuine affection. They are a necessary part of his life and from them he draws help for daily living. The same may certainly be said of your loyal church-goers and church members; but with you, unless I am wholly wrong, the place and the group are intima-tions of a wider and larger reality. The Church of England in its

[1] *The Epic of America*, by James Truslow Adams, pp. 198-9. Little, Brown, and Company, Boston, 1932.

totality is felt as present in each parish church; Nonconformity in its entirety in each chapel. At this point our religious life is far more parochial and provincial. There is no clause in the Apostles' Creed more difficult for the typical American to understand than that which makes mention of 'the communion of saints', the one clause above all others which ought to give the least difficulty to a believer. Belief in God may present grave difficulties to many minds, yet any man of quick imagination should be able to envisage that

> One great society alone,
> The noble living and the noble dead,

which the poet celebrates. For most of us the remnants of a 'swaggering individualism' put this idea beyond our imagining.

Therefore we find it hard to understand a rallying cry which has become a commonplace in Christendom to-day, 'Let the Church be the Church'. We do not quite know, in the terms of our own life, what those words are meant to imply. Legally the churches of America are voluntary associations of individuals formed for particular and restricted purposes. The church, therefore, does not represent, as a centre of social relationships, the only association to which we belong. It is one of a number of societies in which we have membership. There are the professional groups, the Chambers of Commerce, the labour unions, the political parties, the country clubs, the bridge clubs, the athletic clubs, the Rotary and Lions and Kiwanis. We are like fragments seen in a kaleidoscope; at one moment we are formed in a given pattern, the next moment we are rearranged after a different pattern. We may hope that any serious minded American Christian would say that his church is for him the most significant of all the voluntary associations to which he belongs; he cannot say that it is the only association to which he belongs, and in many instances he would have to admit that some other relationship has primacy. The American has been driven to this interpretation of his church by its status before the law. It enjoys the rights and immunities assured to any reputable body formed for sober purposes; it enjoys no special privilege. It is one with colleges, art galleries, opera houses and philanthropic agencies.

In short, the 'social contract' theory of the church has been forced on us by our separation of church and state and the resultant equality of all denominations under the laws of the land. We should have to remake our minds after an elder pattern to recover what has been sacrificed by the American solution of the age-old problem of church and state. When our continental friends tell us that, if Christianity is to survive, the church must again become the church, their warning and summons presuppose a theory of the church which either ante-dates or post-dates our American experience thus far. The words seem to require a conception of some single, self-sufficient society which asks and receives a loyalty that excludes all other loyalties.

One can understand that to members of a monastic order, the world forgetting and by the world forgot, the church can be the church. One can further understand that any church, even the most diminutive of our strange sects, which lays prophetic claim to catholicity, must 'be itself' at all costs. Again, one can understand how, in a society like ours and presumably in yours as well, a church may be expected to communicate its truth and thus its definition of duty to all the rest of one's associations. His church ought to make the shopkeeper a more upright business man, the doctor a more sympathetic practitioner. At this point most modern Christians part company, whether rightly or wrongly, with Roger Williams, who held that the trades and professions have an independent status and do not need the sanctions of religion. Our present interpretation of the relation of our churches to the other societies to which we belong does not deny these societies their warrant or their worth, but neither does it excommunicate them. At this point the minds of England and America are nearer each other than either is to more recent religious thought on the continent. Our continental fellow-Christians seek a reaffirmation of the primacy of the Christian religion, and with their desires we agree. But, however it may be with you, the formula 'Let the Church be the Church' implies either an ecclesiastical monopoly of all life's loyalties or some schism between this single institution and all other institutions which we in America find it hard to grasp in theory and should find it even harder to translate into action.

CHAPTER VIII. *AMERICAN THEOLOGY*

In their description of the religious life the classic books of Christian devotion distinguish between the way of Mary and the way of Martha. They incline to side with Mary, but are quite aware that her way of life is kept wholesome only as it is constantly corrected by that of Martha. The rival claims of the contemplative life and the active life have never been settled; presumably they cannot be and probably they ought not to be settled. They represent a tension which is required by the very conception of the religious life, the relation of the world within to the world without. For each one of us this adjustment is determined in part by his own temperament and in equal part by the culture to which he belongs. So far as arguments are concerned, the case is non-justiciable and such adjustment as we make is a compromise, not a theoretical solution of the problem.

We Americans are predominantly sons of Martha. For the purposes of the conversation implied in these pages, we are reassured when we realize that this is in some measure true of you also. Even if we may not cite Kipling's outspoken preference for Martha's sons, since he was not primarily concerned with religious matters, we remember that your English mystics—Richard Rolle, Walter Hilton, Julian of Norwich and the like—had a strong strain of saving Anglo-Saxon common sense, which is by no means always present in German and Latin mysticism of the Neo-platonic type.

Meanwhile, one of the stumbling stones in the way of the ecumenical movement is the distaste and the distrust which continental churchmen have for American 'activism'. The word so used is a term of blame rather than of praise. At a preliminary committee meeting before the Edinburgh Conference on Faith and Order a crusty old German Lutheran said that he would as soon think of asking his ten-year-old daughter just back from Sunday School for a theological opinion, as of asking any American. Under such circumstances we find it a little difficult to speak out naturally, whatever concession we may be willing to make as to the validity of the indictment. In general, we admit its warrant. We are not a reflective society. There is a marked absence among us of persons living the contemplative life. Of the Roman Catholic orders, those concerned with propaganda and good works are in the great majority. Benedictines, to say nothing of Trappists, do not flourish here. As for our Protestantism, it is happiest when it has 'something to do'. This is, indeed, the indictment which Father Tyrrell meted out to all modern Protestantism, yours as well as ours. Ask any modern Protestant, he says, what the genius of Christianity is, and he will cite you the example of Jesus: 'Circuibat benefaciendo: He went about doing good. "Doing good" seems to be the whole of the matter; more especially that sort of good that involves "going about"!' Those two sentences are a devastating caricature of American Protestantism. We understand 'doing good', particularly that kind of good which involves a great deal of going about, preferably in Pullman cars and on the fastest liners!

Confessedly, we are better at concrete gadgets than at abstract ideas. We can conceive and construct a gyroscope which goes around an incredible number of times per minute; we find it harder to understand Francis Thompson's mystic, who

> Round the solemn centre of his soul
> Wheels like a dervish.

One of our essayists has said that more brains are shown and used by any eighteen-year-old boy repairing a Ford motor in a country garage than are manifested on the floor of the United States Senate in a discussion of international affairs. The difficulty is, of course, that the boy is dealing with ponderables and the senators with imponderables.

We may not lay claim, then, to more theology than we have, nor can we pretend to be a society of meditative recluses. Yet we have not lived a wholly thoughtless life. In particular the colonial period saw, at least in New England, a wealth of hard thinking and good writing. The works of John Cotton and the Mathers rank high in the total body of Puritan letters, whether as recorded chronicles or as theological speculation. Our Thomas Hooker does not suffer by comparison with your Richard Hooker.

Both were concerned with the problems of church polity and church discipline; each was a man of parts.

It will be impossible within the limits of these pages to attempt anything like a review of our denominational theologians of the last hundred and fifty years. There have been many of them; they have served their several causes well; their names are remembered and revered among us. Failure to cite them here should not be interpreted as a disparagement of their works, but the names would mean little to you. Certain generalizations, however, may be made as to the formal religious thought of America.

We were at the first, and in no small measure continue to be, dependent upon Europe for our systematic theology. In most of our older churches the creeds, articles, confessions which were brought from Europe still remain in force. The Book of Common Prayer of the Protestant Episcopal Church carries the XXXIX Articles. The Apostles' Creed and the Nicene Creed are duly said. The Westminster Confession is still the norm for Presbyterianism. Lutherans continue their historic reference to the Augsburg Confession. The problem of subscription in these, and other kindred instances, is the same with us as with you. In so far as the world-view of the modern sciences, the cosmology and the critical history of later times are no longer that of earlier centuries, literal subscription to these older formulae becomes increasingly difficult for many a candidate for ordination, and even for prospective church members.

There is no single satisfactory solution of this problem. Much of the strength of the Christian religion down the centuries has been manifested in its ability to ensure the continuity of western life. Whatever its defects, Christianity has proved to be long-lived. For those who understand and rightly value this survival power of the church, the creeds and confessions are the most patent vehicles through which this indomitable will-to-live has expressed itself. To abandon them would seem to imply a conscious and deliberate break with the past, an interruption of the organic life of the church, century after century. The old formulae are reaffirmed, therefore, in defence of this principle of continuity rather than as contemporary statements of scientific truth.

Another school of apologists, and this is on the whole a considerable body, is prepared to subscribe *ex animo*, following the now historic example set by Dr Hensley Henson some years ago. For substance of doctrine, as against secular alternatives, the old formulae are accepted as being more nearly right than any modern substitute which might be drafted by a present-day committee. Thus a Harvard colleague, himself a mature man who has spent half a lifetime thinking of these matters without identifying himself with any church, says, 'The intuitions of Catholicism are right. Its reasons for defending them and its method of explaining them are wrong.' The problem would seem to be, therefore, that of eventually discovering a contemporary apologetic for the classical intuitions of Christianity.

Still another group accepts all this doctrinal apparatus from the past as being the creation of faith rather than a transcript of fact. Its truth, so construed, is in the strict sense of the word, the truth of poetry. This was the strategy proposed by the Roman Catholic Modernists forty years ago, a procedure which was declared by the Holy Father to be not a single heresy but the sum of all heresies. The Modernist movement, at least in Roman Catholicism, has been driven underground for the time being. Yet private conversation often discovers a good deal of residual Modernism in Catholic circles, biding its time. Theoretically there is much to be said for this subtle apologetic, which would enable those who use it to make the best of both worlds, the world of religious faith and the world of scientific truth. But this procedure was, and probably for indefinite time to come will be, too sophisticated for the plain man to understand. Ours is a prose age, which can no longer understand that the truth of poetry may be of a higher order than that of fact. And, as has been pointed out more than once, this Modernist apologetic may serve as a warrant for staying in a church if you already belong to it; it is hardly a reason for joining a church or taking orders in the first instance.

By these various ways the historic faith is accommodated to modern thought, and continuity is ensured. Few Protestants are prepared to say that the new views were part of the primitive deposit of faith, implicit from the first but only now becoming explicit. The evangelists knew nothing of Copernican astronomy or the evolutionary hypothesis, and the cause of Christianity is not helped by assuming that they did. It seems much more probable, as Father Tyrrell constantly affirmed, that Christianity is a quality of life rather than a fixed system of doctrine. In his interpretation of the place of Christianity in history he used as an illustration the story of the widow's oil in II Kings iv. She borrowed empty vessels from her neighbours round, and the oil ceased to flow only when there was not a vessel more. That, said Tyrrell, is the history of Christianity in relation to the cultures which have surrounded it and the alien systems of thought which it has filled with its own spirit. In short, we are familiar with all that is meant by this problem of theological accommodation or reinterpretation; we have no private answer to it.

Perhaps the next thing to be said of us is that our Protestantism is still closely bound up with the Bible. As has been pointed out, it is the Bible rather than the Prayer Book that is our most familiar friend. There is still a vast amount of biblical Fundamentalism left in America, pledged to a rigid doctrine of verbal inspiration. Twenty years ago the Fundamentalists were very much to the fore in an attempt to ensure their hold on the more conservative denominations. The Baptists, in particular the Southern Baptists, were vocal and active in this endeavour. Presbyterianism was also agitated by the issue. Few conspicuous victories were won in General Assemblies and Conventions, and, save for one or two minor secessions, the national bodies survived the controversy intact. But Fundamentalism was by no means defeated; it simply withdrew to its own bases. In great sections of the country it is still the rule of faith and conduct. Biblical literalism, however, has never realized that no historic document is self-explanatory and that all such documents require interpretation. But by a wholly unconscious act of self-deception, which is made possible by an ignorance of what is at stake, Fundamentalists are able to satisfy themselves that in any given instance their particular interpretation is a transcript of the letter of Scripture. The doctrine of the verbal infallibility of the Bible has never been defeated by frontal attack.

Once the literalist position is abandoned in favour of more

modern methods of interpretation, the Bible becomes another kind of book. Many Protestants think that it becomes not only more intelligible, but more significant. Liberal Protestantism has accepted this method, and its processes are followed unashamedly by its preachers and by teachers in the church schools. In biblical studies after this kind we have been, however, mainly dependent, as you also have been, upon prior work done by the Germans. Our academic affinities during the latter half of the last century were with that country rather than with England.[1] Our scholars took their cue from German predecessors. They translated German works, elaborated German theses, and occasionally ventured boldly forth on independent ventures in the German manner. The result has been a wealth of serious and useful books on the Bible, but once again, no American name survives which can rank with those of the German pioneers.

It was an unfortunate thing for the cause of modern biblical scholarship that those who were so employed were known as 'higher critics'. The term implies, of course, a technical distinction between the 'lower criticism', which is concerned merely with textual matters, and a total appraisal of a body of literature with respect to its authorship, date and content. To the pious mind it was bad enough to be a critic of the Bible at all, since the word commonly implies an adverse judgment rather than positive appreciation; it was doubly bad to be a self-styled 'higher critic'. Equalitarianism resented the implications of the term as being arrogant and impious. The cause of biblical learning in America would have made much more rapid progress could our scholars have been known as humble reinterpreters of the Bible, rather than its 'higher critics'.

As for the social gospel, we have also had our bold spokesmen. Proponents of that gospel held the middle of the religious stage from the 1890s until the first World War. What they had to say differed little from what men of like mind were saying in

---

[1] When I came back to America in 1907 as a returning Rhodes Scholar, after three years in Oxford, I was asked by one of our leading church historians why I had wasted my time going to England, when I might have gone to Germany. President Eliot of Harvard was said to have taken much the same disparaging view of the scholarships.

England. What they said needed saying, and they never lacked courage. Their utterances were often unwelcome to their middle-class congregations and sometimes cost them their professional lives. Yet they made much headway against the dead weight of indifference which they faced and finally reconciled their hearers to the necessity, if not the wisdom, of hearing them through. The conventional American Protestant of a generation ago was in matters economic and industrial a conservative person. His minister, however, prepared him for change. The radical re-organization all life required by the depression and then by the needs of a war-time economy has gone far beyond anything which the social gospellers of a generation ago could have anticipated. Not all these latest changes have been inspired by a distinctively Christian ethic, or addressed to the ideal of a Christian community. But the inertia of the middle classes, which even more than the transgressions of notorious million-aires was the major form of resistance met by those who preached the social gospel, is now largely a thing of the past. The American to-day knows, however little he may like the fact, that hereafter the pattern of social life in the Western world will be different.

Mention should certainly be made of the missionary move-ment which, in the swing back from the secularism of the late eighteenth century, began to appear with the early years of the nineteenth century. Home missions might have been taken for granted as a natural concomitant of the westward movement of the population. Foreign missions, however, could not be so construed, yet if there be any such thing as precedence in such matters, that was granted to them as a matter of course. The great foreign missionary societies have been, in a wholly proper sense of the word, more aristocratic organizations than the home missionary societies. They represented, in Nietzsche's phrase, what was often 'an aristocracy of suffering', and they were—in the nature of the case they often had to be—the guardians of a purer gospel than was current at home.

Until most recent years a quality attached to our foreign missionary movement which was lacking in the sister movements in England. The Empire has given you for generations a concern for a wider world than that of which we have been, at least until most recently, habitually aware. Going out to India, for example, has been a matter of course with you for centuries. Members of the Indian Civil Service did not feel particularly exiled, and so far from shrinking from such service, young men sought it as one of the prizes to be had at the end of a successful university career. If one's country has an empire, such a duty and such an opportunity are part of the day's work. What was true of the secular arm, was equally true of the spiritual arm.

All this was for a hundred years no part of our mental second nature. The missionary who went to India, or China, or Africa, or .the islands of the sea went to a 'heathen' land. Even though a British Raj existed in some such land, it was a high, far-off affair with which the American missionary had few contacts or none. He lived with the 'heathen'. And until our foreign missions began to coincide with our occupation of the Philippines, after the Spanish-American War, there was no question of possible mixed motives in the venture. Our missionaries went out to save souls—souls which, according to the elder theology were eternally lost, in want of the gospel. The need was urgent, and the motives were sincere.

The foreign missionary was a person set apart. He had for the churches at home something of the attributes of 'the religious' in Catholic circles, a touch of saintliness not always apparent in the 'secular' clergy and the laity at home. People felt about him what all of us now feel about Albert Schweitzer, that he had a passionate single-mindedness which their divided minds and loyalties lacked. That fact irritated them, as it always must do, and they took refuge in loud insistence upon the priority of the claims of home missions. But against the heroic example of the foreign missionary such compensatory considerations made little headway. Foreign missions had the prior claim on the resources of the churches at home, and that priority was always conceded.

For us, too, letters from the mission field and the tales of missionaries back on furlough furnished for years an element of wonder and wild surmise by no means satisfied by the more prosaic reports from the home field. There is a latent wanderer in us all, and this globe-trotting proclivity found vicarious satisfaction in the stories that came back from 'Greenland's icy mountains, and India's coral strand'. If Newman was warranted in defending a 'legitimate rhetoric' in narrative, the missionary societies were equally warranted in stressing the wholly 'legitimate romance' in their ventures far afield. Foreign missions were the precursor of whatever internationalism there is in the Christian mind to-day. No American Christian who believes in them and has supported them can really be an isolationist. They bred a sense of obligation to distant peoples, and even a sense of strange identification with such peoples.

Latterly, however, the foreign missionary movement has lost something of what was once its unique place in our religious life. The movies can give you pictures of strange lands and cultures more dramatic than the single 'shots' once available in the stereopticon slides loaned you by the missionary society. Where the missionary pioneered, there the bagman for American business has followed to confuse the issues. More particularly the airplane and the radio have abolished distance, and countries once far off are brought near. Wendell Willkie's *One World* renders certain types of missionary appeal ancient history. The wonder and the romance are not wholly gone even from that book, but the vehicle is non-theological.

With the liberalizing of our theology and our unwillingness to condemn and commit the 'heathen' to cosmic darkness, and with the readiness of many of our missionary societies to work within the religious cultures to which they go and to accept rather than to refuse what seems good in those cultures, the awful urgency of the foreign missionary programme, as at first conceived, is at least modified. Furthermore, the pitiable spectacle of Christendom over the last thirty years has not only given non-Christians doubt as to the practicability, if not the finality, of the Christian religion; it has bred a new humility in the churches of the West. We are perhaps more aware than ever before of the need of a newly born Christianity the world over; we are dogmatically less self-confident than once we were. In these latter respects, then, our great foreign missionary movement is passing through a period of transition. The occasion is still as great as ever it was; the premises and the processes are changing.

For the remainder of this chapter I am proposing to concern

myself with two American thinkers who stand, it is true, far apart in time, but even farther apart in their premises: Jonathan Edwards and William James. The choice of James is self-explanatory; it needs no defence. The choice of Edwards is perhaps more indefensible. Yet if you could be persuaded to dip into some of his pages you would find them interesting. Edwards is significant because he represents the mature sophistication in America of the Calvinistic system. In some of our more conservative denominations Calvinism still remains nominally, if not literally, in force. But even in those liberal bodies, which have given up the premises of the system, its general cultural conception of religion survives.

Puritanism in England never had, as it had here for over a century, a monopoly of your theological thinking. It had to reckon constantly with all that was implied by the Cavalier tradition, as with the strong strain of semi-Pelagianism in the English temperament. On the continent Calvinism was also constantly challenged by other types of Reformation theology and never had the field to itself. In New England, however, until the middle of the eighteenth century, its skills and subtleties could all be devoted to an interior elaboration of the system.

Jonathan Edwards marked the end of the period and was himself its fullest and final product. American critics are inclined to say that of all the speculative thinkers whom we have produced Edwards is probably the most distinguished. He was a Congregational minister in Massachusetts during the first half of the eighteenth century (1703–58). Most of his professional life was spent in the town of Northampton. His later years coincided with the 'Great Awakening', a revival of religion which ended the sterile period at the beginning of the century, and much of his thought was given to the probable results of that historic movement. His works stand only once removed in their excellence from Calvin's *Institutes of the Christian Religion* and remain among the classics of post-Reformation theology. Edwards on the *Freedom of the Will* is the *magnum opus*. We all know that we ought to read it in its entirety; few of us have done so! His treatise on *Original Sin* is perhaps less original than the title might suggest, but wholly correct, given its premises.

Edwards was a man with one idea and one only, the vindication of the sovereignty of God. 'God's design in the creation was to glorify himself.... The absolute, universal, unlimited sovereignty of God requires that we should adore him with all possible humility and reverence. It is impossible that we should go to excess in lowliness and reverence of that Being who may dispose of us to all eternity as he pleases.' Christian theology has never gone in this direction beyond the point at which Edwards arrived. The doctrine got into difficulties, not because it lacked the passionless consent of the human mind to the starry heavens without, but because it did violence to the moral law within. This 'Sultanic' conception of God, as some one has called it, rode roughshod over all moral distinctions between man and man. It is true that the devout Calvinist always faced the possibility that he might be 'damned for the glory of God' and in theory professed his willingness to accept that destiny. In practice, and for reasons which are never quite made clear, he seems to have assumed that personally he was to be a recipient of the grace of God and an instance of the limited divine election. Numerically, the odds were against him, since, as Edwards says, 'the bigger part of those that heretofore lived are undoubtedly gone to hell'. Like Pascal, however, the devout Calvinist apparently thought that the 'wager' was worth making.

Edwards's sermons, as read at this late date, are like black and hardened lava. One is aware of the white-hot, volcanic mood in which they were conceived and preached. 'The God that holds you over the pit of hell, much as one holds a spider or some loathsome insect over the fire, abhors you, and is dreadfully provoked; his wrath towards you burns like fire; he looks upon you as worthy of nothing but to be cast into the fire; he is of purer eyes than to bear to have you in his sight; you are ten thousand times so abominable in his eyes, as the most hateful and venomous serpent is in ours.' No one can begin to understand Calvinism unless he accepts its minor premise; that if we all get what we deserve we shall, for Adam's sin, go straight down into the eternal torments of hell. Only a wholly arbitrary act of God saves any of us. His grace is his own affair; he is not accountable to us for its operations. It is, however, no wonder that the citizens of Northampton, particularly those who had a healthy native palate for life's cakes and ale, tired of these sermons as a too constant fare. Edwards finally had to move on and spent his last years among the Indians in western Massachusetts.

Yet all the while it seems as though Edwards's own heart were pleading against his head. Although he never modified his theology in the interest of what we should now call psychology, he left us, as footnotes to his own thought, two considerable works which have a curious modernity: his treatise on the *Religious Affections* and his *Thoughts on the Revival of Religion in New England*. Edwards was by no means a cold and calculating thinking machine, he was also a man of strong feelings and deep affections. In these two works he turns from an intellectual account of religion to its emotional aspects. In so doing he anticipated much of the theological thinking of a later time. In treating of the whole problem of religious feeling he was a psychologist before psychology had become a self-conscious science. If it be true that the basis of all science is accurate observation, Edwards was a psychologist of the first rank. In his unerring fidelity to the diversified facts of our emotional life he reminds us of Saint Augustine in the *Confessions*; in his interpretation of the facts he was a forerunner of William James. These two works ought to be rescued from neglect, if not oblivion, and re-read to-day. Their shrewd judgments would be as applicable to the Oxford Groups as to the Great Awakening. They cannot, however, be dipped into and dismissed; they must be wrestled with.

During the latter half of the eighteenth century American religious thought began to react against the pitiless objectivity of Edwards's celebration of the Sovereignty of God. The gentler gospel of the Wesleys influenced us somewhat. More particularly the newer doctrines of man, which derived from John Locke, became the order of the day, theologically as well as politically. God became not merely benevolent, lending his sanctions to our inalienable right to the pursuit of happiness; he was also in process of becoming the soul of republicanism. That story must be reserved for our final chapter.

Meanwhile the permanent and still most important influence

of Calvinism on American life is to be sought and found not in its theology, but in its cultural conception of the relation of religion to life. At this point even those churches which are now theologically emancipated remain Calvinistic. Since this situation is a contemporary fact and not a remote historical fact it deserves brief elaboration.

We have said in an earlier chapter that it is not easy for the American to divorce his church from the other 'voluntary associations' to which he belongs, and thus to isolate it after the Catholic or Lutheran pattern. His inability to do so is not wholly due to the institutional consequences of the separation of church and state. It is due also to the influence which the Genevan pattern of life had upon us at the first, and still has. Neither church nor state had for Calvin, in his initial experiment with a Christian society, the self-sufficient independence which they have had in other systems. Both were the instruments and the agents of a theocracy. Since Calvin's overruling and determining idea was that of the sovereignty of God, all other ideas, together with the institutions which incarnated them, were made subservient to it.

There never has been in America, and there is not now, that felt distinction between the sacred and the secular which is a commonplace in most religious circles. Robert Frost, writing of the stones tumbled off the wall around his farm by the ice of winter coming out of the ground in spring, says, 'Something there is that doesn't love a wall, that wants it down'. Something there is in American life which doesn't love walls. There is a residual Leveller in most of us. We instinctively wish our life to be all of a kind. It has been said of the three watchwords of the French Revolution—Liberty, Equality, Fraternity—that England has come the nearest to realizing the ideal of liberty, France of fraternity, and America of equality. There is much truth in the observation, and our American equalitarianism is not merely a matter of individual human rank; it extends also to our institutions. We bridle when any one of our institutions sets itself up above another; they ought all to be servants of a common cause.

Equation of the sacred with the secular may be achieved in either of two ways: secular concerns may be elevated to the level of the sacred; sacred things may be debased to the level of the secular. Ideally a religious equalitarianism presupposes the former process. Such was the aim of the prophets of Israel. 'In that day shall there be upon the bells of the horses, HOLINESS UNTO THE LORD; and the pots in the Lord's house shall be like the bowls before the altar.' Actually matters are more likely to go the other way: things sacred lose their distinctive quality and are subtly secularized.

The most common and perhaps the most sober criticism of our American culture as a whole rests upon the assumption that all things holy and lovely tend with us to be vulgarized. Perhaps the most conspicuous example of this cultural vulgarization is that which is necessitated by a commercially supported radio. There are many unlovely phases of our life which we would prefer, if possible, to conceal from you when you visit us, but we cannot silence our broadcasts. The BBC, though it may be decorous to the point of dulness, saves you from our perpetual prostitution of great art to the manners of the advertising man. You could have had in peace time some intimation of our daily radio fare by listening late at night to Radio Luxembourg and its constant concern for liver pills. When on a memorable Sunday afternoon in December 1941, the stated programme was interrupted by an announcement from the White House that the Japs had bombed Pearl Harbour, this momentous news was followed at once by the summons, 'Give mother foot-ease for Christmas'. Our commercial broadcasting companies claim that by selling time on the air they are able to command artists who would otherwise be beyond the resources of a governmentally controlled radio. This may well be so. Yet the total potpourri, which fills all the entr'actes and intermissions of an opera or a symphony concert with the celebration of oil and motor cars, tobacco and cosmetics, is equalitarianism with a vengeance.

Such, also, is the most serious criticism commonly brought against American religion: its sanctities are too often and too shamelessly accommodated to the secularity of the common mind. The mood of our church services, the style of our sermons, even the stuff of our faith are levelled down to the vernacular of every day. There is among us an uneasy suspicion that the process has already gone so far that we may have lost, perhaps beyond recall, a feeling for that 'wholly other' which all great religion requires. Certain also of our own theologians have voiced this suspicion unequivocally:

The plain fact is that the domestication of the Protestant community in the United States within the framework of the national culture has been carried as far as in any western land. The degradation of the American Protestant Church is as complete as the degradation of any other national Protestant Church. The process of degradation has been more subtle and inconspicuous, but equally devastating in its consequences for faith.[1]

Our situation is not, however, quite as simple as it may seem, for back of our equalitarianism there lies the old prophetic ideal of the whole of life lived as a single consistent experience. In fact we may have levelled religion down too far, but in theory we still cling to the hope that we may also level common things up. Hence one of the more marked differences between the religion of America and that of the old world: the idea of the church is not and never has been the centre of our religious interest. We are more interested in the kingdom of God in its totality.

Among the best modern statements of this equalitarianism, which would lift secular things to the level of things spiritual, is one which was given us some years ago by Mr H. G. Wells. How far his words represent with you a tradition or an ideal is for you to say. Meanwhile they are faithful in their letter, as well as their spirit, to the aims of countless American Christians. The fact that their realization may still be far off does not deprive them of their felt validity. This is the way the average American, at least all the more liberal among us, thinks of his Christianity:

The Kingdom of God is to be in the teaching at the village school, or in the planning of the railway siding of the market town, in the mixing of the mortar at the building of the workman's house.... There is no act altogether without significance, no power so humble that it may not be used for or against God, no life but can orient itself to him. To realise God in one's heart

[1] *The Church Against the World*, by H. Richard Niebuhr *et al.*, p. 162. Willett, Clark and Company, Chicago, 1935.

is to be filled with the desire to serve him, and the way of his service is neither to pull up one's life by the roots nor to continue it in all its essentials unchanged, but to turn it about, to turn everything that there is in it round to his way.... Many men and women are already working to-day at tasks that belong essentially to God's kingdom, tasks that would be of the same essential nature if the world were now a theocracy; for example, they are doing or sustaining scientific research or education or creative art; they are making roads to bring men together, they are doctors working for the world's health, they are building homes, they are constructing machinery to save and increase the powers of men.... Such men and women need only to change their orientation as men will change about at a work-table when the light that was coming in a little while ago from the southern windows, begins presently to come in chiefly from the west, to become open and confessed servants of God. This work that they were doing for ambition, or the love of men, or the love of knowledge, or what seemed the inherent impulse to work itself, or for money or honour or country or king, they will realise they are doing for God and by the power of God.[1]

Our Calvinistic preoccupation with the kingdom of God gives to American Christianity another of its characteristics, its ethical concern. At this point our Calvinism, whether that of earlier times or later, goes back to its origin in the prophetic conception of religion found in the Old Testament. Puritanism, whether ancient or modern, is said to have 'an interfering spirit of righteousness'. The phrase is a literal transcript of the mind and method of American Christianity. On the older and more evangelical of our denominations this interference is addressed mainly to private habits. It is responsible for our ever renewed prohibition campaigns, for anti-tobacco crusades, for bans on dancing and card playing and theatres and even the 'movies'. Despite the conquests of Hollywood there are among us many sectarians who have never seen a moving picture. This has been the traditional area to which the interfering spirit of righteousness in the sects has addressed itself. Among more liberal churches the same spirit has now been redirected to political, economic and

[1] *God the Invisible King*, by H. G. Wells, pp. 105, 106, 109, 110. The Macmillan Company, New York, 1917.

industrial wrongs. Be it in a narrower or a wider application of this temper, the habit of interfering with the morals of society is with us second mental nature. That is why, unless we have been remade after a wholly different manner, we seem to you to be always preaching to other nations about the conduct of their affairs. We are merely addressing to other peoples that interfering spirit of righteusoness which at home we address to ourselves and to one another. The interference may be as inept as it is unwelcome, but it is not pharisaically meant. These are the terms in which we understand religion best.

As with all matters of second mental habit, these native processes of the American mind may have lost their original meaning and intention; they are, however, survivals among us of one of the major emphases in our total Jewish-Christian tradition. It is encouraging to find that a sympathetic observer of our institutions does not feel that our equalitarianism and our levelling have cost us the whole of our heritage from 'prophetism'. André Siegfried is one of the most discriminating contemporary critics of American life. In this connection he says of us:

If we wish to understand the real success of American inspiration, we must go back to the English Puritanism of the seventeenth century, for the civilization of the United States is essentially Protestant.... We must go even further, and realize that America is not only Protestant in her religious and social development, but essentially Calvinistic.... Calvin looked upon doctrines as a means to an end and taught that the duty of the individual was not to concentrate upon himself, but rather to cooperate in furthering the will of God in this world. Born anew through grace, the Calvinist has a mission to carry out; namely to purify the life of the community and to uplift the state. He cannot admit two separate spheres of action, for he believes that the influence of Christ should dominate every aspect of life.... This supremacy of conscience is the essence of religion in its purest form.....The American Christ is not the sentimental mystic of tradition, he is a leader, a sort of superman. For some time it has been common to represent him as the perfect type of social citizen, an efficient producer, almost as the successful and honest business man.... At times it seems as if the object of religion were no longer to kindle mysticism in the soul and spirit, but to enlist them and organize their energies. In this it is the most powerful lever for production that the world has ever known.[1]

For better or for worse, such is the residual Calvinism in American religion. Christianity so construed lacks certain qualities which a 'high religion' must have, but it still preserves something of the prophet's concern for righteousness, which, as has been previously said, is one of the premises in our Jewish-Christian heritage.

There remains now for final consideration the most distinctive contribution which America has made to the religious thought of the present century; that first proffered and still classically represented by William James's *Varieties of Religious Experience*. Canon Streeter once said, in conversation, that this was the most important book which had been written about religion during the first quarter of the present century. I passed this verdict on to Mr Ellery Sedgwick, who was for years editor of the *Atlantic Monthly*, and he said, 'I will go farther, and say that this is the most important book which has been written on any subject in my lifetime'. The importance of the book may easily be missed. It was, and still is, important in itself; it was even more important in what it implied and in what it anticipated.

At the time James wrote the *Varieties* orthodox religion was very much on the defensive. Historic Christianity had always presupposed an intelligible and credible external universe to which man might relate himself. This universe had expanded so rapidly that its boundaries were lost in the immensities of time and space. Men were confronted with what Tyrrell calls 'the cold and shelterless deserts of astronomical space'. With Pascal, 'the eternal silence of these infinite spaces terrified' them. The remorseless progress of the doctrine of evolution only complicated the problem for the believer. There was, in Huxley's phrase, much 'botheration about Colensoism'. The story is a familiar one, as familiar to you as to us, and needs no elaboration. It looked as though traditional religion would have to give up all its more remote outposts, and might indeed find its central position seriously threatened.

[1] *America Comes of Age*, by André Siegfried, pp. 33 ff. Harcourt Brace and Co., New York, 1927.

To all who were haunted by such dread James's work came as an unexpected and powerful ally. The book was novel to the point of seeming bizarre. At the same time it gave great succour to those who feared that their last sanctities might be invaded by agnosticism, if not outright atheism. James said, in substance, 'Whatever may be true of the universe around us, the happenings in the minds and hearts of saintly persons are indubitable and ineradicable. They are a part of human experience; they are data which cannot be denied and they are important data, perhaps the most important with which man has to reckon.' Therefore he rested the case for religion upon experience, especially upon the experience of single individuals. So far as the outer world was concerned, he could safely play with the idea of a 'pluralistic universe'. The religious universe was another and more intimate affair. He was to this extent a child of the romantic movement and would have agreed with Coleridge,

> I may not hope from outward forms to win
> The passion and the life whose fountains are within.

James's definition of religion is restricted in its scope: 'Religion shall mean for us the feelings, acts, and experiences of individual men in their solitude, so far as they apprehend themselves to stand in relation to whatever they may consider as divine.' Notice that James does not guarantee in any given instance the objective reality of that which the believer considers as the divine. But the fact that he does not give his *imprimatur* to the supposed object of any such act of faith still leaves him with what he regards as a body of significant subjective experience.

James was not a churchman, though he was a faithful chapel-goer at Harvard. He was not interested in what he thought of as the chronic religion of institutions; only in those individuals in whom religion 'burned as an acute fever'. 'Churches when once established live at second hand upon tradition...personal religion should still seem the primordial thing.' Nor was James a technical theologian, and it is one of the paradoxes of our life that the most considerable single contribution which America has made to modern religious thought should have been that of a man who was professionally unversed in systematic theology.

There has never been a second William James among us, though he has had countless disciples and interpreters. In one sense of the word he prevented successors from going on with his work because he harvested the best of a long-standing crop. On the other hand he gave great heart to the troubled and doubting, and encouraged defenders of the faith to pitch their camp in what he believed to be the inviolate and invulnerable recesses of the inner life.

We owe it to him that twentieth-century modern American theology, until Karl Barth came over the horizon, concerned itself primarily with the field of religious experience, and with an attempt to make the case for religion on that ground alone. The psychology of religion became the pearl of great price for which we were willing, if need be, to barter away all other theological disciplines.

These major motifs in James's lay theology were and still are congenial to the American temperament. His unashamed individualism is an aspect of our culture which has already been stressed. If carried to the extreme, it invites every man to become his own self-sufficient sect. Again, the importance which he attaches to experience as the rock on which religion is to rest matches an emphasis which is wholly familiar to us. Admission to membership in most of the congregationally ordered denominations has always traditionally rested upon the candidate's ability to give satisfactory proofs of his own spiritual state. His account of his saved condition, and therefore his fitness for church membership, was and still is a highly subjective matter. Furthermore, the trust which James vested in pragmatism was calculated to commend him to the practical temper of our people. If the tree produces good fruit, the assumption is that the tree itself is good. We are a practical people, and, if a religion works, we are not inclined to press the matter further. 'Religion thus makes easy and felicitous what in any case is necessary.' The result is that we have all but forgotten how to 'enjoy God forever', but, with all our defects, we do not fail to make use of him. Religion commends itself to the average American as a means to an end rather than an end in itself. It makes for good government, for honesty in business, for integrity of character, for obedience to law, for world peace, therefore it is to be professed and practised.

In the vernacular of the market place, you can 'sell' religion to any American if you can prove to him its usefulness for other ends in which he already has a prior interest.

For these reasons the psychology of religion, as a theological discipline, has been carried much farther in America than in any other land in Christendom. Indeed, it has been so constantly employed as a means of vindicating religious faith that for the moment its permutations and combinations seem to be all but exhausted. Much precise work has been done in the field, and the general findings will remain part of the permanent stuff of theology hereafter. The believer himself cannot be dissociated from that in which he believes. The motives for his belief and its modes are inwardly conditioned. All this is a highly subjective interpretation of religion, yet a time had come in the long on-going history of Christian thought when this emphasis was not merely needed, it was in its own right over-due.

The science of psychology, however, has latterly been more interested in abnormal than in normal phenomena, and the interest now taken both in the realm of the unconscious and in pathological states of mind threatens to carry this discipline into more problematical areas. The latest secular assumptions seem to imply that religion is largely a matter of primitive thrusts over which we have little conscious control, or of morbid psychoses which are hard to cure. Religion would seem thus to be an ineradicable strain of the residual savage in man, or an incurable disease. In short we are quite familiar in American theological circles with our Freud and Adler and Jung. Meanwhile the inward citadel and sanctuary to which James recalled us, and where he bade us take our stand, now threatens at the hand of the newer psychology to become an intolerable chamber of horrors. Jung, in his *Modern Man in Search of a Soul*, makes precisely this admission, If a man 'turns away from the terrifying prospect of a blind world in which building and destroying successively tip the scale, and if he turns inward upon the recesses of his own mind, he will discover a chaos and a darkness there which he would gladly ignore. Science has destroyed even the refuge of the inner life. What was once a sheltering haven has become a place of terror.'

There would seem to be little prospect in America of any immediate further elaboration of the psychology of religion. The concern of that discipline with both our normal and our abnormal states has been staked out and stated. Its hinterlands have been opened up and its underworlds explored. Much remains to be done in the application of its now generally accepted principles to the conduct of life, particularly with reference to mentally 'sick souls'. There is, however, no longer any theoretical novelty in such ventures, though there is much work still to be done in actual practice. One is reminded of Schweitzer's remark, on his return to Lambarene after his first furlough, that the poetry was past and that he was entering upon a prose period of his African adventure. The poetry of the new psychology is over, though its prose application remains.

We seem, in our religious thinking, to have come now to a parting of the ways. At the theological left there is a group of resolute persons who are convinced that we should accept to the full the logic of our liberalism over the last century and a half, and go on to an unashamed humanism. Hereafter, they say, the race must be prepared to make religious shift for itself. In his concern for righteousness man must rely upon his own will-to-goodness. The best exemplars of this humanism are not unheroic, nor are they defeatists. They would understand the remark accredited to Mr Churchill, when the final news of the fall of France came—they find something rather inspiring in their situation. The vain alliance with nebulous deities is over. Religion hereafter must be a kind of theological Sinn Fein movement, 'Ourselves Alone'.

On the other hand, there are many persons among us who are tired of the summons to self-reliance. They know only too well what Matthew Arnold meant when he said:

> Weary of myself, and sick of asking
> What I am and what I ought to be.

As a friend put it, 'Introspection is of its father, the Devil; it has cost me all the bitterest hours of my life and I am done with it'. All such welcome the prospect of some spiritual and moral 'power not-themselves' to which they may give themselves.

They are turning away from a too subjective account of religion toward a divine world without, toward what one of our thinkers has called 'the Determiner of Destiny' into whose keeping they may commit their lives.

The immediate novelty in the religious thinking of America is therefore not that which is represented by William James or Sigmund Freud, it is rather that which we associate with the name of Karl Barth. Barth has many disciples among our younger theologians, and even those who do not accept the letter of his dogma are in accord with the direction taken by his thought. There is abroad the suggestion that we should return to the Protestant confessions of the sixteenth century and even to the Catholicism of Saint Thomas. The positions of these thinkers of an elder time often receive restatement in the vernacular, and in many quarters they seem to be accepted as the only available cure for what is felt to be the all but fatal disease of liberalism. The more arresting and piquant theological writing of the time is in this vein.

Our immediate theological situation, then, is this: our most vocal theologians—one might almost say, most vociferous—are either at the humanist left or the neo-orthodox right. There remains a great middle body of persons, traditionally Christian, who are candidly perplexed and inarticulate. They have no effective spokesman. The present situation represents our native habit of going to extremes. We have not mastered the virtue of moderation: we are drunkards or teetotallers; we do not understand temperance in thought and conduct.

So far as the neo-orthodoxy of the time is concerned, it seems to many of us too much like an unashamed retreat to capture our whole-hearted consent. We sometimes wonder whether it actually is an affirmation of strong faith, whether indeed there may not be in it a 'veiled backward glance of agnosticism', and thus a subtle form of self-deception. In so far as Barth is accepted as the prophet of the movement, he is much too sophisticated for the average American layman. He may be an exciting figure in the theological schools; he is not in the least intelligible to plain people in a parish church. If he is translated into their language, the result is too much like an ancient incantation, too little like the sanctified common sense which is for the average American his final court of appeal.

On the other hand there is little immediate prospect that any great number of professed believers will follow the lead of the humanists, whether that lead be into a promised land or a desert. Common sense says, 'This is not what we mean by religion, or what we suppose religion to be. If humanism be the truth, then another name should be found for the redescription and re-orientation of our inner life. Let us get rid of the word "re-ligion" as well as the word "God", if both together are under like condemnation, and go on hereafter with an unequivocal vocabulary.'

At the two extremes, therefore, our religious thinking is at the moment sharply divided, and the proponents are moving farther apart. Whether American religion in its totality will cast its lot with the one or the other of these positions remains to be seen. My own impression is that eventually the now inarticulate middle group may find voice and may achieve, if not some synthesis of these two trends, then at least a working com-promise. The idea of religion presupposes the paradox of God and man met in one experience. When either seems to mono-polize that for which religion is supposed to stand, the dual quality which we associate with the experience is impaired. Neither the absolute sovereignty of God nor the final self-sufficiency of man preserve that which the idea of religion re-quires. It may well be that this clash of minds in modern America will issue in some clearer formulation of a contemporary theology. In any case our mind seems to be alert, not sunk in lethargy.

CHAPTER IX. *RELIGIOUS EDUCATION*

This is with us, as presumably it is with you, a stubborn and as yet an unsolved problem. The words themselves, thus related, are by no means self-explanatory. I once ventured to remark to a group of persons professionally concerned with the techniques which now bear this name that we had taken two of the most difficult words in the language and married them, apparently on the familiar theory that it is cheaper for two poor persons to live together than apart. My remark was not favourably received.

The Gospel says that unless we are born again we cannot enter the kingdom of God. The meaning and the modes of this rebirth are open to many interpretations. A minimal interpretation of the experience would seem to suggest that in maturity we should be able to satisfy ourselves afresh as to the truth and worth of religious ideas for which in childhood and youth we were as yet unprepared, and which at that period of life we had accepted on the authority of our elders. Most of the losses which the Christian Church suffers arise from the inability of mature individuals to reassure themselves as to the validity of dogmas taught them at an earlier time. This attrition suggests the unwisdom of teaching children and young people doctrines which are not assured in advance of verification thereafter.

There is much talk, mainly originating within conventional religious circles, of the pain which modern men are supposed to suffer at the loss of their religion. On this matter we have some realistic and accurate words of Leslie Stephen, which are probably nearer the fact. He is speaking of his inability, when the time for decision came, to take orders.

Many admirable people have spoken of the agony caused them by the abandonment of their old creed. Truth has forced them to admit that the very pillars on which their whole superstructure of faith rested are unsound. The shock has caused them exquisite pain, and even if they have gained a fresh basis for a theory of life, they still look back fondly at their previous state of untroubled belief. I have no such story to tell. In truth, I did not feel that the solid ground was giving way beneath my feet, but rather that I was being relieved of a cumbrous burden. I was not discovering that my creed was false, but that I had never really believed it.[1]

Whether this eventuality was Leslie Stephen's fault or the fault of his youthful instructors is beside the mark. Those of us who have had to do with young people over the last twenty or thirty years recognize its fidelity to a situation with which we are only too familiar.

Our American churches had, for nearly two hundred years, a tried and proven device for dealing with the problem—the 'revival'. At a critical moment in his experience emotional and moral pressure was brought to bear upon the wavering individual, intended to bring him into line either as a fresh recruit or as a penitent and returning prodigal. The first American revival was a strange spontaneous affair, the Great Awakening of the mid-eighteenth century. It was a reaction against the sterile dogmatism and the platitudes of the then current Calvinism. It did not altogether deny the premises of Calvinism, and kept a single-minded faith in divine election, but it seemed to open a way for that election to operate more effectually than before. The success of the Great Awakening was such that it set a pattern for church procedure thereafter in most American denominations. In all the more evangelical churches the revival became the recognized means for recruiting church members. The revival in Wales at the beginning of this century is perhaps the best parallel in your recent history to what was for years a convention with us. That revival, like our Great Awakening, was an unpredictable affair, taking place among an emotional people. Its causes and effects are still only imperfectly understood.

Many American churches expected until most recent times to conduct once a year a series of revival meetings or to join with neighbouring churches in such a common venture. For this purpose professional evangelists were brought in from outside. Through the last century the revival kept something of its

[1] *The Life and Letters of Leslie Stephen*, by F. W. Maitland, p. 145. G. P. Putnam's Sons, New York, 1906.

original sincerity, but like all usages, hardened into custom, it became standardized and was eventually stage-managed. Its practitioners were persuaded that the end justified the means, and allowed themselves methods of manipulating their hearers which were both psychologically and ethically dubious. They did not believe, with Browning, that it is 'an awkward thing to play with souls'. Indeed, one gets the impression that they unwittingly enjoyed the sense of power which attends the control of other lives.

Dwight L. Moody was the best of the more recent American revivalists. No one questions his sincerity, though there have been many high-brow critics of his taste. After one of his sermons a literary purist said, 'Mr Moody, I noted fifteen mistakes in grammar in your sermon'. To which Moody replied, 'I am using all the grammar I have for God, what are you doing with your grammar?' Moody had a single-minded love of God and a catholic love for humanity; his sole aim was to mediate the love of God to men. After his time the professional breed began to disimprove. Billy Sunday seems to have been, for the present at least, the last of this particular succession. His theology was too crude, his methods too sensational, and his preliminary commercial demand upon the communities to which he went much too shrewd, to command the moral confidence of our people as a whole. Billy could sober up a drunkard, at least for the time being; of that there was no doubt. He could by his high-pressure psychology incline the wavering to the side of the saints rather than the sinners, but the whole transaction was too theatrical and too calculated. In spite of much moral good which he undoubtedly did, he defeated his own ends, and discredited the tradition in which he stood. He represents the final degeneration of what had been one of our major religious institutions.

The American scene has been so often 'burnt over' by revivals —to use a metaphor which comes from our familiar experience of forest fires and prairie fires—that there is little standing timber or dry grass left among us to kindle in precisely this way. This is one of the reasons why, in spite of its American founder, the Oxford Group Movement has not had in America the success which apparently it has had in England. Even though the techniques of Buchmanism were addressed to the upper social classes—the Salvation Army in a dinner jacket—rather than to the down-and-out, many of the old psychological skills of the American revivalist survive in the movement, and we here can still identify them in their new dress. With us the Groups have failed to make the slightest impression upon the great middle body of non-liturgical American Protestantism. Their American constituency has been largely among Episcopalians, supplemented by recruits from non-churchgoing circles. To all those for whom revivalism had been a familiar feature of church life, and for whom it has now become a spent force, the Groups had little novelty to offer. The movement has succeeded mainly in liturgical churches which have in the past consistently refused to practise or to participate in revivals of the conventional type. To the members of such churches the Groups have apparently come as a new experience; religion may be something more than decorous attendance at Morning and Evening Prayer. As for the official interest which the Church of England, in some quarters, has taken in the Groups, I have been told by one who ought to know, that the church realized in retrospect that it had made a mistake in the case of Wesley, and was determined not to make a second mistake of the same sort and possibly of the same dimensions, in case the Groups were destined to become a major fact in the religious life of our time. This issue will be for you to decide. Meanwhile, with us, Buchmanism, for all its apparent novelty, was an old story. We are tired of religious revivals as we have known them in the last half century. Their theology was often incredible; their applied psychology was filled with emotional dangers; their influence was too ephemeral; their permanent residue was too meagre; their mechanism too obvious, too well oiled; and their commercial instinct much too highly developed.

The passing of the religious revival from the American scene has deprived our churches, however, of what has been for at least a century the one most familiar means of recruiting the ranks of members, both young people and lapsed adults. We have been faced therefore with the necessity of finding some other means of winning and holding members to the churches.

Among all but the most backward churches it is now agreed

that education ought to be, and probably is, the best way of interesting our people in religion and of identifying them with one or another of our many denominations. Our efforts, therefore, have been turned from the religious revival to religious education.

At this point the state can be of little help to us. You use the term 'public schools' to describe what we know as 'private schools'. The public school is, with us, the tax-supported institution maintained by and for the whole community. In practically all states these schools provide primary and secondary education; they are our grade schools and our high schools. In many states, indeed in nearly all, save some on the northern Atlantic Coast, state universities have come into being, carrying the process of education on to the A.B. degree, through four years of undergraduate college work and even further, if the student desires professional training in law, medicine, education, engineering, or one and another of the industrial skills. These tax-supported institutions make few charges, if any, for tuition to a resident of the state. A boy in Illinois may start in the kindergarten and graduate from the University of Illinois a lawyer or doctor, having paid only the most nominal fees for instruction anywhere over the twenty years required by the process.

Given the separation of church and state in America, no public school or state university may offer anything approaching to religious instruction. A studied secularity is maintained from first to last.[1] It is true that certain minimal practices are here and there allowed and even required, but these are of a formal and neutral kind. The constant bone of contention is the use of the Bible at the opening session for the day. In twelve states such reading of the Bible is required in the lower-grade schools; in twenty-four states it is permitted; in other states such reading has been pronounced unconstitutional and is prohibited by law. The Supreme Court of the State of Wisconsin has declared that the

[1] It is said that in certain states, such as Virginia and Texas, which have a fairly homogeneous Protestant population, the high schools are now venturing a limited amount of religious instruction. If so, such a venture is a radical departure from what has been hitherto the fixed convention. Whether such experiments can succeed remains to be seen.

reading of the Bible—presumably the King James's version—to non-Protestant children, makes of the school an illegal place of Protestant worship.

In states which permit Bible reading in the schools, but where there is a strong Catholic minority, such reading is objected to on the ground that the King James's version is a Protestant book. Whether Catholics would approve the use of the Douai version is another matter. In states where the Jewish element is large the use of the New Testament is regarded as in excess of that which the law should permit. On this whole matter it may be said that the usage in any given state is determined by the religious complexion of the major part of the electorate. In states which have some .approach to racial and religious homogeneity, serious objection to a minimal practice is seldom raised. But even such practice must be kept well on the safe side of anything like a denominational interpretation of the Bible, and thus of the suspicion of propaganda. A little resolute agitation on the part of determined secularists or of minority sectarians, who claim that the principles of religious liberty are thus liable to violation, will reduce such practices as there are to the vanishing point.[1]

From the standpoint of convinced believers public education in America is, therefore, in sad default at what they regard as the most important part of all education. They have only one redress, to found and maintain their own schools. The Catholics are the group most largely driven to this alternative, though the Lutherans also in proportionately smaller numbers accept the same necessity. Such schools, if they are to do public duty in the total field of education, must satisfy responsible boards of education that the instruction they give in secular fields conforms to accepted standards. They may not, however, receive any public moneys for their support. Catholics are thus laid open to what they regard as unjust double taxation in the matter of the support of schools; they must pay their part for the support of public schools which their children do not attend, as well as the costs of the

[1] Cf. *The Pastor's Legal Adviser*, by Norton F. Brand and Verner R. Ingram, pp. 37 ff. Abingdon-Cokesbury Press, New York and Nashville, 1942.

parochial schools which the church prefers them to attend. This is felt to be a genuine grievance, but no legal redress has as yet been found. The Catholic Church maintains in America some 6000 parochial schools with about 2,000,000 children in attendance. Other churches maintain their own grade schools and secondary schools in much smaller numbers. The average American Protestant, on the other hand, is content that his child go to the public schools, indeed seems to prefer that he should do so. His preference is prompted by his equalitarianism, and by a 'low-church' rather than a 'high-church' interpretation of the whole nature of the church and its relation to other institutions round about.

Some easement of the situation is being provided by a practice with which you also are familiar. The laws of a few states permit public schools to excuse pupils during school hours for religious instruction to be given by their own denominations. The state of New York has recently conceded such released time. Instruction may be given in a nearby church, in some neutral centre, or occasionally in rooms rented in the schools by the churches for this purpose. At the best, any such arrangement is a makeshift. Apparently it is no more successful with you than it is with us, if recent prolonged correspondence in the *Spectator* may be trusted. To put it on no other grounds, it seems to presuppose an utter ignorance of the minds of children.

The problem becomes more complicated, and in a way more serious, at the level of higher education. There are 500 or 600 accredited institutions of higher learning in the United States. Of these more than 300 are church colleges, originally founded by one or another of the denominations and still traditionally identified with a parent church. Over 100 are Roman Catholic. In the more conservative and centralized churches such as the Lutherans the connection is still close and the control direct. In the more liberal Protestant Churches the tie is weakening. Most of these colleges were Frontier ventures and therefore lie west of the Atlantic seaboard; they are in force in precisely those areas where the great state universities have now become popular centres for undergraduate life and work. The denominational colleges were usually first on the ground, pioneering in the field a century ago, but most of them are inadequately endowed. Financially they are badly handicapped in comparison with the universities; their equipment is poor, much of it already falling into disrepair; their salaries are low; their curricula limited. Many of them are trying to meet this situation by imitating in miniature the elaborate programmes of the state universities in the hope that they may thus attract students. Such readjustment prompts them to stress a denominational catholicity if not a candid secularity. This mistaken strategy is costing them the confidence of the churches which founded them, and is discouraging further financial help from what has been hitherto their recognized source of support. The mortality among the small denominational colleges of America promises to be high in the near future.

The problem of religion in the state universities is a difficult one. Some of these universities enroll 10,000 to 15,000 students; they are candidly coeducational. The administration can allow itself at the best only an occasional and neutral recognition of religion. A commencement ceremony may warrant a prayer by a minister; there may even be a sermon for the graduating class, delivered in an auditorium or an armoury (all state universities make provision for military drill and ROTC training), since no such institution would be allowed to build its own church or chapel.

It is of course utterly impossible for a teacher, even in a state university, to deal with the history of the sixteenth century or to lecture on the poetry of Browning without making some reference to religion, but instruction in these fields has to be as non-partisan as possible. The instructor must conceal his own private convictions and affect the would-be dispassionateness of the pure scientist. It is only fair to say that if anything approaching religious propagandizing is prohibited, anti-clericalism and aggressive atheism are likewise prohibited. Young people in our state universities run little danger of being religiously corrupted by the instruction they receive; though there may be slight prospect that they will be evangelized. Officially, and at this level, anything like religious zeal is out of bounds.

The major denominations accept this situation and are attempting to meet it. In most of the larger state universities they make provision for the religious care of their own young people by off-campus centres and extra-curricular activities. They put up attractive churches nearby a university and supplement them by adequate parish houses for their student work. They staff these denominational foundations with alert young ministers who are familiar with the religious difficulties of modern youth, both theological and moral. With one or two exceptions these church centres have no academic status, though they are usually recognized by university officials as providing an easy and welcome solution of an otherwise awkward problem. Meanwhile students who have been accustomed to go to church when at home find in the university town a near-by church of their own denomination manned by ministers who understand them and speak their language. This whole development in the state university communities has grown up during the last twenty-five years. It apparently represents a redirecting to the student world of certain activities developed by the denominations during 1917–18 in their war-time attempt to meet a religious need in our training camps not fully met either by the chaplains or by the YMCA. We have then, in America at the moment, the rather curious paradox of denominational colleges soft-pedalling their religious tradition in an attempt to be cosmopolitan, and state universities providing by vicarious means an opportunity for the cultivation of the religious life and the maintenance of religious habits, which in theory are no part of their concern. The religious condition of our denominational colleges is by no means as wholesome as tradition suggests it should be; the religious situation in the state universities is by no means as secular as the letter of the law would seem to require. A boy is not as sure of keeping his religion if he goes to a church college, or as sure to lose his religion if he goes to a tax-supported university, as the theory in either case might suggest.

In the older private colleges and universities, mainly along the Atlantic seaboard, the problem is entirely different. These institutions are for the most part not coeducational. Men go to Harvard, Yale, · Princeton, Columbia, Dartmouth, Amherst, Williams, and the like. Women go to Wellesley, Smith, Mount

Holyoke, Radcliffe, Vassar, Bryn Mawr. These institutions have a longer rather than a shorter history; nine of the men's colleges go back to colonial times, some of them to the very beginnings of our American life. Higher education for women did not become an accepted fact much before the middle of the last century, and when our women's colleges were founded, they were modelled on precedents set by the men's colleges.

Since these institutions rank high, they have no difficulty in meeting whatever academic standards a state law requires. For the rest they are free to order their affairs as they choose. Though many of them were religiously conceived—in the first instance for the training of ministers—none of them is any longer chargeable to a denomination or to the totality of denominations. Few, however, disregard religion, either in theory or in practice. Most of them have their chapels and maintain regular religious services, always on Sundays and often on week days. Attendance which was once compulsory is now for the most part voluntary. Harvard pioneered by giving up compulsory chapel in 1886, but there has not been a Sunday or a week day in term time since when morning worship has not been conducted. Once the rebellion against compulsory chapel has been won, not a few of the students return of their own accord to the voluntary chapel services as being a matter of good custom in the community. The attendance is by no means that of a majority, but it is not less in relation to the whole number than is the churchgoing in the world outside. In any case the services are kept up, and full official provision is made for their maintenance. More often than otherwise there is a chaplain in residence, who is a recognized member of the faculty.

These services, however, are not allowed to become the tacit property of any denomination. They gather, as college preachers, ministers from all the major Protestant denominations. They tend also to include an occasional liberal rabbi. A Catholic priest is sometimes invited to be the preacher, but his ability to accept is conditioned by the consent of the local hierarchy, and such permission is usually refused. Theoretically a Catholic priest cannot participate in a formal service of worship other than that of his own church. Therefore, welcome as such a preacher might be in some of our more liberal institutions, Catholics are usually self-exiled from a share in these religious rites.

In our own University the Harvard Memorial Church is in charge of a Board of Preachers, consisting of a resident professor, himself an ordained minister, who shall serve as chairman, and five members from outside the university, representing at least that number of Protestant denominations. Our terminology is rather stilted, but the pattern is not unlike that of a cathedral chapter with a dean and canons. Few of these chapels have any denominational affiliation, and few of them have ever been formally consecrated. They are in theory neutral ground; in practice interdenominational meeting houses. Their services of worship are, however, mainly given to 'the preaching of the Word'. The ecclesiastical difficulties which still attend corporate interdenominational communion are such that the student who wishes to communicate regularly is best referred to a local church of his own denomination.

The American college chapel, so conducted, is open to two quite opposite appraisals. Persons who hold that religion must have the cutting edge of keen dogmatism say that these chapels are so dulled as to be almost meaningless. They suspect the religion mediated by such means of being some lowest common denominator which arouses no enthusiasm. Others think of these chapels as being pioneering ventures in church unity, well in advance of any other single usage in the community outside, and thus as 'houses of the interpreter' where the many denominations may achieve a better understanding of one another and perhaps some increase of Christian charity. There is a measure of truth in both verdicts. Meanwhile my impression is that chapel-going among American college students in our private universities, though by no means the general practice, is appreciably better than that in the Oxford colleges and at St Mary's Church, as I have seen it in recent years. Again, this may be merely another phase of the American lag.

When it comes to instruction, our private colleges and universities are quite free of the restrictions imposed by law on tax supported institutions. They may teach what they will. Few of the older and larger institutions pay formal academic respect, in their curricula, to their ecclesiastical origins or original religious purpose. The courses of study are secular to the extent that they are no longer predominantly theological. On the other hand, there is entire freedom to give full recognition to religion, as a massive historical fact and a cultural influence of the first magnitude. In general the treatment of the subject is sympathetic rather than hostile. In some of the newer institutions there may be an inclination on the part of young intellectuals on a teaching staff to testify in a lecture room to the joys of their own emancipation and to dismiss all religion as an outworn fetish. This is not, however, the dominant temper of a faculty. The American pattern of life suggests in these matters a willingness to live and let live. One sometimes thinks that the cause of religion would be better served in our private universities were there more open criticism of religious conventions in the classroom.

Meanwhile, the normal college course for the American undergraduate does not restrict him as closely to marked out lanes as is the case in an Oxford Honour School or a Cambridge Tripos. Whatever his 'field of concentration' for the A.B. degree (not B.A. !), he has some chance to browse in 'electives'. Thus, a man concentrating on physics or chemistry may well include in his programme a course in history or literature or philosophy. Another man will concentrate on one of these latter fields. The announcements of courses in philosophy and history and letters-in-general unashamedly include many religious subjects. Biblical literature; English literature of periods particularly concerned with religious issues; outline courses in the histories of Judaism and Christianity; church history at the critical periods; the history of religions in general, beginning with primitive religious practices in the remote past (or in remote places in the modern world) and coming down through the major classical and non-Christian religions; the psychology of religion; the philosophy of religion—all these are familiar items in the lecture announcements of any given year. Nor are such announcements made in vain; there is a substantial response from students, who either make one of these fields that of their own concentration, or who elect a course or two to supplement and perhaps to correct a too restricted interest in some other area.

Altogether the American college student in the private universities has an opportunity to get, if he wishes it, decent and intelligent instruction on religious matters. No single lecturer would think of using his classroom as a recruiting station for his own religious convictions, and all together attempt to be as fair-minded as is possible. Such procedure, again, may be open to the criticism meted out to the college chapel: it is too neutral to serve the cause of personal religion effectively; it needs the supplementary process by which, in Saint Augustine's words, 'One loving heart kindles another'. Yet the student in any one of the institutions named above, as in many another, can get, in the terms of modern intelligent thought, some understanding of all that is meant by religion as one of the two or three determining factors in the making of history and the o lering of society. I have the impression that in this respect our students are better placed than yours. The equality of all denominations before the law, and the want of any single dominant nation-wide denomination, enables the private colleges and universities to deal with religious subjects on the common basis of scholarly procedure. It goes without saying that in such institutions the instruction, if it must wear a label, is vaguely that of a liberal or modernist Protestantism. This, indeed, is the familiar charge constantly made against it by persons of Catholic or Fundamentalist sympathies.

As for the rest of the problem of religious education, it is one to which the churches are seriously readdressing themselves. One of the milestones in American religious thought is a little book published nearly a century ago by Horace Bushnell, a distinguished Congregational minister, on *Christian Nurture*. He parted company with the idea that to be fully Christian one must experience a conscious rebirth in maturity—a rebirth traditionally anticipated as the result of conversion at a revival meeting—and said in substance that children are born into the church, already members of the Christian family; therefore their birthright status should be acknowledged from the first. There remained, to his thinking, the problem of so nurturing them through childhood and youth that, without undue emotional disturbance or intellectual revolution, they should grow up in the church toward the fulness of the stature of Christ. This book, non-Episcopal in its origins, was instantly fastened upon by the Episcopal Church as a welcome statement of its own convictions and has become one of the classic manuals within that church. Bushnell's ideas were revolutionary for his own communion, since tradition had previously required conscious experience of something like a spiritual rebirth in late youth or in early maturity.

At the present moment the more sober and less ecstatic types of church expect their children to grow up into the Christian life, and thus into church membership as a result of their training in church schools. The old Sunday School was a hit-and-miss affair. Its only text was the Bible, and the Bible was far too often taught as being uniformly inspired, a high plateau rather than a mountain range with its valleys and its peaks. Not only so, it was taught as though the bare facts, once imparted with a casual moral appended, were themselves immediately serviceable to little children. As a result children came to know many names, places and stories which lingered in their memory as verbal tags thereafter, but which had little relation to life. The mere biblical fact was expected to work like a doctor's prescription, and little distinction was made between the needs of children and adults. In particular no care was taken to indicate the development of religious ideas or the progressive elevation of moral standards as the total narrative proceeded.

Against this whole inaccurate and indefensible presentation of the Bible modern liberal Protestantism is now in revolt. The findings of accredited biblical scholarship are translated into the vernaculars of childhood and youth. The child is given from the first a sense of perspective in his Bible study. Furthermore, the modern church school curriculum does not restrict itself to the Bible. It goes on into church history and often deals with the lives of saints, scholars, ecclesiastics, missionaries, social reformers, all of whom have forwarded our understanding of Christian principles and their application in each new age.

In the attempt to get this task well and truly done churches have turned to our schools of education to learn whatever is known about reliable pedagogical methods. Our departments of education in the American universities and our teacher's training schools have been for a half century more concerned with method than with substance. Child psychology is their premise and point of departure. They tell us that the course of study should be, in the current jargon, 'student-centred' rather than 'subject-centred'. This emphasis is itself a transcript of our hereditary individualism and our recent preoccupation with psychology. The pendulum has swung so far that many curricula are primarily determined by the immediate interests and capacities of the child rather than by any felt obligation to a body of truth which should be passed on from generation to generation. Modern American education tends to be too subjective, and therefore by no means a process of acquiring substantial knowledge. Some years ago a cheerful girl presented herself to the warden of a women's college and was greeted with the question, 'Well, now that you are here, what do you wish to do?' 'I want to learn to express myself', said the freshman. The warden gently suggested, 'Oh, my dear, don't you think you could find something more important to do than that?' The warden was the custodian of an elder tradition, the girl was a product of all that is implied in the Montessori method. Again we have the rival claims of the world within and the world without. The issue can never be settled in theory. In practice American education, running true to the national culture, has swung well to the subjective left.

Most schools for the training of the clergy now have a formal department of religious education, in which professional attention is given to the preparation of the clergy for decent conduct of their church schools. There are in addition many independent institutions training students, usually young women, for paid professional positions in our larger parishes as directors of religious education. All this is a vast improvement on the casual practice of the past, with its misinformation and innocent ignorance of anything like modern biblical learning. As a result the mind of a child now going through a well-organized church school in a liberal parish is not loaded with a cargo of misinformation which will have to be jettisoned at a later time. What is taught ought to stand the test of a later and more mature knowledge of the facts.

There remains, however, one residual doubt as to our modern programmes of religious education. For their pedagogical techniques they depend upon secular institutions. The deliberate aim is to make our best teaching skills available for church schools. The result has been a levelling out—we will not say for the moment whether a levelling up or a levelling down—of the whole educational procedure, both sacred and secular. In their moods and methods the Sunday School and the day school tend to be identical, the former adopting the manners of the latter. Nor does a difference in subject matter automatically preserve for religion those qualities which we associate with it. If it be true that our American services of worship tend to be vulgarized, it is equally true that our Sunday Schools tend to be secularized. Somehow the necessary element of contrast has been sacrificed in the process of accepting and applying approved methods of modern pedagogy. Indeed, the subject-matter seems at times to fall wide of the accepted areas of the sacred. Thus, an Episcopal bishop has recently said that in the Sunday School which his child attends the child is learning to draw airplanes and trucks (lorries), while he has to go to day school to learn to sing hymns! Certain churchmen, fearing the consequences of this subtle secularization of the up-to-date church school, despair of it altogether, and are replacing it by formal services of worship for children, believing that intimations of religion are better conveyed by simple acts of adoration, praise and thanksgiving. In short, we are as yet very far from having solved the problem of the religious education of our children.

No account of religious education in America can be complete without some brief reference to the training of the clergy. If we have any reason to be apprehensive about the future of organized Protestantism in America, that reason is to be found in the lack of anything like a proper professional training of our clergy as a whole.

The prosaic truth had best be told at once, and then interpreted, for we can, in some measure, explain that which we may not deny. America saw a few years ago an epidemic of 'surveys'. These surveys represented a desire on our part to obey the ancient injunction, 'Know thyself'. Until most recently we have not had either occasion or time to know ourselves. Hence the survey of one after another of our affairs, conducted by trained investigators. Thus, the Institute of Social and Religious Research, a well financed and well staffed organization, recently made the first thoroughgoing attempt which we have ever seen to find out something about the Protestant ministry of the United States in its entirety. The results were published in four considerable volumes. The work is now ten years old, but there is no reason to suppose that its findings are not still substantially true to the present facts.

A preliminary word must be said as to the process by which the American student is prepared for a profession. That process is, when in full force, rather longer with us than with you. After leaving the high (secondary) school, the student goes on to a four years' course in college and receives the A.B. degree. This degree does not represent any appreciable amount of pre-professional training for which he receives academic credit thereafter. If he plans to be a doctor, he will be well advised to take as much work as possible in biology and chemistry. If he is going to be a lawyer, he will naturally do some work in constitutional history. If he is going to be a minister, he may perhaps concentrate in philosophy or history or the social sciences. These undergraduate studies do not, however, appreciably shorten his studies thereafter in a professional school. He must expect, whether in law, medicine or theology, to spend three and sometimes four years in the post-graduate professional school. There is no chance in Harvard, for example, as there is in most English universities, to read theology as an undergraduate candidate for the bachelor's degree in Arts, and then go on to some diocesan seminary for a further final year. Seven to eight years after leaving the secondary school are required by institutions of the first rank before our students are through with formal studies leading to the professions. There is abroad a widespread feeling that the average American boy is delayed too long in getting to the practice of his profession. There would seem to be waste time and effort somewhere along the way. We shall probably see the process speeded up hereafter by some overlapping between the colleges and the professional schools.

We have in America what is all but unknown among you in

England, a group of theological schools which are graduate departments of private universities, or are closely affiliated with such universities. Thus: the Divinity Schools at Harvard and Yale; Union Seminary in New York, affiliated with Columbia University; the University of Chicago Divinity School, with which three other schools have now become associated to form a single faculty. These schools are all interdenominational in practice, and enrol students from most of the larger Protestant denominations. Men go from these schools direct to the ministries of their several churches. It is true that many church leaders prefer a man to be trained in a church seminary, but a certain type of student is attracted by the great universities, and by the non-sectarian nature of their divinity schools.

Meanwhile, each of the denominations has its own standards and usage in the matter of academic tests for ordination, and, save in those instances where church control is exercised over both a college and a theological school, the theological schools are not in a position to force their standards upon the churches. With the best will in the world they may set a high academic standard; the churches are free to accept or to ignore these standards as they choose. In recent years we have seen the organization of an Association of American Theological Schools which has attempted to set minimal standards for the entire group of institutions, some 150 in all. An accredited list of the better seminaries has been prepared, and those which fall below the required level of academic decency are encouraged to bring their curricula and degrees up to the norm. Yet once again there is no ecclesiastical pressure which can be put on an institution by this Association; the only pressure is that which we commonly mark and dismiss as 'moral'. Presumably some unaccredited theological schools are thus shamed into raising their standards. Perhaps the main difference between the accredited and the unaccredited schools is this: the former require for admission the A.B. degree from a reputable college; the latter, which for the sake of convenience may be called 'Bible institutes', require no college degree and are willing to accept students direct from secondary schools. In the figures which follow, however, these Bible institutes are listed as theological schools.

As far as we can now determine, by the aid of figures in the federal Census and the findings of the survey just mentioned, 22 per cent of the ministers in America are graduates of both college and seminary, 29 per cent are graduates of either college or seminary, and 49 per cent are graduates of neither college nor seminary. This means that half the clergy of the United States have never had any professional education, and no general education beyond the high school level. The bare recital of these figures is humiliating and disquieting. State boards are requiring ever higher standards for the practice of law and medicine, as well as for the teaching profession, but over standards for the ministry the state has no jurisdiction. Churches may do as they please. This retrogressive movement of one of the historic professions away from the other professions with which it is usually linked, and away also from the steadily rising level of public intelligence throughout the land, must make any thoughtful American wonder what the future of our Protestant Christianity is to be.

The averages given above represent, however, extremes which are very far apart. Of the major Protestant denominations in the United States the Lutherans require and succeed in getting, to a degree not realized by any other body, a full college and seminary training for their ministers, representing seven years of study. Only a fraction of their clergy, less than 10 per cent, have had neither college nor seminary training. Then follow the Reformed Church, the Northern Presbyterian Church, the Episcopal Church, and the Congregational Church. By the time we come down the scale to the last of these denominations we have reached a body in which half its ministry has had the full college and seminary course, a quarter of its ministry has had one or the other, and a final quarter has had neither.

At the other end of the scale we have the southern churches where the percentage of untrained ministers is highest. There are, for example, some 40,000 Negro churches in the United States, Baptists being in the great majority. There is little opportunity in the south for the higher education of the Negroes, and their churches are therefore dependent upon such ministers as they can recruit from their own circles. Less than 10 per cent of the Negro

Baptist ministers have had a full college and seminary training, 80 per cent have had no higher education at all. The figures for the Negro Methodist Churches are only slightly better. Nor is the situation appreciably improved in the Southern Baptist Church (white) or what was, before the recent union, the Southern Methodist Church. Their percentage of fully trained clergy is still very low. Among the Disciples of Christ, a denomination previously mentioned, hardly 20 per cent of its ministry has had what may be regarded as a normal academic preparation for the profession.

Behind these disquieting facts there lie, as their past occasion, two causes. The first was the prominence of the lay reader and preacher on the Frontier. In the days of rapid expansion westward the elder churches in the east could not find missioners enough to send out in the covered wagons and on the flatboats. Therefore local communities had to raise up laymen from their own numbers to serve as their ministers. Let it not be forgotten that, during all the earlier years at Plymouth, the Pilgrim Fathers were without a settled minister and the laity conducted their own services. This has been a necessity with which, generation after generation, American Christianity has been familiar, perhaps only too familiar.

, Furthermore, the individualistic polity of churches congregationally organized enables any single company of Christians to call and to ordain their own minister. Over most of our history the local church has sought the counsel of sister churches in the immediate vicinage before proceeding to an act of ordination, but in theory the right of the local church remains unimpaired. Of churches organized on this polity the Baptists are by far the most numerous, and the fact that in the north only some 35 per cent of its ministers have had a full professional education—the figure is about 15 per cent for the Southern Baptists—suggests a probable close connection between the polity and the standards for the ministry. A pious and personable layman, aware of a call to the ministry, would probably be able, under such circumstances, to receive ordination at the hands of a congregation, backed by near-by churches which understand and wholly approve of such procedure. We have therefore, in the United States, a large percentage of ministers who must be academically reckoned, despite their ordination, as lay preachers.

This situation is not of itself all bad. A devout and earnest layman is often a better minister of religion than a perfunctory clergyman. The Society of Friends in all its elder meetings depends solely upon a lay ministry, and no one questions the propriety or the efficacy of that ministry. Many of our small sects in America follow the Quaker pattern and make no pretence whatsoever to ordaining a ministry. They hark back to the anti-clericalism of early Anabaptism, and stand thus well over at the Protestant left.

Practically, the usage thus far has enabled churches to come into being and to thrive on our Frontier, in want of duly trained and accredited ministers. The churches of our west and south-west have had to do for themselves precisely what the churches of the east had to do in colonial times, in want of clergy sent out from the old countries. If need be, an American congregation can make ecclesiastical shift for itself, and the necessity has been until most recently a constant one. Not only so, but this easy identification of the laity with the ministry—which is after all only an honest expression of our Protestant faith in the priesthood of all believers—has given the American laity as a whole an interest in our churches and a stake in their conduct which must account in part for their vitality.

The difficulties which one can see ahead arise in part from the gulf which must slowly widen between what the founders of Harvard called 'an illiterate ministry' and a progressively literate citizenship. These uneducated ministers are, in the main, spokesmen for Biblical Fundamentalism. They know little or nothing of the findings of modern science, and care less. They take their stand upon the letter of the Bible. Not only so, but there still is in some of our larger denominations an hereditary antipathy to an educated clergy. This again is a cultural matter. It is, on the part of those who have never had any higher education, a defence mechanism by which they justify their illiteracy to themselves. Here we have our equalitarianism levelling down the learning of a people, rather than levelling it up. The inspiration of the Holy Spirit is invoked to do duty for book-learning. While the

operations of that Spirit are by no means restricted to the channels
of theological seminaries, it is doubtful whether the clergy may
make the bland assumption that a lack of all theological learning is
of itself a guarantee of the gift of the Spirit. Anti-intellectualism
still survives in many of our more conservative bodies, particularly
in communities where higher education has not been the order
of the day for youth. Mr Moody honestly used all the grammar
he had for God, and every one honoured him for so doing. But
the deliberate cult of ungrammatical speech and an uninformed
mind is not necessarily an assured means of access to the world
of the Spirit.

In those denominations which set high standards for the training
of ministers, and which maintain reputable theological schools,
there is no grave shortage of candidates for the ministry. We lack,
it is true, men coming in large numbers from our more privileged homes, but we are rid, at the underprivileged bottom of
the scale, of men who drift into the ministry because they can
think of nothing better to do. The United States is known to you
as a country rolling in wealth; the stipends of our ministers are
no part of that legend. The average salary of all ministers in the
United States is less than $1500. Even in a state like Massachu-
setts, where the scale is high, the salary of ministers in the major
denominations does not average over $2500–$3000. For a man
who must plan for the support of a home, the education of
children, provision for illness and old age, there are countless
industrial jobs and professions which will yield more income than
the ministry can give him. The American youth who enters the
ministry does so at a financial sacrifice and solely because of his
concern for the cause of religion. We may be mistaken in our
appraisal, but it is our conviction that, at present, in the denominations which are making serious efforts to maintain the
standards of their ministries, the mean level of intelligence and
ability in the student group of any given seminary is higher now
than it was twenty-five or fifty years ago. We may miss some
of the outstanding men at the top, but we are rid of the academic
problem children at the bottom. If there are not as many
'alphas' as there once were, there are fewer 'gammas'; and
'beta minus' tends to become a straight 'beta' rather than a

'gamma plus'. These are the men whom you will find in our city parishes in the north—sincere, competent, keen, and single-minded. You would not suspect and you certainly would not meet the illiterate type described earlier unless you were to travel far afield and off the beaten paths. Our hope is that the decently trained men may leaven the whole lump, and by their example persuade backward denominations to raise their academic standards for ordination. An illiterate ministry is, in the end, doomed. Most denominations are coming slowly to realize this truth, but they have heavy arrears to make up before they can bring their ministry abreast our American professions as a whole.

CHAPTER X. *THE NEGRO CHURCHES*

No account of American Christianity will be even imperfectly complete which does not make full and grateful mention of the Negro and his spirituals. The cabins and churches in which those moving songs were first sung deserve a chapter for that reason alone, if for no other reason. This haunting folk-music represents one of the two or three original contributions which America has made to the total Christian corpus.

Spirituals were formally introduced to us many years ago, as they were introduced to you, by the Fisk Jubilee Singers (of Fisk University, a coloured school in Tennessee), who were given audience by Queen Victoria. Since that time the recovery and the rendering of the spirituals have become both an academic quest and a semi-religious cult. It is one of the paradoxes of the present situation that the modern emancipated Negro is more and more unwilling to sing these songs in public, since they were the product of slave days and are felt to carry with them still the pathos and the stigma of slavery. Yet no Negro artist, let us say Roland Hayes whom you have often heard, would care, or dare, to finish a programme without a few concluding spirituals. Whatever his own personal affection or disaffection may be, something more than the voice of an individual artist is heard when he sings, 'Were you there when they crucified my Lord?' He is the voice of a race, the cry of a people.

Not only so, but we white people feel about the Negro that he is American in a way that many later comers are not. If Catholicism takes pride in the pattern for American life said to have been foreshadowed by the Maryland colony, the Negro takes pride in the fact that one of the first Americans to fall before British muskets in the Revolution was a certain Crispus Attucks, who was shot down in that brawl calling for police action which is now dignified by the name of the 'Boston Massacre'. Attucks was a Negro. Incidentally, the anniversary of the 'Massacre' is still solemnly observed year by year in Massachusetts, and more often than otherwise is made the occasion for a proclamation by

the Governor, reminding us of the price which we paid for our
liberties. One cannot wholly suppress a suspicion that this pious
pronouncement may have a political eye squinted toward the
Irish vote.

Meanwhile, the Negro has grown up with us. He was, as
Booker Washington used to say, the one immigrant who had
been 'invited' to come to this country. His history goes back to
colonial times. For better or for worse he is one of us: originally
both in north and south as a member of the household or as a
valuable possession; eventually as the occasion for a great war.
He was often cruelly abused as property, while as a cause he
remains an ideal still to be realized. Yet there he was and here
he is, part and parcel of our life. Take out of the record our own
tributes to him—'Old Folks at Home', 'Massa's in de Cold Cold
Ground', and 'Old Black Joe' were written and composed by a
white man—and you have taken away something that is part
of our national heritage, a mode of our thinking and feeling
rather than their content. Lithuanians still seem rather alien; the
Negro is an aspect of ourselves.

Yet there is no blinking the fact that he is to-day perhaps our
major domestic problem. There are 13,000,000 of him, a tenth
of our population. In a state like Mississippi he is in the numerical
majority. In the south he is still largely disfranchised by various
police measures and legislative dodges which prevent his getting
to the polls. The more accurate word would probably be 'un-
enfranchised', since he has never been allowed to realize fully the
rights which, by Constitutional amendment, were assured him
by the northern victory in the Civil War. In recent years neither
of the two major political parties has ever dared to tackle the
Negro problem candidly, making some proposed solution a
plank in its platform. Bills in Congress having to do with relief
of more aggravated situations, such as lynching and the poll tax,
usually have a stormy passage or fail to pass. Much good work
is being done by patient and right-minded individuals in both
races, but the leaven of their influence still has a sodden mass of
prejudice and perplexity to permeate. We are concerned with
the problem and unhappy over it. We often prefer, at a safe
distance and without direct responsibility, to celebrate the

sorrows of India. We get thus a vicarious sense of being true lovers of liberty. One sometimes feels that if at least a share of the righteous indignation which we can easily muster for your Indians were to be soberly addressed to our Negroes, our ancestral passion for freedom might become rather more realistic and a little less sentimental. In short, we do not yet know the answer to our Negro problem, but at least we know it as such.

The problem has become increasingly acute in recent years. The Solid South is traditionally Democratic. The Negro had, or thought he had, the northern Republicans—'Marse' Lincoln's party—to thank for his emancipation. Therefore, while living in the south, he looked to the north with a childlike trust which, alas, has not been redeemed by the event. The first World War brought a large number of Negroes north as industrial workers. Their advent into our cities created a new housing problem. A whole area of Chicago, for example, not far south of the centre of the city, which had been a shabby genteel residential district for whites passed suddenly and almost totally into black hands. There was much friction at the boundary lines between the white and black sections of the city. A similar and much worse situation has developed in Detroit during the present war, where a Government-built residential quarter, presumably intended for white workers, has been allocated to Negroes. Detroit has latterly had the worst race riots we have seen for many years. Apparently northern cities do not know how to assimilate this unexpected influx. A curious situation has, in the meanwhile, developed in Harlem, the Negro section at the northern tip of Manhattan Island in New York. Many of the tenements are owned by Jewish landlords, who have a watchful eye for the letter of their leases. There seems to have sprung up in that section a localized race antipathy in which the white Gentile is not involved; it is solely a Negro-Jew issue vigorously pressed on both sides. A similar situation obtains in Chicago. If the truth be told, the northern, white, Gentile Protestant gets a curious sense of relief from this report of a race problem for which he cannot be held immediately responsible, whatever his initial and ultimate responsibility may be.

The main gravamen of these industrial newcomers in the north is, however, that of discrimination against them on the part of the orthodox labour unions. The northern white worker fears the advent of cheap black labour and resists its recognition. The American Federation of Labour does not accept Negroes as members of its unions. At this point the unorthodox CIO (over which John L. Lewis ruled for many years) has tended to cast its lot with the Negro. The affinities of the leftist unions of the CIO have been with communism rather than with genteel socialism, and communism trades upon a professed indifference to racial distinctions. White workers of the CIO have made a point of fraternizing publicly with Negroes, and the prospect that our whole Negro population may go communist has frightened the conservative white world, capital and labour alike. Much of the latest recrudescence of anti-Negro sentiment in America is due to the economic situation, rather than to traditional insistence on social observance of the colour line.

Negro leaders are now telling us that the experience of their people in the north over the last twenty-five years has disillusioned them. Their naïve confidence in the Republican party has been destroyed; their idealization of the north has been brought to a rude ending. The minds of these industrial workers in the north are said to be, in many instances, turning wistfully back to the southland. They have the feeling that, in spite of the disabilities they have suffered at the hands of the former master race, southerners probably understand them better than northerners, and that the sober hope of a final solution of their situation is to be sought in the south, rather than in the north. It is further said that this divorce of the Negro mind from its sentimental attachment to the Republican party may well encourage southern Democrats to take a more liberal and sympathetic attitude toward the Negro. To-day he is not necessarily a political opponent. Some go so far as to prophesy a possible realignment of parties in the south as a result of this frustrated northern trek of black workers over the past quarter of a century. The whole issue has been complicated by these more recent experiences and has now become a national problem, rather than a sectional problem.

Meanwhile international affairs over the past twenty-five years have added to the Negro's sense of grievance. During the first

World War we had 400,000 Negroes in the armed services, and of this number 200,000 saw active service in France. There was a difference of opinion in the white GHQ as to their effectiveness in action, and, on their part, a vague feeling that they were too often assigned to duties behind the lines rather than in the front line.

The Abyssinian *débâcle* made a profound impression upon the American Negro and stirred him deeply. He seems to have cherished a passionate hereditary idea that Abyssinia was the one ancient Negro state still remaining independent and inviolate at the heart of an otherwise conquered continent. Both as a memory and as a hope Abyssinia was a symbol of racial liberty and self-sufficiency. He overlooked its ruthless slave-driving and idealized it out of all relation to the actual fact. Nevertheless, its cynical conquest by Mussolini—the helpless League standing by and consenting to its death—consolidated Negro sentiment in this country against the white man's world and ways, as nothing else had done for half a century.

It is too early as yet to appraise the consequences of the present war upon Negro opinion in this country. The draft has impartially gathered him, together with his white brothers, into the Army. It is commonly said that he is not as welcome in the Navy, save in a menial capacity—perhaps in a ship's galley. As to his place and part in the Army, the end is not yet. Much will depend upon the opportunities finally given him as a soldier, and his ability to vindicate trust placed in him. He is not, temperamentally, a fighting man, and has perhaps more to learn than has the ordinary white man. Meanwhile, his presence in England, alongside our white troops, has given you a much too accurate impression of the racial antipathies here in America. We would have preferred not to have hung out this particular bit of our as yet unwashed linen in your back yard.

Given the economic and political disillusionment which the Negro has suffered in recent years, and his uncertainty as to whether he is to receive, as a soldier, a whole-hearted vote of confidence in the present war, his visibility in this area is low. The present situation may be described, and for the moment dismissed, in brief bitter words, spoken off the record by one of the wisest and best of the Negro leaders in this country—an educated and devout Christian: 'For the first time since the Emancipation Proclamation the American Negro doubts whether the United States really gives a damn for him, or his wife, or his children, or the future of his race'. Such is the present problem put to us and stated for us by a tenth of our people. The Republican party, which seems to have learned little in the last half century, is sentimentally sympathetic but also ingloriously apathetic. The traditional dependence of the Democratic party upon the white southern vote holds out at the moment little promise of easement.

And now—the religion of the Negro.[1] That religion would seem to be wholly indigenous. Various attempts have been made to seek and to find its origins in the far-off forests of Africa. Vachel Lindsay's stirring poem, *Congo*, is a cultural transcript of these efforts. Thus far, however, such ventures have proved little or nothing. It is true that from time to time secret Voodoo practices are reported in the deep South. These practices have been transplanted from the West Indies; they did not come direct to us in the old-time slave ships. It is further true that much of the emotionalism which we associate with Negro religion may have to be explained in the terms of its primitive origins in Africa. Meanwhile the formal content of the religion of the American Negro, his theological ideas and his churches, is a transcript, modified for his own uses, of the religion of his white masters in the days of slavery.

The Catholic Church disallows, in theory, all racial discrimination. It further holds that a Christian may not be owned as a slave. This doctrine was not able to stand up against the demand for slave labour in the south, though the church required that some religious instruction be given slaves. Meanwhile Catholicism had in many ways, in its missions to the native Indians of both continents, a better record than that of the Protestant Churches. It has been strangely less concerned for the Negro,

[1] The standard volume on this subject has been for many years, *The History of the Negro Church*, by Carter G. Woodson, Associated Publishers, 1921, which may now well be supplemented by *The Negro's Church*, by Benjamin E. Mays and Joseph W. Nicholson, Institute of Social and Religious Research, 1933.

even though the distinction between a red man and a black man has no warrant in the faith. That faith in its entirety has been recently reaffirmed by a distinguished American Jesuit.[1] As Father LaFarge points out, the failure of the Catholic Church to make any great headway among present-day Negroes is due to the suspicion on their part that it is primarily a white man's church, which can never become their own as certain Protestant denominations have become. The Negro's distrust of Catholicism, rather than the indifference of the Church itself, apparently accounts for the relatively small number of Negro Catholics in the country—only some 300,000 in all, as against 6,000,000–7,000,000 Protestants.[2] The Negro, having been propertyless over most of his life in America, now takes special pride in the ownership of his own church buildings. Catholic practice, which vests title to the property in the total church rather than in the local congregation, deprives him of one of the deepest sources of satisfaction in his corporate religious life.

As for the earlier Protestant Churches, their usages varied in the several colonies. If missions to Negroes did not imply manumission—and this point was often safeguarded in the statutes —certain churches were willing to attempt the Christianization of the slave. The Society for the Propagation of the Gospel, founded in London in 1701, extended its mission beyond the colonists to Indians and Negroes as well. It did courageous and charitable service to this cause. The one province which took a whole-hearted interest in the spiritual needs and the moral state of the Negro was, as one might expect, Pennsylvania, but its Quaker principles and practice won it much ill will in other colonies. It is, of course, the distinction of the Society of Friends to have pioneered in the anti-slavery movement. The name of John Woolman will never be forgotten among us. By the end of the eighteenth century slave-holding had ceased among Friends. The New England Yearly Meeting for 1782 could

[1] *The Race Question and the American Negro*, A Study of the Catholic Doctrine on Interracial Justice, by John LaFarge. S. J. Longmans Green and Company, New York, 1943.
[2] This is the figure given by Father LaFarge. The Census reports a much smaller number.

report no slaves known to be held by its members. In 1784 only one slave was left in the Philadelphia Yearly Meeting. Friends were at this point eighty years in advance of the country as a whole.

Yet the single mind and the good will of Anglicans and Friends failed of the response they deserved. A modern Negro historian tells us why this was so. Both were at a cultural disadvantage in attempting work for the Negro. The rituals and the dogmas of the Episcopal Church baffled him, and he found the quietism of Quakers equally hard to understand. The one was too elaborate; the other too mature in what must have seemed to be its over-simplification of the spiritual life. Even to this day, the historian tells us, Negroes think of the Presbyterian and Congregational Churches, as well as the Episcopalian, as 'intellectual' denominations, and are repelled by the much learning which they impute, perhaps overgenerously, to these bodies.

In the years immediately following the Revolution there was in all churches an uneasy feeling that the glorious principles of liberty were not as yet accommodated to the awkward fact of Negro slavery, and this uneasiness prompted, both in the homes of the masters and in their churches, some attention to the religion of their black property. At home in the big house a white mistress would often teach the children from the cabins to read, to read above all else the Bible. In some instances Negroes were admitted to white church services, though they were relegated to an upper gallery. The term 'nigger heaven' still lingers on among us as a designation for any top gallery in a theatre or public hall. In other instances white preachers were appointed to minister to separate Negro congregations.

As the lot of the slaves worsened toward the middle of the nineteenth century, the attitude of the Negro toward white churches was determined primarily by the position which any given denomination took on the fact of slavery. The New School Presbyterians, as we have already seen, tried to dodge the issue and succeeded in remaining undivided until the onset of the Civil War. The Episcopal Church in the south never considered slavery a sin or made it a matter of discipline. Of the major bodies, the Baptist Church, running true to form in its theoretical devotion to the principle of liberty, seemed to the Negro to be the most sympathetic. While the polity of the Baptist Churches did not allow a national organization to impose its ruling upon individual churches, and thus to discipline the membership of a whole denomination, many individual churches, particularly in the north, were outspoken in their opposition to slavery. It is to this fact, probably more than to any other, and to the ease with which such a church may be organized, that we owe to-day the great predominance of coloured Baptist Churches over their nearest numerical rival, the Methodist. Eighteenth-century Methodism had been equivocal; Whitefield had been a slave holder, and had advocated both slaves and rum as a means to the economic betterment of Georgia. Wesley himself, as we have already noted, had no sympathy with the Revolution and its corollary concern for liberty. It is true that after the Revolution the Methodist Church joined with Baptists in fostering sentiments which proposed equality of whites and Negroes in the churches, but with the waning of Republican ardours these sentiments were conveniently forgotten.

During the middle years of the nineteenth century the Negroes in the south were neglected religiously by their white masters. First they were relegated to the fringes of white congregations and later segregated in their own churches, though still ministered to by white preachers. In so far as these ministers contented themselves with the 'pure gospel', separate coloured churches were tolerated.

There was, however, candid opposition to a Negro ministry, since it was feared that such ministers would use their pulpits as a vantage point from which to incite insurrection. It is true that the first independent Negro Church in the United States was one founded in South Carolina in 1773–5. But such churches were not generally encouraged in the south as long as slavery was in force. Emancipated Negroes in the north were in the meantime free to go ahead with the organization of their own churches and began to do so soon after the Revolution. The Abyssinian Baptist Church in New York, to-day the largest single Negro congregation in the United States, was organized in 1808. The African Methodist Episcopal Church was founded in 1816. White neighbours cooperated with their Negro fellow Christians in making considerable gifts for the building of churches and the payment of ministerial salaries. By common consent in both Methodist and Baptist circles it seems to have been tacitly agreed that whites and blacks were better off worshipping apart. After the Civil War the ex-slaveholders of the south were quite willing to be rid, in their churches, of members whom they could no longer control, and were wholly content to 'let my people go' —as the words of the spiritual have it.

The Negro fastened at once upon the Baptist precedent as giving him his best pattern on which to organize his own churches. The independency of this type of church did away with any ecclesiastical overlordship, and thus with all reminders of past servitude. Moreover, white Baptists, despite the formation of their own southern pro-slavery church, had manifested over many years more concern for the principle of freedom than any of the other strong denominations. The independence of the local congregation, the absence of any elaborate ritual or involved theology, and dependence upon the Bible as the seat of religious authority—these and other kindred characteristics fitted the Negro's temperament and needs. Here was a church in which every man was equal to every other man, and in which the dream of freedom could be speedily fulfilled in fact. It is no wonder that this denomination took so quick and deep root in the minds and hearts of a freed race, or rather, that the emancipated blacks were rooted so soon in its faith and polity. By far the largest number of Negro Churches in the United States are to this day Baptist in their organization and connection. The Methodist Church is next, but numerically it follows afar off. Thus it is said in the south that if you find a Negro who is not a Baptist, you can be sure that there has been a Methodist raiding in the vicinity. In so far as Methodism supplements the Baptist bodies among Negroes, its appeal to them rests upon its concern for immediate experience and its permissive sanctions given to the more uninhibited type of emotionalism which we associate with the camp meeting.

The Negro Christian has still to be won in any numbers to the ritualistic, doctrinal, 'intellectual' type of church. Denominations so designated attempt to carry on sober and conscientious work

among Negroes, mainly in the field of higher education, but
their success has been meagre as far as numbers are concerned.
The conventional Negro preacher still prefers to boast that he
'has not rubbed his head against any college walls'. As with the
more obscure white sects, the cult of anti-intellectualism is
plainly a form of psychological and social compensation.

His church has meant more to the American Negro than any
other institution with which he has been connected. Even in
slavery days it had tended to become a thing by itself. With his
emancipation it furnished him at once his first and best opportunity to find himself and to express himself in the terms of
corporate life. 'The Negro', says one of his recent historians,
'must eventually rely solely upon himself, and not until he
emerges from a state of dependency can he hope to secure the
recognition of other groups. The white man is rapidly tiring of
carrying the so-called burdens of the Negro. The Negro home,
church, school must, as fast as possible, become sufficient unto
themselves.' His schools become self-sufficient only slowly,
because of his poverty. He by no means always owns his home;
he is more often than otherwise a tenant farmer or a share-
cropper. But his church is his own. To the building of its
edifice, the maintenance of its fabric and the support of its
ministry he has given freely. It has been to him the one sign and
seal, above all the other aspects of his life, of his emergence from
servile dependency to self-respecting independency.

So also with the ministry, which has been for nearly eighty
years the most obvious opportunity for leadership open to any
single ardent Negro. If Adler be right in saying that the secret
springs of life in our humanity are to be identified with the
promptings of the will-to-power in us all, then the ministry
offers the Negro his best chance to gratify that will. American
testimonials, whether concerned with white men or black men,
tend to stress the 'capacity for leadership' in the recommended
individual. So much is this true of us that, if these testimonials
are to be taken at their face value, our land must be by this time
fairly well depleted of persons who, *faute de mieux*, have to be
designated merely as followers. Oxford upper common rooms
are only too familiar with this bit of American jargon, as they

review the papers of Rhodes Scholars applying for admission to one and another of the Colleges. The prospect that any one of us may become a 'leader' lingers on as a heritage from Frontier days. The Negro, so far from having an immunity to this idea, is particularly liable to it. The one inviting way out and way up and way ahead for the aspiring Negro has been for years the ministry. Until most recent time the leaders of the race have uniformly been its preachers. It is only latterly that Negro doctors, lawyers, educators, journalists, poets, playwrights, actors, and musicians have begun to come into public notice. To a degree which has been true of no other stock in the country, the church has been the peculiar possession of this people, and their clergy its acknowledged spokesmen. The minister, in spite of much secularization among the more emancipated coloured classes, is still all things to his race, and not a man with a restricted professional function.

Meanwhile, the religion of the Negro remains reminiscently that of slavery days. Politically the race is only as yet imperfectly emancipated and enfranchised; economically great parts of it are in semi-serfdom; intellectually it is deliberately kept illiterate. In a recent year America as a whole spent an average of $101 on each of its white pupils in tax supported schools; $12.50 on the Negro. In the same year Mississippi spent $45 on each of its white boys and girls; $5.45 on its Negro children. The more serious institutions of higher learning conducted by white people for Negroes, or maintained by Negroes for themselves, are making an effort to bring the people as a whole abreast of something like a mature modern interpretation of religion. They are pioneering into a future which is still remote. Let any Negro who has taken a theological course in a northern seminary go back to his own people in the south, and he will be met by the indifference and suspicion of his congregation. There are in the north Negro churches which now tolerate, even though they may not heartily welcome, modern Protestantism. In the south, however, the coloured Baptist Churches get little encouragement to move in even a mildly modernist direction, since the powerful environing white southern Baptist Church is in America the recognized citadel of biblical Fundamentalism.

One of our more progressive Negro educators has given us an appraisal of the mass religion of his people. 'Their ideas of God adhere strictly to traditional, compensatory patterns. They are traditional in the sense that they are mainly those of orthodox Christianity as set forth in the Bible, with primary emphasis upon the magical, spectacular, partial, revengeful, and anthropomorphic nature of God as revealed in the Old Testament;... ideas of God that are being rapidly discarded in an age of science.'[1]

The Egyptian bondage of God's people, the exodus from Egypt, the passage of the Red Sea, the destruction of Pharaoh's host in that Sea, the wanderings in the desert, and the final crossing of Jordan into the Land of Promise—these were the parables of life which furnished the constant themes for sermons and spirituals. In the days of slavery there seemed little hope of deliverance here on earth. Emancipation could come only as death struck his shackles off the slave and released him into another and happier world. Jesus was, for him, no cold Christ in a tangled Trinity, much less an inspired ethical teacher; he was the friend who had gone before into a Father's house to prepare for his black brothers their place. Neither the theologian nor the moralist can ever quite feel the imperious force of the simple summons, 'Steal away, steal away, steal away home to Jesus'.

There is no point at which the liberal Protestantism of America is farther removed from traditional Christianity than at this point. In a little monograph, *War and Death*, written during the last war, Freud says that modern man is essentially dishonest in the presence of death. He keeps the idea at arm's length during his lifetime, and concedes it only with perplexity and resentment as it finally forces itself upon him in the circle of his home or in his own person. He does not know what to think of it, because for so long he has studiously avoided thinking of it at all. Therefore all that may lie beyond the inevitable mediatorial fact of death is even further removed from his mind. However these things may be with you, they are only too true of us. American Christianity is for the most part two-dimensional, extending only in contemporary space. If it lacks the depth and perspective

[1] *The Negro's God*, by Benjamin E. Mays, p. 14. Chapman and Grimes, Boston, 1939.

given by an awareness of history, it lacks even more markedly the traditional Christian reference to all that is meant by eternity. We pride ourselves on our intellectual courage and candour and realism. At this point, however, we are timid and wholly unrealistic. A committee of one of our major orthodox denominations, charged with preparing religious pamphlets for use by soldiers, recently rejected a manuscript which had been submitted to it, on the ground that, 'It speaks of death too often, and fighting men will not want to be brought face to face with that thought any sooner than they have to. It is bad psychology to present it to the men.' How far removed that prudential statement is from Henry Adams's account of the refectory in Mont Saint Michel, where the knights sat about the table listening to Taillefer's songs of battle. 'Sooner or later all those men were to die in the large and simple way of the eleventh century.... First or last the whole company died in fight, or in prison, or on crusade, while the monks shrived them and prayed.' Granted that the average American still hopes that the time may come when he need not die in vast numbers in precisely those ways, the fact remains that he much prefers not to think of dying at all, even in any other way.

It is at this point that the Negro spirituals are perhaps our most moving statement of an inescapable fact and a serene hope. Somehow, not even our classic hymns of heaven have the untroubled conviction of the spiritual. 'I walk in the moonlight, I walk in the starlight, I lay this body down.' There is in those words a calm self-possession which might strengthen less confident souls. I have read countless books and lectures on the immortality of the human soul. Nothing which I have ever read moves me and reassures me as does Paul Robeson's rendering of 'Deep River, I'm goin' to cross over into camp ground'. This may be sheer sentimentality; I can merely record the fact. I can match that haunting song only with Bunyan's line about 'all the trumpets sounding on the other side'. More than one American finds, therefore, in these simple lyrics about camp ground an expression for doubts and hopes and longings which the conventions forbid his mentioning to others, if not even conceding to himself. He allows himself this furtive theological self-indulgence on the ground that all such sentiments are just Negro spirituals, nothing more.

The emancipated Negro, like the modernist Protestant, has foreshortened the picture and has attempted to restate his hope of heaven in the terms of an earthly Utopia. We can hardly blame him for so doing. The symbolism remains the same: bondage, flight, freedom, wanderings, and arrival in a land of milk and honey. These transactions now take place in the terms of present life. Thus, a brilliant Negro journalist, writing of his people to-day, takes the title for a recent book from one of the old, familiar spirituals, *Good Time A-Coming*. The question is, how long the old symbols will last, wanting the depth of earlier faith and feeling. They were in the first instance religiously conceived; they have less expectation of life when restated economically and politically. Can they survive indefinitely the subtle erosion of secularism?

Indeed, the whole problem of the future religion of the Negro moves in this area. As with the Jew, so with the Negro; once he breaks with his orthodox ancestral faith in its literal forms, he is like a released pendulum which swings to the other end of the arc. It is difficult to arrest him at that point which we might call the golden mean of modernism. Many if not most of the Negro leaders to-day, particularly those who have put their racial treasure in the keeping of the communist party, are frankly irreligious and anti-clerical. There is in their verse and prose— much of which is very powerful—a strain of bitterness, of cynicism, and nascent revolution. The Negro population in the north, particularly its upper circles in the great cities, is in an inflammable condition, and firebrands of their own kind are not wanting to kindle them. The conventional fabric of democracy is in more danger from this type of man than is the sanctity of that southern womanhood which dares not walk abroad alone on a dark night. A modernized Christianity for their own people still seems to these radicals too reminiscent of the old anodyne of heaven offered the slave as an opiate, too half-hearted in its vindication of a professed concern for liberty, equality and fraternity. Way back in the 1830s Harriet Martineau noted the advertisements in the New Orleans papers of the sales of occasional lots of 'pious negroes' as being an especially good bargain. They would give no trouble here and now. The modern radical Negro agitator regards his pious brothers as one of his liabilities; they are an obstacle to the full and final freedom of the race. This menace of Negro radicalism to our conventions, if it be such, is however still peripheral, not central. It comes from the intellectual fringe, not from the heart of the people, with whom the old other-worldly symbols still keep valid meanings.

There is one other aspect of the religion of the Negro which deserves mention—his monumental patience. One is reminded of the line in Synge's *Riders to the Sea*, in which the old mother says, 'There's nothing more the sea can do to me now'. There is nothing more that America can do to the Negro than it has done. Racially he knows the worst, and through it all he has endured. The acquiescence of the Negro in whatever befalls him may be dismissed as a striking example of that slave morality from which the world's would-be supermen are seeking to deliver us all, white and black alike. But the temper of which we are speaking is not that of a false humility. The Negro has to a marked degree a native dignity, which no affront or cruelty has ever destroyed. He is in this respect not unlike the American Indian, and here, if anywhere, the myth of the noble savage would seem to have a warrant in fact.

This patience is precisely the quality in his own people which annoys and baffles the leftist agitator. It bears the name of 'Uncle Tom-ism', and against all for which Uncle Tom stands he is in revolt. He will have none of it.[1] At this point the higher education of the Negro has come to a parting of the ways. The one greatest name the race could boast a generation ago was that of Booker Washington. He stressed the necessity for vocational education in agriculture and industry; he did not think the time

[1] Thus, the issue of *Time* for 13 March 1944, reports that a plan of the Metro-Goldwyn-Mayer studio to produce an elaborate screen version of *Uncle Tom's Cabin* has been abandoned, largely because of the opposition of the Negro press, which agreed that the story was socially significant in its own day, but was likely at the present time to increase racial tension.

was ripe for the Negro to aspire in any numbers to the professions, or to public office. He believed that, once the Negro had proved that he was an economic asset and not a liability, he would have a stronger case. This programme seems to the more restless members of the race merely a perpetuation, in slightly altered terms, of the social conventions of slavery and from such a policy they dissent. Their dissent took form in 1909 with the formation of the NAACP (The National Association for the Advancement of the Coloured People). This association proposes to bring the Negro abreast the white man in all walks of life. Needless to say it has set itself a long hard task, but it now has much white backing in the terms of both men and money. Thus there have come into being a number of colleges and universities committed to the full professional education of the Negro, so that the race now has a small group of lawyers and doctors, as well as ministers, fully qualified according to the highest standards. In such institutions Uncle Tom is an outmoded ideal, not a classic hero.

The race as a whole, however, still keeps much of its old-time patient dignity. It is for the most part silent and non-resistant when insulted and injured. At its best it does not cherish resentment. It knows now that it can endure all things. It has waited so long that longer waiting asks for no new access of virtue, since the needed virtue is already second mental and moral nature. This is the temper which the Negro minister, whether fundamentalist or modernist, constantly preaches to his people. In the recent Detroit race riots Negro ministers seem to have been more effective than the police and the military in calming their people. If, as is said, 'man is the animal that can wait', the Negro is at this point a mature human being. The patience of this people is a rebuke and an example to much of the well-meant, but short-sighted ethical impatience of our white world. It is not apathy; it is not indifference; it is not servility; it is a kind of spiritual vigil, as of those who watch for the morning and wait for the consolation of Israel. If any one in our impatient America is fitted by his history to understand that majestic phrase in the Apocalypse—'the kingdom and patience of Jesus Christ'—it is the Negro.

Note. The Negro problem is one which it is difficult for any American to approach dispassionately; yet there is no domestic problem in greater need of dispassionate consideration. Recognizing this fact, the Carnegie Corporation recently invited a Swedish scholar, Gunnar Myrdal, to spend some time here studying the whole situation. Dr Myrdal is a social economist, a professor at the University of Stockholm, economic adviser to the Swedish government, and a member of the Swedish Senate. He had a fellow countryman as his assistant. Their findings have just been published in two volumes: *An American Dilemma*, The Negro Problem and Modern Democracy, by Gunnar Myrdal. Harper and Brothers, New York, 1944.

CHAPTER XI. *AMERICAN CATHOLICISM*

It has been said that no one can hope to understand a religion unless he has first professed it and then left it. If that be so, all Protestants should have an hereditary understanding of Catholicism denied to Catholics themselves. As for American Protestantism, nothing could be further from the truth. Many otherwise fair-minded Americans close their minds against all that is implied by Catholicism; they will hear no good of it and will have none of it. Even at this late date the Roman Church is felt to be an alien fact. We have a blanket term for the many manifestations of this frame of mind—'Nativism'.

In spite of patient attempts on the part of men of good will on both sides of the line to cross the border which divides them, the Protestant and Catholic sections of the community live mainly to themselves. Though the two groups meet in business and in the practice of the professions, there is no general social give and take. Meanwhile, the Catholic Church is much the largest of our many denominations, the most powerful single church in the land.

The average Protestant householder knows Catholicism only outwardly: by its substantial churches; by the crowds pouring from its doors at the end of a Mass; by the police directing traffic at such a time—an attention seldom given to a neighbouring Protestant congregation and, if the truth be told, not always required by its smaller numbers; by the arrangements which must be made to allow maids to attend Mass; by early dinners in Lent or during a Novena preaching mission (by the way, what is a Novena?); by vague rumours that the *Index Expurgatorius* is not unobserved on news stands or in bookstores; by disgruntled comments in conservative clubs at the growing strength of the Irish vote; by the loyal patronage which parish priests accord professional baseball games; by the intransigence of the Church in the matters of birth control and divorce, and its scepticism as to the 'noble experiment' of prohibition. In all these respects we look at Catholicism with mixed emotions of envy and perplexity. Its customs are not ours, the two ways of life do not always 'mesh' like well-oiled gears. There is, however, one thing we cannot do: we cannot ignore that which we do not wholly understand. The massive fact of American Catholicism is too considerable to be dismissed by studied indifference.

It is a difficult and delicate venture for any Protestant to attempt to write fairly of Catholicism, doubly so in America. Therefore, with the generous permission of both author and publisher, I am proposing to use as the basis for this chapter a recent book, written by an English Catholic now living here, which has received both the *Nihil Obstat* of the 'Censor Librorum' and the *Imprimatur* of the Archbishop of New York.[1] The book has for your purposes the advantage of not being written by an Irish apologist. Statements of fact, and all direct quotation unless otherwise specified, come from this book. I shall refer to the author as our 'chronicler', and shall introduce my own comments by the gambit 'one' or 'we'. In this way I shall hope not to make the author himself chargeable for my Protestant second thoughts.

Catholic historians take much pride in the fact that the discoverer of America, whoever he may have been, was a Catholic. It could hardly have been otherwise, whether the time was the year 1000 (Leif Ericson) or the year 1492. If for the purposes of convenience Columbus be accepted as the discoverer, it is a matter of regret with Catholics that, save for a possible error in navigation and the threatened mutiny of his crew, he might have reached the North American mainland. A miscalculation seems to have brought him farther south than he intended, and he made his landfall in the Bahamas. From there he turned still southward rather than northward, and his subsequent voyagings, as well as the conquests made by his successors, took him across the Caribbean to Mexico. The open road thereafter led to Peru. If Columbus had kept his course and sailed straight westward he would have landed here, and our history might have been quite other than actually it has been. It is all rather like the problem to which G. M. Trevelyan once addressed himself, what would

[1] *The Story of American Catholicism*, by Theodore Maynard. The Macmillan Company, New York, 1941.

have happened had Napoleon won at Waterloo? Reminiscent pride is also taken in the fact that the earliest attempts at a settled English colony in North America were made by a Catholic proprietor, Sir Humphrey Gilbert—first on the coast of Maine in 1584 and later on the Virginia shore in 1585. Neither survived.

Permanent and successful Catholic colonization in what is now the United States was begun in Maryland in the second quarter of the seventeenth century. We have already cited Sir George Calvert, created Lord Baltimore in 1625. He died shortly after his charter was granted, and title to the province, as well as the duty of developing the territory, passed to his son, Cecil Calvert, the second Lord Baltimore. For public purposes the name Maryland was chosen as a gracious tribute to Queen Henrietta Maria; it was tacitly interpreted as being also an act of homage to the Queen of Heaven, and was undoubtedly intended to allow this dual ascription.

The crown knew full well that Sir George Calvert proposed to provide in the New World an asylum for English fellow Catholics, but the crown would hardly have dared to sanction a purely Catholic colony, even had it cared to do so. While the proprietorship was Catholic, and local privileges were accorded the faith of the proprietor, colonization, so far from being restricted to Catholics, was thrown open to all sorts and conditions of men. The chronicler affirms that Calvert's 'intention was to prove that it was possible to have Catholic and Protestant living in amity, side by side on a perfect equality, and to provide a model that others might follow'. Hence Catholic apologists maintain that Maryland foreshadowed from the first what was to become the American pattern for church and state. Here, we are told, rather than in Massachusetts or Virginia, we have the true anticipation of our present ways of life. 'It was Catholics who first thought of America as a place where Protestants and Catholics alike could enjoy religious liberty. In this Calvert was perfectly disinterested.'

Whatever the generous and prophetic intention of the first Lord Baltimore may have been, it is agreed that his son did not allow sentiment to obstruct business. 'Cecil Calvert was in some respects a driver of hard bargains—a cold, cautious, efficient man, with an eye always open to his own profit.... He was not an idealist with his head in the clouds.' He therefore accepted the conditions under which development of any proprietary province was possible, a welcome to one and all. His need for so doing was the greater because the English Catholics of the time were not, as a class, persons driven out of the homeland by dire economic necessity. Nor was there, at the moment, any naked necessity of fleeing outright persecution. The original Catholic colonists were gentlemen, often persons of appreciable substance, but they did not come in great numbers. There were only some twenty of them in the original exodus, with an indiscriminate following of two hundred and fifty indentured servants. Therefore immigrants of other faiths had to be welcomed to work the land.

There is no question, whatsoever, that, so long as Maryland continued in her original form, religious toleration was the order of the day. By comparison Massachusetts Bay was a centre of bigotry, and even Rhode Island was imperfectly emancipated. Roger Williams may not have had a heavy hand; he had however a sharp and bitter tongue. The one other American province which might be compared with Maryland was that which at a later time William Penn founded in his own name. Thus our chronicler says, 'the great idea of religious liberty... remains the chief glory of Maryland. Even though it seemed to have been destroyed before the seventeenth century was out the Maryland concept lived on, to be taken up again after the Revolution. And although religious liberty would doubtless have been established as a natural concomitant of the political liberty won at that time, it was Maryland after all, that had provided a working model. Here already was the American Church; here already Catholics were living as Americans.' It is impossible to overestimate the importance of those early days in Maryland, not merely for what they were at the time, but even more as being the source of that whole-hearted identification of themselves with the life of the country, the unashamed enthusiasm for its opportunities and its institutions, which has been characteristic of American Catholics to this day.

However, the relative paucity of Catholic settlers and the

influx of colonists of other faiths, or of no faith, complicated the Maryland situation from the first. In particular the Virginians looked with apprehension at a Catholic province abutting on their Anglican preserve and encouraged their own kind to cross the border and challenge their rival neighbours. Sooner rather than later the majority of Maryland freemen were Protestants, liable to the ministry of those whom our chronicler calls 'bigots' The fortunes of the English Civil Wars were to be reflected in the course of Maryland affairs. For a short time all Catholic practices were prohibited. But Cecil Calvert succeeded in making terms with Cromwell and toleration was restored as the order of the day even during the latter part of the Commonwealth, to say nothing of the Restoration. The period of nominal Catholic ascendancy in Maryland ended, however, in 1702, when the Church of England was by law established in the province.

The Toleration Act of 1689, while it gave relief to many sectarians in other colonies, was of no help to Catholics. Precisely the contrary was true, since Papists, together with persons who did not believe in the Trinity, were denied its benefits. There followed then in all American colonies what is still known as the 'penal period' of our Catholic history, a period which ended only with the Revolution. Priests were forbidden to say Mass in Maryland. Pennsylvania was more lenient: churches and chapels could be built and public services held. This fact brought a number of German Catholic immigrants into Pennsylvania in the early years of the eighteenth century. As for much-vaunted New England: Massachusetts was implacably Protestant, and even Rhode Island remembered Roger Williams's words about the 'Romish wolf' gorged with 'huge bowls of the blood of the saints'. The few Catholics who came into those areas had little encouragement to profess their faith, and less opportunity to practise it publicly.

The major problem over all the colonial period was that of an adequate priesthood. Calvert had originally committed care of spiritualities in Maryland to the Jesuits, but members of that order were in difficulties with the secular priesthood at home, and Calvert's initial confidence in his clergy eventually changed to distrust. He made little or no provision for their maintenance and let them shift for themselves. They were therefore left without the decent subsistence allowance made to the clergy of other colonies and provinces where there was an actual or nominal establishment. It says much for the devotion of the Jesuits that in the face of the proprietor's antipathy they persisted in remaining in Maryland as private persons, doing such work as they could. Attempts to bring out secular priests from England found few volunteers, and the ministry of the church throughout colonial times remained in Jesuit hands. It is said that up to the time of the Revolution every Catholic priest in the colonies had been a Jesuit. Their numbers were however small, and their work was handicapped by the restrictions imposed upon them by the Toleration Act. A good many south Irish had come out during the Cromwellian period, but they had to go untended by clergy, particularly in New England. 250,000 Catholic immigrants are reported to have been lost to the church during the eighteenth century, lapsing for want of any proper provision for their spiritual care. By the time of the Revolution there were only some 25,000 professed and practising Catholics in the colonies: 16,000 in Maryland, 6000 in Pennsylvania; the rest widely scattered and isolated.

The Toleration Act undoubtedly cost colonial Catholics many of their rights and privileges, but it was not the main source of Protestant antipathy. That antipathy was still the dread of Spain and France. Spain kept her toe hold in Florida. Georgia was in part colonized as a buffer state. Violent anti-Catholic 'Georgia sermons' were preached in England to encourage the settlement of this last of the thirteen original colonies. The Spaniards moved west across the Florida peninsula to dispute and divide with the French all the northern coastline of the Gulf of Mexico. Border raids back and forth between English to the north and French and Spaniards to the south were the order of the day. This menace of an alien culture to the south was ended only with the Louisiana Purchase in 1803. A little surviving strip of the east coast of Florida remained in Spanish hands for another sixteen years. Thereafter Catholicism of the Spanish type withdrew to Mexico and South America.

During the first half of the eighteenth century the French peril from Canada to the north was becoming more and more acute. The Indians living along the Atlantic seaboard had tended at first to be friendly to English colonists. They welcomed the prospect of allies who would help them defend themselves against the much more powerful tribes farther inland. The strongest of these hinterland groups was the confederation of the Five Nations, known as the Iroquois. They lived on the upper reaches of the St Lawrence and in what is now northern New York. The intercolonial wars along the disputed border of French and English possessions lasted nearly a hundred years, culminating in the French and Indian War (1755-63) in which the Iroquois fought on the side of the French. This war was, of course, the American version of the Seven Years' War in Europe. Protestant sermons at the time abound with references to the popish tortures devised for Protestants by the horrid savages. The French era in Canada ended in 1759 with Wolfe's capture of Quebec, though formal cession to England was not made until 1763. A few years after Canada had become English the colonies were outraged by the passage of the Quebec Act, granting full religious liberty to Canadian Catholics. The prospect of a possible extension of such liberties within their own borders stirred new fears in the minds of Protestants in the American colonies. The passage of this Act undoubtedly added fuel to the fires of rebellion already kindled.

It remains, therefore, something of a riddle why Catholics in the thirteen colonies threw themselves so whole-heartedly into the Revolution, as they undoubtedly did. The assumption is that they saw in the prospect of American independence an immediate opportunity to gain for themselves liberties which they had long been denied. At the time of the Revolution there were only two colonies in which they enjoyed anything like toleration. The chance of local freedom apparently took precedence in their minds over what might have been a felt obligation to the world strategy of Catholicism. Moreover, they were already potential American citizens, and they fought to translate that possibility into achieved fact. How far a reasoned and reflective theory as to the nature of their faith carried them in the revolutionary direction is a matter upon which there may be a difference of opinion. Our chronicler says that Catholics in the American colonies supported the Revolution 'because the principles of the Revolution were so closely consonant with Catholic political philosophy.... The Church has always maintained that, whatever be the accidental inequality in gift and station between man and man, they are all essentially equal in the sight of God. It is only upon such a doctrine that democracy can repose. For despite the Declaration of Independence, with its "self-evident truth" that all men are created equal, the thing is not self-evident at all. It is really a mystical doctrine, and the one institution we can be perfectly certain will never renounce that doctrine is the Catholic Church.' Protestant reviewers of Mr Maynard's book have questioned this statement.·

American Catholicism, as we now know it, begins with post-Revolutionary days. Carlyle says in his *Heroes and Hero-Worship*, that we have often seen an age calling for a great man and going down to ruin because no such man was forthcoming. Roman Catholicism in America at the end of the eighteenth century called, above all else, for a great man. Fortunately it did not call in vain. He came in the person of John Carroll. Carroll belonged to one of the old aristocratic Catholic families of Maryland. His cousin Charles Carroll, a great landowner who was known as 'the Duke of Norfolk of Maryland', had signed the Declaration of Independence—its only Catholic signatory. Carroll himself had gone for his education to France, where he had become a Jesuit; he had then lived for a time in London; and had finally returned to this country before the Revolution. He was the one obvious man to attempt the consolidation of American Catholicism after the Revolution.

The Papacy, operating at a distance, was at first reluctant to appoint bishops in America. There was little assurance that such persons would run true to ecclesiastical form so far away from headquarters. Moreover, if the truth be told, most colonists, Anglican and Catholic alike, having drunk the heady wine of liberty, were reluctant to concede residual obligations to the Old World. The best that Carroll could do for his first five years in office—1784–9— was to get himself appointed 'Prefect Apostolic' —a missionary bishop without a see. This equivocal status did not assure him of the respect and obedience of his clergy. His

position became ecclesiastically sure only in 1789 when he was
made Bishop of Baltimore. His jurisdiction extended for the
moment over the entire land, though other bishoprics were
subsequently established, sooner rather than later.

Carroll was faced with what our chronicler happily and accurately calls 'the Church Turbulent'. He had two main tasks
confronting him: first, the vindication of decent ecclesiastical
control of his parishes; second, provision of an adequate clergy.

The first problem was by no means simple. In want of bishops
the Catholic laity had often taken the conduct of parochial affairs
into their own hands. This was, in the most instances, particularly
true of the ownership of church buildings. Parish trustees held
title to the property and were loath to relinquish a right which
of necessity had been vested in themselves. Carroll had to concede
this right for an interim period, a right which in theory should be
vested in the larger body. At the time, moreover, lay trustees
were backed by the law of the land which made the local congregation the owner of its church building. Following the lead
suggested by their title to the property, trustees then went on to
claim the right to choose their own pastors. Compromise at this
point led Rome at a slightly later time to go still further and allow
the American clergy, as a special concession, the right to elect
their own bishops. The dubious precedent thus set eventually led
to what was to become the most serious crisis in the whole
history of American Catholicism, an attempt to set up an Independent Catholic Church of America, free of all reference to
Rome. Continuing concessions to trustees in the appointment of
their clergy, and to priests in the election of bishops, particularly
in the southern states, gave to this bold and seditious idea much
apparent prospect of success. 'Historical truth demands the admission that it was the Irish who were the great trouble makers
at the time.' The issue seems to have arisen in the first instance
because of the mutual jealousy of French and Irish prelates. The
Archbishop of Baltimore was at the time (1817–28) a Frenchman,
Ambrose Maréchal. Impatient Irishmen in Norfolk, Virginia,
anxious to be free of French domination, sent a statement to
Propaganda in Rome announcing that, 'in consequence of our
inalienable right of patronage our first bishop will be elected by

us'. The Norfolk party was subsequently joined by a similar group in Charleston, South Carolina. Maréchal proposed to replace an Irish priest in that congregation by a Frenchman. A plot was hatched to have a certain Dublin Franciscan proceed to Utrecht and there get himself consecrated Bishop of South Carolina. On his arrival in the States he was to consecrate other bishops. The Norfolk-Charleston cabal looked to nothing less than 'the monstrous proposal that the South set up its own Church independent of Maréchal and therefore also of the Pope'. The proposed scheme was, primarily, an extension of the principle of local trusteeship which logically led on to these extremes. The success of the Revolution, the temper of the times, and the republican enthusiasm of newly arrived Irish priests all gave political occasion, if not ecclesiastical warrant, to the plan. The danger was averted by Bishop John England of South Carolina, who devised a 'Charleston Constitution' which nominally preserved the rights of parochial trustees while actually reserving ultimate authority for the episcopate. The final stage of this drama was known as 'Hogan's Schism'—the man who gave it its name being 'a stage Irishman' who sided with his trustees against his bishop and was in due time suspended. He seems not to have been a great loss to the church, since his assets were apparently physical rather than spiritual. He had a magnificent head of hair, a fair and ruddy complexion 'which was not impaired even by the liberal use of the bottle', a glib tongue and a plausible way with women, who professed to sense 'a spiritual effulgence' emanating from him. The whole incident shows how widely the principle of independency in church matters had spread through America, and, in Hogan's case, how defenceless the congregational polity is in the presence of a plausible scoundrel. Many a Protestant Hogan continues, to this day, to foist himself upon a bewitched and uncritical congregation. Against such misadventure the polity of independency offers only ineffectual safeguards. But, since the days of Hogan's schism, there has been no serious question of an Independent American Catholic Church.

The other problem which Carroll and his successors had to solve was the staffing of their parishes with an adequate clergy. After the Revolution English priests were disinclined to come out here. This was natural. We had been seditious and, what was worse, successful. There were already a number of German priests on the ground in Pennsylvania, but they restricted their ministry to fellow nationals. The great influx of continental Catholic priests at the time was that from France, clerics who were fleeing the secularized order which followed the French Revolution. At first Carroll was inclined to welcome them. They were men of deep piety, intellectual distinction, and cosmopolitan culture. Thus, French Sulpicians were encouraged to start a seminary in Baltimore. This venture languished, not merely because of the language difficulty, but also because the gulf between the educated staff and the uneducated students was too wide and deep to be crossed by the ordinary skills of pedagogy. Carroll was satisfied that, if these 'edifying and inoffensive' Sulpicians could not succeed in America, no Frenchmen could. However, a number of French clerical immigrants rode into high office on the tide of popular enthusiasm for France which was flooding at the turn of the century. Little attention was paid to the fact that they were the victims of the very system which the crowds were celebrating. They were Frenchmen, that was enough for the average citizen.

French bishops became for a short time the order of the day. They did not share, and could not have been expected to share, our short-lived enthusiasm for republican France, and their popularity with the general public waned with our waning sympathy for a changing France. What is more to the point, they were culturally an alien element. To put it on no other ground, they could not speak English, or spoke it only brokenly. The American is to this day a docile person who likes to be harangued in the vernacular by an orator, and, in so far as the faithful were predominantly Irish, a rather sophisticated French priest could not serve their desires, however faithfully he might attempt to minister to their deeper spiritual needs. John England of Charleston confirmed Carroll's initial impression as to the unserviceability of French clergy. 'If Rome wishes to have our religion established here, the reasonable wishes of our people must be taken into account. I am daily more convinced that the genius of this nation and the administration of the French are not easily reconciled.'

The future lay, therefore, with Irish priests who began to come in steadily increasing numbers. The vanguard was not uniformly tractable. Many a clerical buccaneer, who was in difficulties at home, decided to try his ecclesiastical fortunes in the New World. Our chronicler says of the earlier arrivals of this kind: 'A priest was judged mainly by his "gift of the gab". Such being the standard of judgment, it was the simplest thing in the world for an Irish ecclesiastical adventurer, who happened to have a glib and humorous eloquence, to acquire a personal following. So also, he was likely, because of the vanity which is the besetting sin of the orator, to fall foul of the bishop's authority, to kick over the traces and, backed by his admirers, to enter into open schism.' Such was the Hogan type which had first to be disciplined, if not dismissed, and eventually supplanted by a more sober and devout type of priest, a procedure which followed in due time.

In the common American mind the words 'Catholic' and 'Irish' are all but synonymous. Our chronicler generously admits that

taking the history of the American Church as a whole, it is the Irish who have done by far the most to build it up. In the end the American episcopate became almost an Irish preserve, and though this too was to cause some dissatisfaction, it can hardly be denied that the Irish showed themselves to be the men best qualified to captain the Church. I say this because I may be accused, as an Englishman, of an anti-Irish prejudice. Actually, if I have any prejudices, they are in the opposite direction.... Not the least of the contributions of the Irish was their work in Americanising Catholics of other nationalities.

Their ardour and their success in this venture were due to the fact that the Irishman 'takes to America like a duck to water'.

The opening of the Frontier called for Catholic priests, as it called for Protestant circuit-riders. There were in particular a number of French settlers left in the territory compassed by the Louisiana Purchase. Other Catholics held over from Canada in the northern areas of what is now the Middle West. Here was an outlet and an opportunity for many of the French priests who had been at the best indifferently successful along the seaboard. A broadsheet circulated in France, seeking recruits for Frontier missions, read, 'We offer you: No salary; No Recompense; No Holidays; No Pension. But: Much Hard Work; a Poor Dwelling; Few Consolations; Many Disappointments; Frequent Sickness; a Violent or Lonely Death; an Unknown Grave.' The tone of these words has to-day a familiar ring. Mr Winston Churchill once said something of the same sort. Mankind never fails to respond to such a summons, and did not fail at that time. The bishops of those outpost sees wrote back in wry humour describing their circumstance. Their cathedrals were little wooden chapels; their episcopal palaces log huts of a most primitive kind. Bishop DuBourg of Louisiana, in acknowledging the gift of a bedstead, says that his palace is too small for such a decorative piece of furniture and that he has exchanged it for bread. Whatever the relative merits of their divided faiths and the success of their rival missions, those devoted priests shared a common lot with the 'Methodist and Baptist rabble-rousers' on the Frontier.

There are no reliable statistics as to the growth of the Catholic Church in America during the first half of the nineteenth century. There were perhaps 100,000 members in the year 1800. By 1850 the number is estimated in the *Metropolitan Catholic Almanac* as 1,600,000. The formidable Catholic invasion began in the 1840s when the potato famines in Ireland drove about a quarter of the population of that unhappy island to these shores. They landed in our coastal cities, and there for a time they stayed. They had no money to go farther, and in the cities they have remained. It is one of the paradoxes of our immigration that a people so largely rural in the Old World should have become so predominantly urban in the New World. Perhaps they wished to be near one another, and all together near a church and a priest. Perhaps their mode of life in Ireland gave them no training or fitness for the types of agriculture which this country allows. Perhaps they had had enough of bogs and boulders and bleak glens. If one has toured the west of Ireland, one can understand the seduction of the stirring life and the bright lights of a city after the grimness of Connemara or Donegal. It is the tourist who is most sensible of the charms of the west of Ireland.

German Catholics in Pennsylvania tended to move west and to continue to live on the land. French Canadians have come down from Quebec, not merely into the mill cities of New England, but into its lumber camps and on to the wide acres of the potato farms in Maine. The Portuguese are by now in almost sole possession of the cranberry bogs of Cape Cod. Italians flourish on the fringes of our cities as prosperous truck-gardeners. In short, many of the other Catholic immigrant stocks have carried over into their life here the habits of a European life spent in bread labour on the soil. Not so the Irish. With us an Irish farmer is all but unknown. The American Irishman lives in the cities; he loves the cities; in many instances he runs the cities.

The Irish began their life here, when they first came in great numbers, as hostlers and coachmen, as labourers digging ditches for water mains and gas pipes, as track layers on ever-extending railway systems, as house servants in our homes. They lived at first in ramshackle cabins on the fringes of the towns and cities; this 'shantyland' was their first staked-out claim among us. They were pitifully destitute and often unhelped in their distresses, save by their own kind. No city was prepared to assimilate them quickly, and each newly arriving ship brought still more of them. That was eighty or a hundred years ago. While it is true that there is no Catholic community or country in Europe which has not contributed to the total complex of our present-day Catholicism, and that the church does its best to minister to each race with a priesthood drawn from its own ranks, the grand strategy of the American church has been for the most part in the keeping and control of the Irish hierarchy.[1]

The third and fourth generation of Irish have come very far from their meagre beginnings here. The opposition of the church

[1] 'Over a hundred native Irishmen have been made bishops, and those who were Irish in blood, though not by birth, at least double this number. It is unquestionable not only that they have supplied the majority of the members of the American hierarchy but that they have occupied the most important sees. New York has always been held by an Irishman (except for Dubois); Boston (except for Cheverus and the Marylander Fenwick) has always been so held; Baltimore (except for the Frenchman Maréchal and the Englishman, Whitfield) has been an Irish preserve. The same thing is true of the other great dioceses.... Upon the whole it is incontestable that the guiding hands of the Church in the United States have been Irish.' Maynard, *op. cit.*, pp. 506, 507. This statement covers a period of nearly 150 years.

to mixed marriages has kept the stock relatively pure. There has been little cross-breeding, racially or ecclesiastically. They marry within their own circle. Meanwhile they have made their steady way ahead in the economic and political worlds. There are still vast numbers of them left doing the humbler forms of hand labour. For the most part, however, their trend is socially upward, and the more menial tasks in the community have been delegated to those who have come after them. To-day the Irish are found in all our professions, alert and competent. They are especially to the front as lawyers. Where their numbers are considerable, they abound in our city halls and legislatures. Many a city on the Atlantic seaboard now accepts the fact that it will normally have a Catholic mayor and a predominantly Catholic board of aldermen; many a state is habituated to an Irish Catholic governor and legislature. They go, as a matter of course, to the House and the Senate and the Supreme Court in Washington. There is only one position in the land they have never filled—the Presidency. It is still a vigorous and unspent race among us; its zest for life is often in striking contrast to the seemingly waning vitality of the older American stock, of which our modern novelists make such bitter copy. If the Catholic Irish have got on, one can only say that they deserve to have done so. It is a curiously different people from what it is in Eire. It has passed here through some kind of cultural rebirth.

The advent of these hordes a century ago became the occasion for the emergence of that 'Nativism' which we have already mentioned—an instinctive rallying and closing up of the ranks on the part of the older English stock against persons who were felt to be essentially alien. In the days immediately after the Revolution the Catholic Church enjoyed no little public recognition, if not positive favour. Conspicuous Protestants gave money for Catholic buildings, and on stated public occasions attended Catholic services. The tolerance accorded a small minority at that time was withdrawn as the numbers of Catholics began to assume alarming dimensions a half century later. Nativism first appeared with the 'Know-Nothing' party organized in 1852, which proposed the political proscription of Roman Catholics. There was in that party a reminiscent hostility to any and all European powers-that-be, carrying over from colonial and Revolutionary times; there was also, and much more considerably, fresh apprehension at the sheer mass of the Irish invasion. The Republican party fell heir to Know-Nothingism, so that to this day an Irish Republican is as improbable a person as an Irish farmer. The times saw riots and much mob lawlessness. Catholic churches and rectories were burned. The lurid narrative of Maria Monk led to most indecorous inspections of convents and nunneries.

Nativism has never lacked since that day various societies and journals with an avowedly anti-Catholic bias. The APA (American Protective Association) of the 1880s took up the cause. The Ku Klux Klan, revived in the present century, has been openly anti-Catholic, though it has never matched the excesses of its Reconstruction years in the south. Altogether the record of Protestant Nativism over the past hundred years has not been creditable to our democracy, with its supposed commitment to the principles of religious liberty. These anti-Catholic movements more often than otherwise have been promoted by agitators who saw a chance to get into the limelight or an opportunity to make money on the side. Thus, it is said that the revival of the Klan a few years ago was largely sponsored by firms which sold the necessary regalia, a sheet and pillowcase for the ghostly ritual around a fiery cross, at a pretty profit to themselves. It is only fair to say that when such proceedings get out of bounds and call for police action, the courts will usually deal effectively with offenders.

The growth of the Catholic Church over the past century has been steady. It has kept pace with the corresponding growth in Protestantism, but relatively it has not outdistanced Protestantism. A Catholic Directory credits the Church with 4,600,000 members in 1870; 6,400,000 by 1880. The present figure of 23,000,000 has been reached in the intervening sixty years partly by the normal increase of the original stock, and partly by immigration.[1]

[1] For the figures until 1880, cf. *Christianity in the United States*, by Daniel Dorchester, pp. 614 ff. Hunt and Eaton, New York, 1889. I have not attempted to enter here details as to Catholic immigration from Italy, from the Azores, and from the many countries of eastern Europe. Ac-

Opinion is divided as to the losses which the Roman Church has suffered during the process of transplanting European stocks in America. Those losses were undoubtedly heavy in colonial times, as we have already indicated, because of the lack of parish priests to care for the faithful. Bishop England said, in 1837, that had the church been able to hold all her own people up to that time, the Catholic population would have been, even then, 4,000,000. After 1850 there seems to have been in Ireland an attempt on the part of the church to keep its people at home, lest they be parted from the faith by coming here. Bishop Reynolds of Charleston told a priest going back to Ireland in 1852, 'You will save religion by proceeding, on your return to Ireland, from parish to parish, telling the people not to lose their immortal souls by coming to America'. The editor of *The Celt* (1855) advised his countrymen 'to stay at home because the Catholic Church loses sixty per cent of the children of Roman Catholic parents in the United States'. *The Tablet*, a New York journal (1864), writes, 'Few insurance companies, we venture to assert, would take a risk on the national life of a creed which puts five hundred daily into the grave for one it wins over to its communion; and yet this is what the Catholic Church is doing in these States as we write.'[1]

Plainly the situation has not been as bad as these prudential utterances suggest. The mortality has probably been no higher than in Protestant Churches. Many institutions believe that it is sound strategy to show a deficit rather than a balance, since a balance makes for complacency, while a deficit stirs supporters to make good the losses. This may have been the real aim of the Catholic pessimists just cited. In any case, immigration at the high levels of earlier years is now at an end, and losses to the Church from this cause will be much lighter than they may have been fifty or a hundred years ago. As to the human occasion for these lapses, there is a lethargy in us all, which was betrayed in

cessions from these sources have been considerable, though these strains have by no means remained as faithful to the Church as has the Irish stock. In particular the ties which bind the lower classes only loosely to the church in Italy have not uniformly survived the Atlantic crossing.

[1] Dorchester, *op. cit.* pp. 618 ff.

the remark once made to me by an Irish maid in our own home. She was most indifferent in her religious observance, and I once ventured to reproach her. She had come from a 'wild and windy corner of far distant hills' (Synge) into a crowded city, and she merely said, 'Ah! sure; God won't miss one among so many'. This is the way America affects many a newcomer.

There remains the problem whether or not Catholics will eventually outpopulate Protestants. The prohibition of birth control among Catholics and the prevalence of such practices in most Protestant circles would seem to foretell such a shifting of the ratios of church membership in America. This issue is already known in Canada as 'the battle of the cradle', where deliberate attempts are being made to increase the Protestant birth-rate, so that the western provinces may hold their own against the French stock in Quebec. Catholic families in America are, in the lower social strata, much larger than Protestant families. But one seems to observe that Catholic parents in, let us say, professional circles, content themselves with two or three children rather than ten. On this matter our chronicler candidly says, 'We cannot expect to grow by a birth-rate noticeably superior to that of non-Catholics; at any rate we are not growing that way.' This is in some ways the most surprising statement in Dr Maynard's interesting and valuable book.

As for conversions from Protestantism to Catholicism, I have already suggested that such a move is not, for an Anglo-Saxon, socially as easy in America as it is in England. You have your great Catholic families surviving from the sixteenth century. We never had families of the Norfolk tradition in like numbers and of the same distinction. Furthermore, we have never had in this country any single 'vert' to move the imagination of Americans as John Henry Newman moved that of his contemporaries, and indeed of later generations. In want of any such single commanding figure, whose example might be followed, going over to Catholicism has been a matter of independent action. Making one's submission to Rome asks of the convert in this country a social readjustment of his whole life which is not easy and which requires a depth of religious conviction that is by no means a spiritual commonplace. Of the rate of conversions our chronicler says, 'The number is still so small that it probably does not offset defections'. It is estimated at about 75,000 a year, and many of these are probably from non-English stocks.

Thus far I have followed, I hope not unfaithfully or un-sympathetically, the account of the development of American Catholicism given by Dr Maynard. I should, however, be false to the total religious situation if I did not enter two or three of the conventional Protestant reactions to Catholicism. How far these reactions are warranted, or how far they represent merely racial and ecclesiastical prejudice, are matters on which there is room for a difference of opinion. They are, however, here among us to be reckoned with. The few comments which are to follow are not proffered in every instance as my personal opinion; rather they represent ideas which are familiar commonplaces in Protestant circles.

Many of us miss in American Catholicism any wide concern for the contemplative life. We Americans are too practical, too much given to action without reflection. Theoretically we might expect the Roman Church to correct our culture at this point. American Protestants are still Bible readers. (Here incidentally is one of the differences between you and us. A British chaplain writing back from the front deplores the marked absence of Prayer Books among the men. Were he an American he would deplore the absence of Bibles.) The Douai Bible has been selling at the rate of only about 2000 a year. What are such sales among the millions concerned? In a wholly laudable effort to increase Bible reading among the faithful a group of American Catholic scholars has just put out an admirable fresh translation of the New Testament.[1]

There is among many American Protestants a widespread interest in the classical literature of Christian devotion, much of which antedates the Reformation or is of subsequent Catholic origin. Such persons follow the lead given by Evelyn Underhill in her *Mysticism*. We find little or no such concern among American Catholics. Apparently this type of literature is re-

[1] *The New Testament of our Lord and Saviour Jesus Christ,* tr. by the Very Reverend Francis Aloysius Spencer, O.P. (and editors). The Macmillan Company, New York, 1937.

garded as too sophisticated for the rank and file of the laity, and possibly as too unconventional in doctrine for the secular clergy. One realizes, in discussing such matters with Catholic professors of theology, that the mediaeval mystics were often insubordinate and at times near-heretical. They did not always walk the straight way of obedience and orthodoxy. At this point, therefore, we fail to find in Catholicism what we might expect, a common meeting ground for more meditative minds. André Siegfried, whom we have already quoted, says of the Catholic clergy in America, 'The priest who tries to save his congregation from over-rapid Americanization is himself a complete American in his outlook on life and in his daily habits. He is a business man who dominates his church on the same lines as the most practical modernists.... Like all good Americans, he believes that the intensity of business life is measured by the cubic contents of church buildings, and meditation and mystical repose seem to him little better than morbid manifestations.'[1] And even John Ireland had said, 'An honest ballot and social decorum will do more for God's glory and the salvation of souls than midnight flagellations or Compostellian pilgrimages.'

No church is more vocal in unqualified affirmation of its 100 per cent patriotism than the Catholic. So much is this so that in 1899 Leo XIII addressed to Cardinal Gibbons an Apostolic letter, *Testem Benevolentiae*, warning its recipient and his flock against the perils of 'Americanism'. If American Protestants have any reservation at this point, it is not that the Catholic Church is un-American, but that in some ways it is even too American. Our society has many glaring faults against which Protestantism is in constant and more or less ineffectual protest. Our municipal politics are often a scandal; graft on a police force, corruption in the lower courts, favouritism in the awards of contracts, special privileges for camp-followers are only too familiar. These abuses cannot be corrected in many an American city without the help of the Catholic vote, and when a general clean-up is proposed by a reforming minority, that help is by no means always assured. Let it be said that in the case of many

[1] *America Comes of Age*, by André Siegfried, p. 52. Harcourt Brace and Co., New York, 1927.

scandals of an entirely different dimension and in higher places
—for instance, Tea-pot Dome—the Catholic Church cannot be
made the public scapegoat.

In matters of national policy the Catholic Church sometimes
seems to many Protestants too uncritically patriotic. This instant
loyalty to the federal government is in part a vote of thanks for
the opportunities which the country has given the Catholic
Church thus far. The utterances of the higher clergy have constantly stressed the entire propriety as well as the inevitability
of an American Catholicism. John Ireland, the famous Archbishop of St Paul, preaching before a Catholic Congress said,
'It will not do to understand the thirteenth century better than
the nineteenth.... We should speak to our age; we should be in
it, and of it, if we would have its ear. For the same reasons there
• is needed a thorough sympathy with the country. The Church
of America must be, of course, as Catholic as even in Jerusalem or
Rome; but as far as her garments assume colour from the local land-
scape, she must be American.' No Protestant sect could be more
unequivocal. What one misses, perhaps, in these utterances is a
strain of sober, critical second thought upon all our American
institutions.

As to the constant guerrilla warfare which goes on at the polls
over matters of faith and practice, nativists seem to assume that
all the rights in these matters are theirs, and thus to resent the
imposition of Catholic ethics upon their own usage. Theoretically, however, there is as much political warrant for the Catholic
campaign against birth control as for the Methodist campaign
in favour of prohibition. If the biblical Fundamentalists in
Tennessee decide and decree at the polls that their school children
shall be construed as the descendants of Adam, who was created
on a given Friday in 4004 B.C., the minority protagonists for the
anthropoid ape have no legal redress. The fact that many
Catholic convictions and practices do not square with those of
Protestants does not outlaw them. The assumption that Protestant ideas and ways should prevail as a matter of course has no
standing in law. This, however, is not to say that a majority vote
in any given locality is a transcript of the truth. Such matters
are never settled by counting ballots.

Protestants have what may well be an unwarranted respect for the administrative efficiency of the Catholic Church. Perhaps that is because we see the church from the outside rather than the inside. At this point our chronicler makes an amusing disclaimer:

Macaulay's thesis, as everybody knows, is that the Catholic Church has survived because of its marvellous organization. Catholics of course smile at this, not only because they know that the life of the church is supernaturally guaranteed, but because (if they have seen much of the working of the machine) they are somewhat sceptical about the supposititious Catholic efficiency. The triumphs of the church have often been achieved in the face of almost unbelievable muddle.... Almost any Protestant church, in short, is better managed than the average Catholic parish.... It might almost be said that it is Catholic *inefficiency* that proves the Church divine.

This sounds a little too much like G. K. Chesterton. Perhaps we have an undue admiration for Catholic administration, but we think of the church as a well-managed and well-run society. In any case its organization allows it opportunity for a long-range, long-term policy denied to more loosely articulated denominations. 'The old firm, doing business at the old stand', keeps its accounts with history in a ledger, not in a day book.

There is, however, this difference between Protestantism and Catholicism: most Protestant discussions leading to the formulation of policies take place in the open. We are allowed to see the processes by which Protestant Churches order their ways. We never know precisely how and why the Roman Church reaches its decisions. We meet the doctrine or policy as a *fait accompli*, we do not see it in the making. It was said of the literary method of Charles Péguy that he asked his readers to share not merely in the repast, but in the preparation of the repast. Catholicism invites the world to partake of its repast; Protestantism asks the world to share in the preparation of the repast. The want of the 'town meeting' mood and manner in Catholicism sets it, at this point, apart from the traditional culture of the country. We feel its habitual method of procedure to be at this point un-American.

Behind and beyond all these reservations lies the deep and widespread belief that the American Catholic is, and in the nature of the case must be, a person whose ultimate loyalty is to a foreign prince—the Pope in Rome. That suspicion goes back to colonial times, with the then dread of Spain and France; yet it has never been finally suppressed. Catholics do their level best to disabuse us of this idea, but there it is in the common mind. The issue came to the front and into the open at the time that Alfred Smith was running for the Presidency. Our chronicler adds, 'It was lucky for the Catholic Church that he was defeated before the depression broke, otherwise he and the Church would assuredly have been blamed for the economic disaster already approaching'. 'Al' Smith's apologia in behalf of his single-minded Americanism, and that of his coreligionists, did not convince a majority of the electorate. Presumably this is the main reason why no Catholic has ever been elected President of the United States— countless voters, whether rightly or wrongly, have a feeling of insecurity at this point. A Roman Catholic is to them a person with a double political loyalty.

There is, moreover, the suspicion that Catholic subscription to the American separation of church and state is an 'interim ethic'. In an article which he wrote in 1909 Cardinal Gibbons said, 'While the union (of church and state) is ideally best, history assuredly does not prove that it is always practically best. There is a union which is inimical to the interests of religion, and consequently to the state; and there is a separation that is inimical to the interests of religion, and consequently to the state; and there is a separation that is for the best interests of both.' Gibbons, says our chronicler, merely thought that, under the circumstances which obtain here, separation of church and state is best for America. The chronicler himself goes on to add, 'The basis decided upon has never been considered by the Catholic Church as being, absolutely considered, the best basis, though American Catholics will not wish any change so long as our society is constituted as it is. . . . According to Catholic doctrine, the union of church and state is still affirmed to be the most perfect solution.' Such a union requires, however, a society predominantly Catholic, and that is not yet in sight in America. It would seem, therefore, that Catholic enthusiasm for the American pattern of life is a matter of expediency rather than principle, a necessary and perhaps a wise compromise required by the local facts. To this extent the Americanism of the Catholic citizen must apparently be taken *cum grano*.

At the present moment American Protestantism is more disquieted over the international commitments of the Catholic Church than over any of the more familiar local issues. The uneasiness is apparent in many sober quarters; it is not a matter of crude mob-nativism. President Roosevelt's action, in sending Mr Myron Taylor as his personal representative to the Vatican, seemed to imply political recognition of the Papacy and aroused widespread formal criticism in many Protestant bodies. Latterly the Catholic Church here has been publicly opposing Protestant missions in the South American countries, and that action would seem to be a departure from the Maryland principle of religious toleration, which is said to have set the formal precedent for Catholic policy in America.

More particularly there is a widespread suspicion that in its implacable hostility to communism Rome has leaned, and may continue to lean, toward dictators and their totalitarianism. We in America have yet to be as fully converted to Russia as you in England have been, presumably for the simple reason that we have not had occasion to be on this soil as indebted as you are to the valour of Russian arms. Even so, our general sympathies with communism perhaps lag behind yours. On the other hand, we have no great affection for—let us say—Franco. Our naïve trust that we may spread the blessings of our kind of democracy over Europe probably bears little relation to what will be the ultimate event. But at the moment there is in non-Catholic circles in America a fear that when the time comes to try to restore some kind of order in Europe the Roman Church may not be found a staunch ally of the American type of democracy as a pattern for other lands to follow. Whether democracy, either of our kind or of your kind, ought to be established or can be established in Germany and Italy is an open question. That is beside the mark. So far as common opinion in America goes, it is our childish confidence that we can communicate the blessings of our kind of life to the rest of the world; indeed, that such is our duty and destiny. Many signs of the time lead us to conclude that, when we attempt to do so, we shall not find the Roman Church at headquarters in as full agreement with our international mission as American Catholicism thus far professes to have been with our national institutions. It is the international aspect of Catholicism which, at the moment, concerns us most. It is not at all clear that the Holy Father and the Sacred Congregation are as whole-heartedly democratic as we might wish.

I append here the text of a succession of prayers, composed in the form of a prose poem, offered by Archbishop Francis J. Spellman at a rally of the Union of the Holy Name Society recently held at the Polo Grounds (a professional baseball field) in New York, which gathered 75,000 of the faithful. It is interesting and suggestive in that it indicates on the part of our official Catholicism that enthusiasm for America, and identification with its life, of which I have already spoken. There may be other countries in which the Catholic Church speaks the vernacular with the same warm approbation. There can be no other land in which the Church says just these words:

Lord, lift this mighty host that is America;
Too oft have we forgot our ancient heritage of faith.
The mess of pottage to our eager eyes was dear;
The gold within our coffers deadened us.
We, who by nature are between the earth and sky,
Earthward have sunk, and drunk of miraged visions.
But now, re-born,
We lift again to Thee our nation's soul.
Behold, we are Thy wheat, nurtured beneath the sunshine
    of the plains;
We are Thy grapes from vineyards,
And timber from Thy forests.
Ours are the iron sinews from out the earth's torn breasts,
And oil from earth's rich arteries.
O God, we build anew and dedicate again to Thee
The host and temple of America.
Many are we, and whole-world wide apart in space;
But one we are to-day, made one by this our common will:
That righteousness shall walk again
Among the sons of men; and welded of our plan,

AMERICAN CATHOLICISM

We would again
Be what our forebears were,
Men who did worship Thee.
And, mindful of Thy Fatherhood,
Could reach a brother's hand to brother o'er the sea.
We found Thy image then in every man,
And, finding, wrote our nation's creed,
A pledge that made us the Samaritan
To the oppressed and lowly of the earth.
In those far days our soul was young and free,
We opened arms unselfishly to all who suffered wrong;
We bowed not in our youth though foe was strong,
For we were strong in loyalty to Thee.
And strong in faith that all men should be free,
And worship Thee in liberty
As conscience should direct.
And now, amidst the ruins of a world that sought
To prosper and to live apart from what was bought
On Calvary by Christ, Thy Son,
Now come we back by that well-trodden way
That prodigals of every age have walked,
Back to our higher destiny—to Thee,
Our Father and our God,
And kneeling in the Valley of our Grief
Re-dedicate (both we who here must work and those, our
     sons and brothers overseas who still perhaps must die),
Re-dedicate ourselves to this great task that still remains,
That on the altar of our common victory,
Not to a god of war,
But to the Lord of Peace
We give ourselves anew within the wounds
Of Him in whom all men are one,
And all may yet redeem their faulty past,
Held in these wounded hands of Christ, our great High Priest.
We are a single host of grateful love for Thee,
A single will for universal peace of men,
A single soul of righteousness to be,
Lord, lift this mighty host that is America,
Reconsecrate us to-day in Thy Son's Holy Name.

Amen.[1]

[1] *The Boston Daily Globe*, 4 October 1943.

CHAPTER XII. *CHURCH UNION*

'What you are speaks so loud that I cannot hear what you say.' You will be quite warranted in applying this candid epigram of Emerson's to us if we try to say anything to you about church union. For whatever we might say would seem to be invalidated at the outset by the preposterous fact of our 256 denominations. What right have we to attempt to throw any light on the matter, when we are walking in such gross darkness?

There is a familiar type of person who, having made a conspicuous failure of his more intimate personal relationships, becomes thereafter an ardent apostle of world peace. Plainly he is trying by this means to reassure himself at the point where his self-confidence is weakest. May it be that our eager American participation in the world-wide church unity movement is a tacit admission of a deep discontent with our own affairs, and therefore an unconscious act of compensation? How little any man understands himself in such matters.

Furthermore, no advocate of church union should take its major premise for granted—that church union is desirable, and that the desire for it is a sign of religious vitality and Christian charity. George Tyrrell thought otherwise:

As the branches of the tree bifurcate and diverge, they grow more characterized and unlike one another. So of the varieties of the religious idea. They do not converge towards, but diverge from, a point of sameness. Schism is their very law. So far as they are alive and vigorous, each pushes forward in its own direction and away from others: reunion becomes less and less possible. The tendency towards reunion among the Christian sects of to-day is the result of weariness and decay; of scepticism as to the values of their several systems. The withered branches break off at their point of bifurcation. Union is restored by going backwards to an original state of indetermination.[1]

In spite of the fact that their author was a 'Modernist', these

[1] *Christianity at the Cross-Roads*, by George Tyrrell, p. 233. Longmans, Green and Company, London, 1910.

words were written in the *fin de siècle* mood of the years before 1914. To-day most of us are satisfied that we should support the church union movement simply because a hopelessly divided church, giving 'an uncertain sound' in the presence of sinister doctrines of anti-Christ, cannot hope to defend and to further the Christian cause. The Holy Church Universal, which once seemed a luxury, is now a moral necessity. Yet we should constantly satisfy ourselves afresh as to the validity of the motives which prompt the movement.

And now, what of America in particular? The facts from which we must proceed are complex and at first sight discouraging. The situation, however, is by no means as unintelligible or as hopeless as it may appear.

In general the small sects, of which we have spoken at some length, live their life quite apart from the larger denominations. Exception must be made, however, in the case of an occasional group of this sort which, for reasons that are not easy to understand, experiences a rather rapid growth in numbers. As such a body grows it ceases to be a society of underprivileged persons and tends to include numbers from the middle classes. In this respect the pattern is that of the earlier and then the later periods of Methodism. In the process of expansion, to use a phrase of the social historian, the sect 'cools off'. Its initial emotional enthusiasm and its anti-intellectualism are succeeded by a greater sobriety and a sincere desire for decent learning. Until its own theological seminaries are founded, candidates for its ministry are sent to the older divinity schools. Tentative alliances are made with national organizations for religious education. At the moment the 'Church of the Nazarene' is perhaps the most signal instance of this process. From its modest beginnings less than fifty years ago it has now become a denomination of 165,000 members, and is making preparation for its own seminaries. This history is, however, the exception rather than the rule with the small sect, which remains for the most part aloof from other religious bodies.

Perhaps the next thing to be said is this—that here in America we are made aware of the large part which racial factors and the history of European nationalism over the last four hundred years have played in dividing and subdividing the churches of the Old World. Conventional books on church history are disinclined to dwell on this fact. The inference is that any such admission might seem to concede a strain of secularity in the character of an institution supposedly divine in its origin and spiritual in its nature. Yet, when the many European denominations are transplanted here, we cannot help noticing in them certain elements which pass unnoticed in the lands of their origin.

Thus, a Norwegian Lutheran visiting America a few years ago found himself in a Minnesota city. A friend was driving him about, showing him the sights. They came to a street crossing where there were four churches, one on each corner. 'This seems to be a very religious city', said the visitor; 'what are these churches?' 'Yes,' said his host and guide; 'that is a German Lutheran church, that is a Swedish Lutheran church, that is a Finnish Lutheran church, and that is a Danish Lutheran church !' The faith and order of Lutheranism, whatever the national designation, represent a single consistent type of Protestant Christianity. The establishment of Lutheranism in many European countries may give the racial and political adjectives local validity, but the terms 'German, Swedish, Finnish, Danish' have no political relevance here, much less any theological warrant.

So, again, with the Eastern Orthodox Church. Orthodoxy in Europe represents not a single type of ecclesiastical imperialism, but a 'commonwealth' of national churches. Given the commonwealth theory there is warrant for the many Orthodox bodies which prevail in the Old World, but there would seem to be no occasion in America for the permanent perpetuation of the 'Albanian, Bulgarian, Greek, Roumanian, Russian, Serbian, Syrian, and Ukrainian' churches, all of which are for the moment entered in our Census.

Presumably these national churches—Lutheran, Orthodox, or of whatever other persuasion—will eventually be merged, each as an 'American' church after its own kind. This is, if we may use the precedent of the public schools, a matter of two generations or three at the most. In all candour we must admit that the eventuality which we foresee may only complicate the total problem. To the German...Danish Lutheran churches, and to the Albanian…Ukrainian Orthodox churches, we shall then have added one more denomination, in each instance an American church.[1] If the World Council of Churches, when it takes final form, is willing to regard the United States as a laboratory where free experiments can be made with elements brought here from the Old World, using reagents provided by this country, then much can be learned from these experiments as to the nature of the whole problem and possible methods for its solution. For experiments can be made here, are being made, and will continue to be made under conditions which do not obtain and perhaps cannot obtain in Europe.

One might cite, in this connection, as a parallel to the religious situation, a passage from a recent and amusing novel, *A Bell for Adano*, which deals with the attempt of a certain Major Victor Joppolo, U.S.A., an official of AMG, to administer the affairs of a little town in southern Italy:

America is the international country. Major Joppolo was an Italian-American going to work in Italy. Our Army has Yugoslavs and Frenchmen and Austrians, and Czechs and Norwegians in it, and everywhere our Army goes in Europe, a man can turn to a private beside him and say, 'Hey, Mac, what's this furriner saying? How much does he want for that bunch of grapes?' And Mac will be able to translate.

That is where we are lucky. No other country has such a fund of men who speak the languages of the lands we must invade, who understand the ways and have listened to the parents sing the folk songs and have tasted the wine of the land on the palate of their memories. This is a lucky thing for America. We are very lucky to have our Joppolos.

You can be as isolationist as you want to, but there is a fact. Our armies are on their way in. Just as truly as Europe once invaded us, with wave after wave of immigrants, now we are invading Europe, with wave after wave of sons of immigrants….

---

[1] Since the above words were written a newly organized Federated Orthodox Greek Catholic Church, with Primary Jurisdictions in the United States, has been announced, which will include the Syrian, Russian, Serbian, Ukrainian, Carpatho-Russian, and Roumanian Churches.

Therefore I beg you to get to know this man Joppolo well. We have need of him. He is our future in the world.[1]

It should not be difficult to translate these words into their ecclesiastical equivalent, and when translated they will give you some suggestion as to the kind of contribution which America may make to the cause of the Holy Church Universal.

As for the immediate situation in this country: in the major Protestant denominations the whole trend is toward federation and union. The two terms should be clearly distinguished. In acts of federation each constituent church retains its own denominational integrity and connection. In acts of formal union, two prior denominations become a single denomination.

Federation is a commonplace with us. The record may appropriately begin with its simplest statement. Many American villages, particularly those where the population is falling rather than rising, are badly over-churched. Each little loyal group taxes itself beyond its resources to maintain its corporate life, but the time comes when further independent survival is economically impossible. The villagers are all neighbours; they meet at their work; they pass the time of day at the post-office and in the general store. They have no need to be introduced and interpreted to one another. They belong mainly to the old Yankee stock. They also belong for the most part to 'free' churches and therefore are not denied independence and initiative of their own. They finally agree to federate. There are no serious theological hurdles to be negotiated, only a few stubborn habits to be accommodated to one another. Thus a fisherman on an island off the coast of Maine confronted with the proposal that his church join its neighbour over the way said, 'Wa-a-ll, I don't know whether we kin do thet or not. They sing three hymns and we sing only two!' Even in its higher reaches the ecumenical movement is not unfamiliar with such persons.

These local federated churches are, in the first instance, the outcome of naked economic necessity. A modest study of the process as it has gone on in two of our states, Massachusetts and

[1] *A Bell for Adano*, by John Hersey, pp. vi, vii. Alfred A. Knopf, New York, 1944.

Ohio, makes it quite clear that nearly all of their local federations came to pass as the result of an attempt to solve the practical problem of dollars and cents. Yet these federated churches go on to report that, having joined, they have discovered unsuspected communities of religious interest, and would now keep together on this ground alone. Meanwhile, the principle of federation allows each constituent group to retain its original denominational connection, so that half of the group will continue to be credited, let us say, to the Methodists and the other half to the Baptists. This process is quietly going on apace in many of our smaller communities. Within its modest dimensions it represents an informal yet concrete adventure in church unity.

Conversely, in rapidly growing suburbs of large cities, a 'community church' is coming into being. The occasion for such a church, if not our American form of it, has become familiar to you with the redistribution of a war-time population. Finding themselves unchurched, accustomed to making their own way in the world, and unwilling, because of their diversity, to be identified with any single denomination, these suburbanites meet and organize a church of their own on the congregational polity. The resultant church is not at first connected with any of the larger denominations. It remains a thing-in-itself. A simple profession of Christian faith and purpose suffices. A duly ordained minister of any one of the major bodies is accepted as pastor. The whole procedure is, in recent and metropolitan terms, reminiscent of the Frontier a century ago.

'Community churches', yclept, may also be found in the down-town areas of great cities. In theory they propose to invite and profess to include persons of all types. In practice they have become meeting places for leftists who still cherish some residual feeling for organized religion. They tend to be socialist-to-communist and pacifist. They minister, therefore, to a single recognizable but limited group in the city. They can be called 'community' institutions only by courtesy.

Sporadic attempts are made to organize all these community churches on a state and national basis. Should such attempts succeed, they would then become our 257th denomination! There was some fifteen or twenty years ago a possibility that churches of this type might multiply rapidly in many places and supplant the older denominations. There seems now little prospect of that eventuality. If the down-town community churches are leftist, those in the suburbs tend toward the right. Furthermore, the social fabric of any one of these parishes is so intimately local, so much a transcript of a single residential area, that as a whole they find little in common. The down-town churches, meeting usually in some public hall, are likely to survive, if they have vigorous leadership. As long as he carries on his ministry John Haynes Holmes, one of our most vivid personalities, will have a following and a hearing in New York City. As for the suburban community church, it will probably identify itself in due time with one or another of the larger denominations, its choice being determined by the previous affiliation of the stronger groups which originally organized it.

The principle of federation is also in force in wider terms. Most large cities, and many states, have their federations of churches. The movement comes to a head in the Federal Council of the Churches of Christ in America, which was organized in 1908. The preamble to its constitution duly stresses its concern for 'devotional fellowship and mutual counsel concerning the spiritual life and religious activities of the churches', but its main task has been 'to secure a larger combined influence for the churches of Christ in all matters affecting the moral and social condition of the people, so as to promote the application of the law of Christ in every relation of human life'. The Council has no ecclesiastical standing under the law as a denomination, and no jurisdiction over its member churches. 'Its province shall be limited to the expression of its counsel and the recommending of a course of action in matters of common interest. It has no authority... in any way to limit the full autonomy of the Christian bodies adhering to it.'

This Federal Council of Churches is, therefore, the American form of the Life and Work Movement; indeed, it antedates that movement by some years. The strength or the weakness of the council—and you may have your choice between these two appraisals—lies in its candid concern for that *activismus* with which our German friends so constantly charge American

Christianity. The pronouncements of the council have tended to be well in advance of the political and economic opinions held by the rank and file of American Protestants. Its public utterances have often been deplored by our more conservative church members, and on this ground at least one denomination withdrew its membership. But the council has done much to prepare our people for a world of social change and to educate them in advance of the event.

In 1940 the council consisted of twenty-two Protestant denominations with a membership of nearly 25,000,000. Therefore it is not a negligible factor in our religious life as a whole. The only large denominations now outside its ranks are the southern Baptists and the Lutherans, neither of whom has ever joined. In economic matters the south is conservative, and the absence of the largest southern denomination may be accounted for on that basis. Lutheran Churches have always held aloof from movements which seemed to secularize Christianity by following the lead of Calvinism. Therefore in remaining apart from our Federal Council they are merely running true to their historic form. It is significant, by the way, that in 1937 Germany allowed delegates to attend the Edinburgh Conference on Faith and Order, but refused to allow attendance at the Oxford Conference on Life and Work. The latter conference proposed to address itself to the problem of church and state, and the Nazi officials declared that subject out of bounds.

American Lutherans are, however, finding it more and more difficult to keep apart and aloof from our Protestantism as a whole, and even at the cost of some modification of its premises, Lutheranism is now beginning to move toward the other churches. Thus, the President of the most influential Lutheran seminary in the United States has recently said, 'In the face of this war what excuse is there for conditions such as exist in the American Lutheran bodies to-day? Other Christians don't know us, and we don't know them. The Lutheran Church of America cannot for our own good maintain the traditional point of view and say, We will have nothing to do with other Christians.... I think we Lutherans will have to act differently in the future than in the past.' Anyone who knows what lies behind these words and what is at stake here can understand how revolutionary they are. Such an utterance is an instance of what I have called the opportunity for free experiment in church union which America offers. The results of any experiment which American Lutheranism may make will not be without significance for parent churches in the Old World.

For many years the Protestant Episcopal Church had only an affiliated relation to the Federal Council. Here again we meet the reluctance of an historic body, with a Catholic as well as a Protestant heritage, to identify itself too soon and too whole-heartedly with a movement which seems in danger of secularizing religion because of its preoccupation with the affairs of every day. The Episcopal Church, however, finally accepted full membership in the council in 1940.

We can get some idea of the activities of these federated movements by reviewing the programme of any one of our state federations. These federations have, for the immediate purpose of illustration, the advantage of lying midway between city federations, which must always be local, and the national Federal Council, which may seem at times too all-inclusive.

Thus the 1943 annual report of the Massachusetts Council of Churches, which includes most of the Protestant bodies in the state, cites the following activities. A Department of Religious Education, headed by a field secretary, works through its several committees concerned with young children, junior high school pupils, youth groups, adults, week-day Bible schools, and vacation schools. A Department of International Justice and Goodwill has as its chairman a distinguished Harvard professor. This committee holds conferences to train leaders of discussion groups in the churches. A further war-time committee carries on work at Fort Devens, one of the largest Army posts in the country, supplementing the duties of the chaplains in the conduct of public services and in visits at the base hospital where wounded veterans from overseas are cared for. A Service Club committee conducts a centre for soldiers and sailors in the heart of the city of Boston, with 75,000–100,000 visitors a year. A Department of Evangelism organizes preaching missions. A Department on Comity advises federated local churches as to the conduct of their affairs. This department also addresses itself, in behalf of the churches, to the housing problem in industrial cities and the problem of the religious care of persons living in newly developed areas. A Department of Social Relations concerns itself with applied Christianity, as expressed in settlement houses, public institutions for the care of the aged and infirm, orphanages and the like. The committee sponsors Protestant chaplains in the two largest hospitals in Boston. A sub-committee on legislation studies proposed state laws as they are likely to affect morals, education and health. A further department addresses itself specifically to the problem of some 60,000 war workers concentrated around the shipyards in Quincy. A Youth Council identifies its seventeen local units with the United Christian Youth Movement. In all these ways the corporate Protestantism of Massachusetts is directly geared to the life of the Commonwealth. Cooperation in the fields mentioned is not only possible, it is effectual, quite apart from any final resolution of the ultimate problems of faith and order which still divide the denominations.

Countless other forms of interdenominational cooperation are in effective force in America. This is particularly true of mission boards, home as well as foreign. There is a determination to avoid needless duplication hereafter. A denomination which insists upon establishing a mission church in a given locality against the better judgment of an interdenominational board of strategy invites serious criticism. We shall have hereafter, whether at home or abroad, much less wasteful competition.

Organizations like the YMCA and the YWCA, though consistently refusing to call themselves churches, rely for their support mainly upon church people, and serve therefore as an expression of a total Christian concern. Incidentally it should be said that the 'Y', though English in origin, has become with us a much more considerable institution than with you. It has climbed well up the social ladder and is now, in many communities, the accepted 'club' for the youth of the upper-middle class. Its buildings are ample, its dormitories excellent, its recreational and educational facilities first rate and its religious programme varied and serious. The Scout Movement, the Red Cross and similar organizations run through all the vertical party

walls which divide the denominations and thus become hori-
zontal, interdenominational strata in our society.

Special mention might be made of one of our bolder and more
recent organizations, the National Conference of Christians and
Jews, which has come into being as an attempt to start a backfire
against the menace of religious and racial prejudice. There is full
warrant for such a society. We have already had ugly incidents:
inflammatory journals, defacing of churches and synagogues,
clashes of street gangs. Just what lies behind these happenings
and what they may portend, no one quite knows. They are,
however, serious enough so that they cannot be ignored. This
conference is laying sober and steady siege to public opinion in
our larger cities. It conducts public rallies, seminars, discussion
groups for the consideration of racial and religious issues. It is
well organized and well manned by liberal and patient spokesmen
for each of the three groups concerned; Catholic, Protestant and
Jew.

In all these ways, then, America has varied and perhaps adequate apparatus for the application of religion to the general life
of the community. Indeed, one might say of all this interdenominational machinery what is often said of our automobiles,
that the machine is better than the ride you can take in it. Our
problem is not to set up still more organizations to serve the
federated conscience of our churches; the problem is how to
bring the conscience of the rank and file abreast the prophetic
blue prints we already have. For the practical purposes of the
social gospel we have, and have had for some years, formal means
by which to serve our common Christian concerns. This volume
would be pathetically incomplete and wholly false to its theme
if, somewhere in its course, it did not make use of the neologism,
'to implement', which is at the moment very much in vogue
among us. This is, perhaps, as good an occasion as any other on
which to do so. Let us say, then, that America has 'implemented'
the Epistle of James with countless contemporary agencies
addressed to our common Christian 'Life and Work'.

When we come to the other aspect of church union, that which
involves 'Faith and Order', the problem is more difficult and the
end is not yet. As was said in an earlier chapter, the only major

schisms which America has seen for the last hundred years were those occasioned by the Civil War in the Baptist, Methodist and Presbyterian Churches. The Baptist and Presbyterian Churches, north and south, still remain divided. The two Methodist Churches were reunited in 1939. In general it is now assumed that the centrifugal schismatic forces in American life were more or less spent when the last of the public lands were taken up in the early 1890s. The exhaustion of those lands marked the end of an era and called for a reorientation of the common mind. Since that time federalization of our life has been the order of the day.

Our churches have moved with the times, unconsciously perhaps rather than wittingly. In any case there is little or no interest in further subdivision of our larger denominations and much interest in church union. Over the last few years countless conversations have been going on between denominations, in the first instance usually between a given two of them, looking to organic church union. There is no major denomination which does not now have its commission exploring that possibility. The most interesting of these ventures is, at the moment, that in process between the Protestant Episcopal and the northern Presbyterian Churches. Nor have these conversations confined themselves to talk; a number of them have issued in the act itself.

We have already noticed that American Lutheranism is over-diversified. In 1872 four Lutheran Synods, with a mission under their joint supervision, united to form the Lutheran Synodical Conference. In 1930 five Lutheran groups united in the American Lutheran Conference. The technical denominational status of the constituent bodies is nominally still preserved, but the drift in Lutheranism is toward unity.

In 1931 the Congregational body, which harks back to its Pilgrim and Puritan origins in early New England, united with the Christian body, a denomination which originated with the Wesleyan revivals of the late eighteenth century and which had been mid-western in its locale, to form the 'Congregational Christian Churches'. The plural word marks the common polity of these two denominations.

We have mentioned the reunion of the northern and southern Methodist churches in 1939. That union included also, at the time, a third and smaller body, the Methodist Protestant Church, which had previously had independent status.

In many ways the most striking and suggestive act of union in recent years is that which in 1934 joined the Reformed Church in the United States with the Evangelical Synod of North America to form the 'Evangelical and Reformed Church'. Dr George W. Richards of Lancaster, Pennsylvania, the long-time President of the Reformed Church Seminary in that community and one of the acknowledged American leaders of the ecumenical movement, was the moving spirit in the union. The whole procedure was ecclesiastically so unique and so character-istic of our American ways of life, that I have solicited his account of the matter, as follows:

Both churches have a Continental background. The pioneers of the Reformed Church came to America in the eighteenth century from the Rhinelands and the German Swiss Countries; an influential minority from France (Huguenots), and from Holland. The pioneers of the Evangelical Synod came into the United States in the nineteenth century and represented the Evangelical United Church of Prussia (1817), a union of the Lutheran and Reformed Churches by mandate of King Frederick William III. The distributing centre of the Reformed pioneers in the colonial period was Philadelphia and the majority of the Reformed churches were located in Pennsylvania. The dis-tributing centre of the pioneers of the Evangelical Synod was Saint Louis, Missouri, the larger number of them settled in the Mississippi valley.

In the latter half of the nineteenth century the two churches through their theologians, ministers, and laymen migrating into the states of the mid-West became acquainted with each other and discovered that there was sufficient agreement in doctrine, polity, and culture, and above all in their European heritage (the German language was spoken by the pioneers of both churches), to warrant a joint meeting of the Committees on Closer Re-lations of Churches which should discuss the possibility of organic union. Formal conversations in joint session were held in 1928. It was mutually agreed that, unless the two Churches were one in spirit, an attempt to unite them on paper would be futile.

Accordingly a Plan of Union was prepared before a Constitution, a statement of doctrine, and a Book of Worship were considered or adopted. This mode of procedure was a venture; so far as we know it was the first to be followed and successfully consummated in the history of Christianity. The Plan was submitted to the supreme judicatories of the churches and they in turn presented it for adoption to the districts on the one hand and to the Classes on the other.

The union of the two bodies was formally and regularly effected in a joint session of the General Conference of the Evangelical Synod and the General Synod of the Reformed Church, 26 June 1934, in Cleveland, Ohio. The General Synod of the *Evangelical and Reformed Church* was constituted on the morning of the day following, 27 June, at the same place. A Constitution, a Hymnal and a Liturgy were prepared by Committees; the Constitution was declared adopted by the General Synod at Lancaster, Pa., 1940; the Hymnal and the Book of Worship were approved for use by the churches by the General Synod at Cincinnati, 1942.

According to the Constitution, the Old and New Testaments are recognized as the Word of God and the ultimate rule of Christian faith and practice. The doctrinal standards are the Heidelberg Catechism, Luther's Smaller Catechism and the Augsburg Confession—'the authoritative interpretation of the essential truth taught in the Holy Scriptures. Wherever these doctrinal standards differ, ministers, members and congregations, in accordance with the liberty of conscience inherent in the Gospel, are allowed to adhere to the interpretation of one of these confessions. However, in each case the final norm is the Word of God....In its relation to other Christian Communions the Evangelical and Reformed Church shall constantly endeavour to promote the unity of the spirit in the bond of peace.'

All told, during the last fifteen years, some ten millions of Protestant Christians have been included in now consummated acts of church union.

There is as yet, however, no blue print for anything like a single American Protestant Church. In this respect the World Council of Churches (in process of formation) is in advance of any goal which we have proposed for ourselves, and may well do us a pioneering service. Meanwhile we are working at the problem empirically, discovering what the total problem is by modest concrete experiment. Such is, after all, the habit of our American mind.

We are less well equipped for a consideration and resolution of the problems involved in Faith and Order than for those of applied Christianity, for the simple reason that most Americans have never really known what the theological and ecclesiastical differences were which long ago and far away gave birth to their denominations, and those who once did know have more often than otherwise forgotten the details. It is here that our lack of anything like a general knowledge of church history and a proper feeling for theology is a liability. Our contemporaneity often prompts us to venture premature solutions of stubborn problems. We cry, 'Peace, peace, when there is no peace', or at least where peace is not to be had quickly and cheaply. Therefore, we are instinctively feeling our way toward church union in the terms of the union of denominations, two by two. There is no reason to suppose that this process will not go forward in America rather rapidly in the next few years. But it will come, in due time, to that point of arrest at which the Edinburgh Conference arrived, and what the procedure will be thereafter is not yet clear.

In its findings the Edinburgh Conference stated that there are two major types of churches: the 'authoritarian' and the 'personal'. These terms were deliberately chosen to avoid the more conventional words 'Catholic and Protestant', 'priestly and prophetic', which may be said to represent the 'objective and subjective', the 'deductive and inductive', interpretations of religion. In the former type the main emphasis is upon the movement from God to man, in the latter from man to God. Neither denies in theory the correlative and supplementary concern, but in practice the emphasis naturally falls upon one or the other of these antitheses.

It would seem, at this point, that we have to do not so much with the fabric of institutions, as with the temperaments of men. One of the most useful pass-keys which we have to the mystery of human nature is that which distinguishes between the extravert and the introvert. The words are new, the facts are as old as man himself, and in any given instance the dominant trait is a physiological and psychological datum. Each of us has to accept the major truth about himself and work with it; if he is wise, he will attempt to save it from exaggeration by deliberately cultivating the antithetical truth. Any one of us knows, however, whether he is by nature an outward-turned person, or inward-turned.

Now it may not be true that an institution is 'the lengthened shadow of one man', but it is true that a given individual is often more at home in one institution than in another. He is at home in the one rather than the other because the institution of his choice gives corporate expression to his own temperamental bias. A science seminar and a poetry club are two different kinds of societies and the members of one would not be at ease in the other. Outward-minded people tend to flock together, so also inward-minded people.

It would be false to the facts to say that all members of authoritarian churches are outward-minded, and all members of personal churches are inward-minded. There has been far too much cross-breeding between churches to allow any such crude generalization. But it is true that the Catholic Mass at one extreme and the Quaker meeting at the other extreme are frequented by distinct types of persons, and that there is a recognizable difference between the transactions on these two occasions. It is further true that in its direction the 'procession' is not the same in both cases. Thus Hugh Benson says that 'Gothic architecture represents the soul aspiring to God, and that Renaissance or Romanesque architecture represents God tabernacling with men'. In the former 'the lines of this world, as it were, run up into gloom'; in the latter 'the round dome of heaven is brought down to earth'. The analogy may be overworked, yet it has its warrant in the dual direction implied by the very word, religion.

In the authoritarian type of church the initial movement is from God to man. The church is thought of as divinely instituted. It has its historic liturgies, its ancient creeds, its apostolic succession. Its life 'comes down', down from a historic past, down from Christ its founder, down from God himself. In the personal churches the movement is in the first instance from man to God. Its members are 'seekers', its congregation is 'gathered'. It prefers immediacy to tradition. It stresses the importance of individual initiative, preferring the active to the passive virtues. Ethics are more to the front than dogmas.

The whole issue comes to a head over the question of ordination. How is a man made a minister? We are confronted here with two types that have always been present in the history of religion, types that have never finally reconciled their differences: the priest and the prophet. The priest represents the objective, extraverted, authoritarian interpretation of religion; the prophet represents its subjective, introverted, personal aspects. The classification is arbitrary and perhaps too crude, since no one man can be wholly identified with the half-truth which institutionally he may serve, yet there is a difference between the two men. The problem is, how to get the priest and the prophet, together with the churches they serve, to recognize each the validity of the ordination of the other. In theory each admits the propriety of the antithetical interest; in practice we have not yet come, as churches, to the point where we are ready to concede it. Specifically, and as matters now stand, we are not able to have corporate communion, in which celebrants and communicants of both types of church can participate.

It would seem, therefore, as though the church union movement would remain stalemated in the presence of this issue unless we can solve the problem of orders. The trouble is that each of us is trying to make his half-truth serve as a whole truth, fearing lest, if he concede the validity of the antithetical type of orders, he may seem to impair the full validity of his own orders. A united church will remain unrealized until the priest and the prophet are willing each to concede to the other the right to serve in both capacities. The thesis and antithesis ought not to be denied or obliterated; they should be preserved. But until they are reconciled in some comprehensive conception of the ministry the church unity movement will mark time at the point of which we are now becoming acutely aware. We Americans have no special insights into this matter or any light to throw upon it. Our authoritarian churches might conceivably draw together into a single communion; so, also, our personal churches. We might thus achieve two major denominations, but how then to unite those two in a *Una Sancta* is still beyond any ecclesiastical wit which we have as yet mastered. For this reason many of us are willing to share humbly and work patiently in the total ecumenical movement.

Meanwhile, I find in *The Church Times* for 16 July 1943, a letter which says:

> Why are we attempting to combine together the Church of England and the Nonconformists? Should we not try for the good of the world, to combine together our brothers in the Roman, Greek and Russian Churches? Is it for the good of England we are striving, or for the good of the world? Which is more important?
>
> The so-called joining together in England can only divide us more from the great churches. I hope that some one will be able to tell me why British unity is more important than world unity.

I do not know how far the writer of this letter represents Anglican opinion. I can understand his awareness of a great military debt to Russia, and I know something of the conversations which have been going on for years between the Church of England and the Orthodox Eastern Church. Furthermore, his disclaimer of insularity and his concern for the good of the world are wholly admirable. But, as an American, I am puzzled and sobered that he should by inference thus exile so much of our American Christianity from the world unity which apparently he earnestly desires. As far as America is concerned, he cannot have the Church of Rome without the Papacy, and unless I am wholly mistaken, the Anglo-Catholicism which he presumably represents is not yet ready to make that submission. As for the rest, the great bulk of our American churches and thus of our Christian people are from his standpoint Nonconformists. If they are to be put out of bounds religiously, the difficulties of the Anglo-American alliance, upon which supposedly so much of our world unity is hereafter to depend, will be vastly complicated. The correspondent in question might well reconsider his proposals in the presence of over 30,000,000 American Nonconformists who, as Christians, hope to have some part in the fashioning of a united world, unless from the outset they are to be put outside the pale.[1]

One final observation might be made on this whole matter of America and the Holy Church Universal. You will have noticed that, save in the case of the Methodist Churches north and south, I have consistently used the word 'union' rather than 'reunion'. The whole idea of a reunion of Christian churches carries with it a connotation which is un-American. The term implies a return to some past state of affairs which presumably ought never to have been abandoned. Thus, the Nonconformist bodies might be expected to return to the Church of England; and all Protestantism eventually to Rome. Willingness to construe church union in such terms would seem tacitly to imply the admission of an initial error in originally breaking away. There is in any plan for 'reunion' just a hint of a penitent prodigal going back to an ancestral home. The home may deny any such interpretation of the event, and may go out of its way to lavish its best gifts upon the returning schismatic sect. Yet there the matter stands. Few of us, for the sake of mere external unity, are prepared to repudiate our own past, to turn state's evidence against so much of the truth, even though it be only a half-truth, as our experience has taught us.

Meanwhile, in America, there is no widespread cultural awareness of any one church to which we might properly return, and with which we might be reunited. The Roman Church, in anything like its present dimensions, is in our experience a later rather than an earlier fact. Our colonial history and the consequences of the Revolution made it impracticable for us to 'return' to the Church of England. Nor is there any sense of some such reminiscent obligation to continental Protestantism. The levelling processes which have been going on, denominationally, over the whole period of our life, make the whole idea of reunion difficult to conceive and thus to translate into achieved fact. Mr Walter Lippmann once said that the legend of the *Mayflower* can no longer provide any basis for a cultural unity in American life; the symbol of that unity must be sought in our

[1] The Protestant population of the United States has already been cited as some 38,500,000. If the Episcopalians and Lutherans be subtracted from this total, we have left over 30,000,000 Protestants who for the purposes of the above argument must be counted as 'Nonconformists'.

future rather than our past. So it is with church union. We habitually think of it as an ideal not yet realized, not as a past fact long lost and now to be recovered. So far as our own affairs are concerned, our relatively brief history determines the manner of our thinking. There never was in America, even in colonial times, to say nothing of the years of our national independence, any undivided church. A few wistful antiquarians may hark back with longing to Massachusetts, or Maryland, or Virginia, or Pennsylvania as they were two or three hundred years ago. But even then no one of them was able to impose the pattern of its religious life upon all the others; much less so now.

All this may well imply in the American mind an imperfect awareness of history, but we have already pleaded guilty to that defect in our mental processes. We have to work with the minds we have, and in spite of many recent rebuffs and much disappointment our mind is still forward looking. Indeed, in thinking of church unity as an ideal to be attained rather than a lost fact to be recovered, we might say, if pressed hard, that we think it possible to exaggerate the degree of unity in the church of the past. During all the centuries covered by the history of the supposedly undivided church schism was present. Thus Professor Kirsopp Lake, leaning over the edge of the pulpit, once said to a group of our theological students, 'It must be a great comfort to any modern minister to realize that, no matter how bad his parish may be, the one which Saint Paul had in Corinth was worse !' The main difference between the history of the church from the fourth to the sixteenth centuries, and from the sixteenth century into the twentieth century is not that there were no schismatics in the earlier period and many schismatics in the later period; the difference is that schismatics were suppressed then, but survive now. The Church Universal, which the ecumenical movement now contemplates, is not for us a church which proposes to suppress all that is implied by schism. It may not revive the Inquisition or renew the wars of religion. It proposes rather to comprehend religious differences. In that sense of the word we are not returning to a past which should never have been abandoned; we are looking to a future which as yet has never been realized. At least, such is the construction which most American Christians place upon the terms 'reunion' and 'union'.

CHAPTER XIII. *SECOND THOUGHTS*

The depths of the seven seas have never been fully charted; perhaps they never can be. Oceanographers send down their apparatus to make soundings, to take temperatures, to net plankton and swimming things, to dredge the primeval ooze, to determine the nature of the sea bottom. That is the best they can do.

The sciences of man make use of a similar process; they call it 'sampling'. When the mass of human data is too great to be compassed by any single type of inquiry, they dip at random into the lives of men and societies for their facts. If the facts show certain uniformities, they hazard tentative generalizations.

These pages have been pathetically incomplete. A detailed history of any one of the churches we have been considering would require not one volume but many. We have had to make use of the 'sampling' method for some intimation as to the nature of the religious situation in America. The areas chosen for sampling have probably been unconsciously determined by my own preferences or prejudices. The result may be therefore a partisan statement. I concede that possibility, which amounts perhaps to a probability. If so, I can only plead in defence Huxley's remark that, if you want a duffer at an inquiry, you should get some one who has no possible interest in the result. In any case there are left now time and space for only a few second thoughts.

I

You will have been struck by the recurring reference to the 'congregational' polity in American church life, known to you as 'Independency'. This type of church is, with you, a minor fact numerically; with us it is a much more considerable fact. Of our 256 denominations 99 are organized on this atomistic theory of the church, the independence and self-sufficiency of the single local congregation. All congregational bodies recognize the correlative principle of the fellowship of the churches, i.e. within a given denomination. These two ideas are supposedly held in equipoise. The weight of tradition is however thrown on the side of the original principle of the independence of the local church.

Of the denominations so organized the most familiar are perhaps the Baptists, Disciples, Congregationalists, Unitarians, Universalists, Quakers and the Jewish synagogues. The statistics of the '36 Census are, as we have indicated, incomplete and to this extent incorrect. They must be compared with the figures in the '43 Yearbook of the American Churches. In any case we can safely say that between 19,000,000 and 23,000,000 persons belong to religious bodies which are organized on the congregational polity. Thirty per cent of all our church people are thus 'gathered' into local churches which are in theory theologically and ecclesiastically self-sufficient. There is no parallel to this situation elsewhere in Christendom. A European scholar among us, trying to grasp this fact, which was entirely new to him, once said, 'Yes, I think I see what you mean. But this congregationalism of yours is not what the world has hitherto called a church; it is anarchy!'

The situation is, however, a faithful transcript of our life thus far. The pilgrim father and the pioneer and the frontiersman had to be individualists. The conditions of their life were reflected in the nature of their institutions. The naked necessity of self-reliance was not only a primal virtue, it became the natural pattern for any given local statement of all that is meant by church and state.

As was said in our first chapter there is a vast deal of parochialism and provincialism left in American life. That fact may still be accepted as a premise which makes easy generalizations about us difficult, if not impossible. Yet the present drift of American life is now away from the isolationism of different areas and toward standardization, centralization, federalization. America is becoming increasingly a land of Ford cars, Saturday *Evening Posts*, Lucky Strike cigarettes, and nation-wide broadcasts. In particular Washington more and more overshadows every town and city, determining from a single centre our entire life as a people. Local jurisdictions, as we have said, still persist, governing many of the details of our everyday transactions, but in the final and decisive matters we become more and more subject to the federal government, with its universal draft laws and tax bills.

We do not know whether this standardization and federalization of our life is to go steadily forward with increasing pace in the direction which it has been taking in recent years, or whether there may be a reaction against it. The shift from the right to the left in political and economic matters so far from retarding the process has speeded it up. The presumption is that this drift is one which is inevitable and therefore cannot be arrested. On the other hand, those who are still the dauntless soldiers of the cause of 'individual initiative' fear that America is in danger of losing the very qualities which have made her what she is. Such persons like 'mourners go about the streets'. They are probably defending a lost cause, but they are fighting a stubborn rear-guard action, often with the best of motives, to save and to reaffirm that individualism in which they honestly believe.

Meanwhile churches congregationally ordered are not a faithful transcript of the kind of society which is rapidly supplanting that of all our earlier years, nor do such churches express, in natural terms the standardization which is increasingly becoming our accepted pattern for living. No two churches, congregationally organized, are alike. Each has its own statement of belief, each has its own covenant between its members, each has its own order of public worship. It is true, that within a given denomination there is probably some total 'sense of the meeting' which gives sufficient integrity to the denomination. Nevertheless, differences exist and are more and more noticeable. The parts of a Ford car are tooled to the fraction of a millimetre. You may buy your car in Maine, but if you break down on a transcontinental journey, you can buy the part needed for repair at any wayside garage in the Arizona desert, and it will be the precise counterpart of that which was originally in the car when you bought it back east. There is however absolutely no guarantee that if you go to church in Arizona you will, unless you are a Roman Catholic or an Episcopalian, find the transactions with which you were familiar in your church in Maine. This cultural discrepancy between the modes of our contemporary life and the polity of a very large section of our Protestant churches is one of which we are now becoming acutely aware.

Such churches are faced with one of two options; they may subtly reorganize themselves upon some much more centralized basis, or they may reaffirm their polity in an attempt to secure what they regard as a still valid principle for the conduct of life. In general our congregationally ordered churches are moving in the former direction. They stop short of any actual concession of authority to their denominational headquarters, but they are inclined to allow headquarters to bring them abreast what they regard as the inevitable, if not ideal, usage of the country as a whole.

On the other hand, many church people—and these the persons who are by heredity or temperament still individualists—feel that the issue is not merely one of cultural accommodation; it is ultimately a matter of religious principle. 'The liberty of the Christian man', the rights of private conscience—these are part of the birthright which every Protestant inherits. They cannot be forfeited without the sacrifice of values to which Protestantism has been for four hundred years committed. Standardization and centralization seem to negate that which has made Protestantism what it is. A Congregational Church is to such persons a corporate witness to these principles and values. The religion of America in the middle distance will be in no small measure determined by the position which churches congregationally organized finally take on this matter. Will they make their submission to all that is meant by the federalization of our national life, or will they resist it? Only time can tell.

II

Next—what of the 'immense and indomitable optimism' of America?

This optimism, like the harsh laws of the Puritan colonies, derives ultimately from the Old Testament. If the Mosaic code gave us the laws, the prophets gave us our Messianic hope. The New England Calvinist may have taken a grim view of the nature of the single individual; he took however an inordinately hopeful view of the future of the society which he was founding here. Consider, for a moment, the invitation extended by colonists already on the ground to prospective immigrants from at home. To-day we should call any such broadsheet publicity, if not propaganda. At that time it was devout profession of faith.

Christ Jesus intending to manifest his Kingly Office toward his Churches more fully than ever yet the Sons of men saw, ... stirres up his servants as the Heralds of a King to make this Proclamation for Voluntiers as followeth.

Oh yes ! oh yes ! oh yes ! All you the people of Christ that are here Oppressed, Imprisoned and scurrilously derided, gather yourselves together, your Wives and little ones, and answer to your severall Names as you shall be shipped for his service, in the Westerne World, and more especially for planting the united Collonies of new England; Where you are to attend the service of the King of Kings, upon the divulging of this Proclamation by his Herralds at Armes....

Could Caesar so suddenly fetch over fresh forces from Europe to Asia, Pompy to foyle? How much more shall Christ who createth all power, call over this 900 league Ocean at his pleasure, such instruments as he thinks meete to make use of in this place.... Know this is the place where the Lord will create a new Heaven, and a new Earth in new Churches, and a new Common-wealth together.[1]

This faith persisted in its most literal form for a hundred years after the settlement of America. Thus, a passage in Edwards's *Thoughts on the Revival of Religion in New England,* 1740, contemplates the possibility, amounting at times in his mind to a probability, that God may be about to complete in America his age-long work in history, by ushering in the new and final order. Edwards searches the passages of prophecy diligently to try to find some intimation there as to the precise place where this fulfilment of all things is to be consummated. He thinks it only fair, since the first creation took place in the Old World, that the second creation shall be allocated to the New World; indeed it may well have been for this purpose that the discovery of this continent so long delayed, has now been made. Is. lx. 9 says that

[1] From *A History of New England, or Wonder-working Providence of Sions Saviour,* by Captain Edward Johnson. (London, 1654.)

the place can be reached only by a long sea voyage. England will not do; it is too near the continent. Moreover, as America has supplied the Old World with gold and silver, so now she may be destined to complete her mission by providing for mankind the final spiritualities. If it be said that the colonies still belong to a 'day of small things', Edwards can only reply that it is apparently God's custom to begin his greatest works in modest terms. Shall not the last be first? And so he comes to his more specific conclusions, 'If we may suppose that this glorious work shall begin in any part of America, I think if we consider the circumstances of the settlement of New England, it must needs appear the most likely of all the American colonies, to be the place whence this work shall principally take its rise!' Whatever any New Englander to-day may think about Edwards's general speculations as to the locale of the new order, he has no difficulty in subscribing to this concrete proposition. There is something, shall we say, incurably Anglo-American about its bland self-assurance. The passage might be a minute at a meeting of the English Speaking Union.

I have cited these two passages because they suggest the nature of the subsoil of our American optimism. With the winning of our independence these tempers were restated in political terms. They were saved from the wreckage of Calvinism and given a new lease of life in the Democracy. The expectation of a Holy Commonwealth to be brought into being on these shores by an act of God was restated as a vote of political confidence in the average man and his corporate ability to achieve a democratic Utopia. The letter of our faith was subtly altered; the temper of our life remained unchanged. This was still 'God's country'.

The twentieth century was well advanced before our optimism suffered any rebuff or rebuke. The Civil War did not shake it; nor the first World War. It was the Depression of '29 and the early '30s that for the first time in our history disquieted the common mind. The sombre gravity of the present World War has not added perceptibly to the previous disquiet. It was the collapse of banks, the evaporation of the savings of a lifetime, the ever-mounting unemployment, the millions of men standing idle in the market place or given relief through arbitrary and artificial jobs which lacked bread and butter reality, the hunger and the bitter cold of the dead of winter in unheated city tenements— it was this, itself an effect of deep unsuspected disorders, which ended in America, probably for good and all, what one might call the age of our naive Messianic hope.

You may expect hereafter to meet a less boastful, less truculent type of American. Our soldiers now, and our travellers here- after, will not cease to be loyal to their country. You will of course have to deal with the occasional 'swaggering optimist'. But he will no longer be a faithful representative of our people. You must bear with him and write him off as the exception, not as an example. Whether it be in our political and economic life or whether it be in our formal religion, we have outgrown the early years when it could be said of us that we were only 'once born souls'. Hereafter—to use the distinction of which William James made so much—we shall be 'twice born'. We shall con- tinue to be hopeful for our country and for the world, but our hope hereafter will not be inexpert; it will lie on the far side of much preliminary discipline in tribulation and patience and experience, following that sequence which Saint Paul cites and celebrates in his Epistle to the Romans.

In this respect, therefore, it will be easier hereafter for the Old World and the New World to understand each other. Europe has known such maturity for centuries. We have grown up to it only within the last few years. But with the end of what might be called the escapist period of American history, which brought us across the ocean in the first instance and then took us across the continent, we now have to turn back reflectively upon ourselves to review our experience. If we are to continue to affirm our 'cheerful faith that all which we behold is full of blessings', we shall do so under conditions which are often perplexing and disquieting. In short, from now on it should be easier for us to understand each other, in England and America, because the 'immense and indomitable optimism' of America has outgrown its adolescence and has come of age.

III

One of our historians says that at some time during the latter part of the eighteenth century 'God himself became republican.... The moral revolution in New England from Puritanism to Americanism transformed God from the Perfect Being of Edwards into the Universal Benevolence' of the theological liberals.[1]

I shall have failed entirely in these pages if I have not succeeded in making plain a contradiction at the heart of our American religion—that between the disparagement of human nature meted out by orthodox theology and the vote of confidence in human nature given by our equally orthodox democracy. One might defend the thesis that the true and operative religion of America is not that of the churches at all, with their pessimistic general confessions, but that of the state with its declarations of independence. The everyday working faith of the average American citizen has been, and in some residual measure still is, that of the liberalism of the last hundred and fifty or two hundred years. To this extent 'natural religion' as proposed in the mid-eighteenth century has for the purposes of daily life supplanted revealed religion. William Ellery Channing said that if Edwards was right in saying that man's place is the dust, then Edwards had written 'one of the most pernicious books ever issued from our press. Happily it is a demonstration which no man believes, which the whole consciousness contradicts....God's sovereignty is limitless; still man has rights. God's power is irresistible; still man is free.'[2]

You, as well as we, are quite familiar with the paradox of a Sunday self-abasement and weekday self-assertion. Reginald Campbell called attention to this paradox years ago in his *New Theology*. He said that on Sundays we get down on our knees in church and confess that we are miserable sinners; but that, if someone were to accuse us on Monday of actually being sinners, we should ask him to particularize, and then probably bring action

[1] *The Puritan Mind*, by Herbert W. Schneider, pp. 201-2. Henry Holt and Company, New York, 1930.
[2] *The Works of William E. Channing*, D.D., pp. 2-4. Boston, 1898.

against him for defamation of character. The problem which we both face is that of the validity of nineteenth-century liberalism as a whole, whether political or religious. The issue is, perhaps, rather more acute with us because we have been more rhetorical in our praise of the premises of democracy, and because liberalism has penetrated deeper into the traditional substance of our theological orthodoxy. Personally, I do not think that the religious issue can be separated from the political issue. These are two aspects of a single interpretation of life and the conventional liberal runs true to form, whether he be statesman or churchman.

It is only fair to say that our present perplexity had been foreseen a generation ago by many of the more discriminating observers of our common life, whether in England or America. Thus Lord Bryce, in a series of lectures given at Yale before the First World War, conceded certain doubts which were even then crossing his mind:

When the struggle for political liberty began by the wresting of power from kings or ruling groups, the war was waged in the name of Rights....Rights to be won were the cry of battle. Rights to be enjoyed were the crown of victory.

In the long conflict the other side of the civic relation fell out of sight. Whoever claims a right for himself must respect the like right in another....Duty is the correlative of Right.

There was in the latter part of the eighteenth and the earlier part of the nineteenth century a faith widespread among educated men, and not wholly confined to those of a sanguine temper, that the government of the people by the people was the chief and sufficient remedy for the ills that had afflicted society....I ask you to note that these Perfectionists based their ideal of Democracy on a view of human nature which had been held neither in the ancient world nor (so far as I recall) by anybody in the Middle Ages....They assumed that the mass of mankind will be Capable Citizens....

There has been disappointment....The citizens have failed to respond to the demand for active virtue and intelligent public spirit which free government makes and must make. Everywhere there is the same contrast between that which the theory of democracy requires and that which the practice of democracy reveals....In no European country—(and courtesy should not have prevented Lord Bryce from including America)—is the average citizen what the citizen of a democracy ought to be.[1]

This is the problem by which we are confronted in both church and state. Our hereditary faith has undoubtedly suffered from becoming a platitude. It has been, as Coleridge puts it, accepted as so true that it has lost the power of truthfulness. We are now fighting to defend it, to vindicate it, and if possible to reaffirm it. Patently, however, its reaffirmation will have to be made in a modified form; the mid-eighteenth century formulation no longer fits the fact.

It should be said that the biological sciences never took the blandly cheerful view of human nature which the Perfectionists took. If not Adam, then the ape and the tiger live on in us, to say nothing, as Bishop Creighton used to add, of that much more intractable animal, the donkey. Patently human nature in its totality is, at the moment, very far from giving a letter-perfect vindication of liberalism. The biological sciences were not taken by surprise by World Wars. Likewise, the newer sciences of the mind have accustomed us to a much more sombre view of human nature than is presupposed by our traditional liberalism in church and state.

The liberal churches, at least in America, have not been conspicuously successful in enlisting the support of our scientists. They are puzzled by their failure to do so. That failure, I suspect, is due to the discrepancy between the romanticism of the non-orthodox churches and the reservations which the sciences of biology and psychology have as to the inherent excellence of human nature. This is, in America, a theological problem of the first magnitude. Can we continue to profess with our habitual cheerfulness our bland confidence in human nature? If not, must we go back, for the want of any other doctrine, to the disparagement of human nature which was the elder fashion? Or, can we perhaps fashion some credible contemporary doctrine of man which shall be at once realistic and reassuring? Much of the religion of America hereafter will depend upon our resolution

[1] *The Hindrances to Good Citizenship*, by James Bryce, pp. 8-16. Yale University Press, New Haven, 1909.

of this issue. If it be said that the whole issue, thus considered, is stated in too humanistic terms, we can only reply that every doctrine of God is, to some degree, conditioned by our experience and interpretation of human life. What we think of God must bear some relation to our ways of thinking of man. Therefore this whole perplexity as to the warrant for liberalism passes over into theology proper.

IV

What about all these peripheral persons whom I have mentioned, and you are as familiar with them as we are, who make no personal profession of religion and yet who are doing much if not most of the serious work of the modern world? We find them in all our professions; we are perhaps most familiar with them in our colleges and universities. They are our scholars: the scientists, historians, philosophers. I have said that, since they are not against us, they may be counted as for us. This is, however, our interpretation of them, not their own account of themselves. They might repudiate our ascription of religion to them, and they would certainly refuse to wear any of our denominational labels. There is among this group little truculent anti-clericalism. We have already mentioned the want of that temper in American life as a whole.

These persons as we know them here are, for the most part, only one generation removed from the church. If, in some moment of confidence one of them tells you his history, you will usually find that he was brought up in childhood and youth in some literal fundamentalism or rigid orthodoxy which his later education compelled him to abandon. The contrast between the world-view proposed by the guardians of his youth and the world-view unfolded before him by science and history in his more mature years was so sharp that there seemed no possibility of reconciling them, and he accepted the only alternative, that of the truth of things as they apparently are. No one can blame him for so doing, and obscurantist sects have only themselves to blame for his defection.

But all such persons have instinctively preserved and continue to practise, in so far as any of us practise it, the traditional

Christian ethic. The story is familiar to you in the terms of the lives of such men as Thomas Huxley, John Morley, Leslie Stephen. That group of men was a generation in advance of a similar group in this country. We have to-day in America many men of this type. They have broken with organized religion, yet they are imperfectly irreligious. They are our humanists *en masse*. And we may not forget what Bishop Barry said not long since, that such humanism is the religion of half the intelligent persons in the modern world.

Is it probable that these persons may become avowed members of some new religion? Is the humanist movement at the ecclesiastical left likely to gather them in and organize them into what might thus become a powerful denomination, perhaps the most powerful of them all, because its members would thus represent many of the best brains and the most disciplined characters among us? Such is the hope of official humanism.

One might wish for the sake of the world's future that this could be so. Yet there is nothing in the history of this type to indicate that it desires to be thus organized or is capable of such organization. The type is not gregarious. It is still reminiscently so afraid of anything like ecclesiasticism that it shies away from all formal societies which might be in any way identified as churches. The generation in question will live out its time without radical departure from the ways of its fathers, though the words of creeds are no longer said. There is, to use a crude metaphor, enough moral money in the bank to last out one generation, but moral money in the bank seldom lasts two generations.

The real problem which such persons create for the formal religion of the land is not that which is stated in their own persons, since they present no problem. The problem becomes acute in the terms of the young people of the second generation, who have no religious memories and traditions behind them. This is the youth which we are now meeting, in increasing numbers, in our colleges and universities. 'Young barbarians all at play'; happy, healthy, admirable, altogether loveable pagans. Mark Rutherford has described them in his picture of Miriam Tacchi: 'She had to encounter life alone, and with no weapons and no armour save those which Nature provides. She was not specially an exile from civilization: churches, philosophers had striven and demonstrated for thousands of years, and she was no better protected than if Socrates, Epictetus, and all ecclesiastical institutions from the time of Moses had never existed.'

In my account of our colleges and universities I said that many of our young people go to denominational churches or college chapels. I do not pretend that they are in the majority. The percentage of these church and chapel goers, in relation to an entire student body, is probably higher with us than with you. But these may be merely the last of that 'lag' which we have already mentioned. Such young people come, of course, from church-going homes where the parents are 'practising'. Their continued practice of religion away from home is partly a matter of conscious loyalty to their own traditions. ·

With the young pagans, who are undoubtedly in the majority, it is otherwise. They have little or no awareness of any historic religion in the background of their own personal life. They are as innocent of theology and ethics as if 'all ecclesiastical institutions from the time of Moses had never existed'. There can have been few times in our era when the continuity of the Christian tradition as a cultural fact has worn as thin as is the case to-day, or when the vital succession is as seriously impaired. How to begin all over again the 'evangelization of the native races' in our colleges and universities is still with us an unsolved problem. The types of instruction which have been previously described do attract, in America, an appreciable number of these 'young barbarians'. They are intellectually curious; they have no studied and reasoned antipathy to religion. In many an individual instance some such student is really wakened up to the whole body of religious fact and truth, as to the freshness of an early world. Some of our best theological students come on to us from college on the strength of just such an experience. They belong to no church, they have no idea in which denomination they will eventually seek ordination. They only know that their minds have come alive to religion as a concern of intense interest, and they wish to pursue the leads given them in college days. They are a small number as yet, but they constitute one of the most hopeful signs of the times in a world which is otherwise so often overcast.

No devout Christian, however, supposes for a moment that the Christian religion is now in process of passing away before our eyes. Merely as a matter of history it is written too deeply into our past to be deleted suddenly and finally. Yet no denominationalist or sectarian can be certain that the particular forms of his faith and practice have a guarantee of immortality in times to come. Sheer stubborn immobility will not suffice. Mere acts of prudential accommodation to advancing scientific knowledge give us only brief respite, and such acts will have to be constantly renewed, if they are our only means of salvation. The solution of our problems must be more vital than that.

We in America have on the one hand a residual and still operative Christianity which is by no means yet spent. That Christianity, however, has been subtly secularized, or at least rendered 'this-worldly' in its interest—so much so that it may have impaired its own spiritual health. Furthermore, our Protestantism is still, in no small part, Fundamentalist, if not obscurantist. At the moment it is moving farther away from the sciences and the sober philosophy of the day. Intellectually much of it lives an isolationist life, apart from the sober brain work of the land. I rather think we have more of these people, relatively, in America than you have in England.

It is conceivable that a religion stated in other than ecclesiastical terms might succeed to that of our churches: the religions of science, and art, and class; more particularly a religion of the state. But the abuses of the latter type of religion in modern Europe disincline us at the moment to deify an administration in Washington. As citizens we are highly regimented at the moment, necessarily so, but in the presence of the state we are not yet idolatrous. Personally, therefore, I see little prospect of any new religion of a secular kind coming over the horizon to supplant what is still the traditional religion of the land. We shall get along, and make our way as best we can, in the terms of the various forms of religion which we now have.

V

A word as to what is happening in our churches and to our churches in another war time.

The churches of America in the uneasy interim between the two wars were very vocal in their professions of pacifism. We too had our debates in which we decided never again to fight for 'king and country'; we had our peace ballots. Pacifist professions were not confined to the historic peace churches, such as the Quakers and the Mennonites. They became commonplaces, if not conventions, in many of the other communions. In particular the Methodist Church was predominantly pacifist, at least in the ranks of its clergy. For this reason, it is said, that church has found it difficult to deliver its fair share of chaplains for the Army and Navy. The number of Methodists who are CO's is also much larger than at any time in the past.

We seem to have been, prior to the attack on Pearl Harbour, drifting into the war, but there was, as you well enough know, much difference of opinion as to the wisdom and the moral necessity of our so doing. Pearl Harbour ended all that. It came suddenly, and with a finality which could not be denied. Furthermore, it precipitated a problem of which we had long been aware, and for which we were not altogether mentally unprepared. Mr Herbert Hoover once said that it should be put down as an accepted fact that, if wars are to come, Japan is for America 'public enemy No. 1'. The Japanese issue was, for us, of prior importance to that raised by Germany and Italy.

Christians, therefore, unless they were prepared to say that their country must be totally demilitarized, and thus undefended and defenceless, accepted the grim necessity of war with Japan and thus with her allies. We might eventually have come into the war as your ally; you will certainly feel that we ought to have done so before we did. We actually entered the war by way of the Pacific, rather than across the Atlantic.

There has been very little rhetoric and sentimentalism in our churches since December 1941. Our mood is not unlike yours, though our extremity has been negligible in comparison. We have had slight deprivations in our domestic life. Our taxes have quadrupled and in certain brackets now match yours. But we have never been seriously threatened by any appreciable force by air or sea. The strategy of our leaders would seem at this point to have been sometimes rather dubious. We were warned of possible clouds of suicidal bombers from overhead, but insurance rates against damage from air raids have never risen above $1 to $1000, and as long as that realistic fact obtained, rhetoric could not prevail against it.

Perhaps we did not suffer enough in the last war—if entering into the fellowship of the world's sufferings be a discipline which no sensitive people should shirk. Perhaps we shall not suffer enough in this war to be able to understand you hereafter, much less to understand the harder-pressed peoples of Europe. Perhaps we shall be condemned to moral mediocrity in the history of the next half century because we shall not have won a place for our-selves in the 'aristocracy of suffering' in our time. One feels that this may be particularly true of our churches. Their untested platitudes will hereafter mean little to those who have been tried by the fires of persecution.

But in the meantime there is in our churches a new sobriety and a lack of flamboyant flag-waving, which is reassuring. The favourite indoor pastime of preachers in the last war, hanging the Kaiser from the pulpit edge, has no present parallel. The preaching which one hears in a college chapel—and this is a fair transcript of what is being said in parish churches—is more simple and morally more earnest than it has been for years. In reaffirming the necessity for personal religion our preachers are not fleeing from the world and its summons, but they are trying to deepen the religious life of individual Christians so that they shall be able, in the first instance, to endure whatever life may yet bring to them personally, and beyond all that, to provide for the days to come a body of Christian faith and practice which is something more than an easily drafted blue print for the Utopia.

It was commonly said, after the last war, that the churches, by their support of the war, had finally forfeited the respect and consent of intelligent and conscientious persons. We had a spate of books to this effect; *Preachers Present Arms* was the most popular. Those of us who were concerned for churches wondered whether this was to be so. As a matter of actual fact the churches of America from 1918 to 1941 began to be really awakened to the highly problematical world in which they were living. There was much self-criticism, there was a deepened sense of moral obligation, and there was a strong desire to get together. Whatever outsiders may have thought and said of us, by way of criticism, those of us who have lived and worked in churches for the last thirty or forty years are prepared to say that both spiritually and ethically, and in spite of many superficial signs to the contrary, our churches were better in the 1930s than they were in the 1900s. They are to-day less perfunctory, less complacent, morally more disquieted than they were thirty or forty years ago. The difference is not absolute, it is only relative; and the progress may not have been very great. For the moment, however, our churches seem to be gaining rather than losing.

When he left this country, George Santayana said that, 'if he looked in the heart of a man and did not find kindness there, he would know he was not an American'. Our easy-going kind-heartedness has been proverbial. One sometimes suspects that Santayana's generous tribute carried with it, also, a tacit criticism. So again, Mr Lippmann, in discussing our foreign policy, has recently said, 'For fifty years no nation has been more liberal in its words...or contributed less to realizing the ideals it so assiduously preached.' The traditional kind-heartedness and the even more traditional rhetoric of America are transcripts of our immaturity. Our hearts have not been hopelessly hardened; we are not as yet a cynical people. Nor have we given up our ideals. But, to cite André Siegfried again, we have in these matters 'come of age'. We are, as Christians, in process of putting away at least some of the childish things which have had to be charged against us in the past.

VI

These pages have tried to be, in so far as is humanly possible, a dispassionate transcript of fact. I have attempted to give you an account of 'how things have come to be as they are', religiously, in the America of to-day. But Christianity is a forward-looking faith, and I should be false to its spirit if I ignored the future, problematical, yet filled with great opportunity for both you and us.

If our hereditary American idealism is to have hereafter a

realistic rather than a rhetorical foundation, we cannot ignore the more disquieting signs in both of our countries. As the war draws nearer its conclusion, the grim economic necessities in both countries can be only too clearly foreseen. The problems of housing, of bread and clothing, and of a decent day's work have already come over the horizon. Mr Tawney tells us that the difference between the trades and the professions is this: that the trades are organized for gain and the professions for service. Christianity is often spoken of as a profession, and it certainly ought never to become the servile handmaid of gainful trade. There is still a gulf between the premises of the secular state and the historic axioms of Christianity. The first duty of the state, in behalf of its citizens, is to attempt to insure its own perpetuity. This accepted duty of self-preservation is by no means the whole mission of the Christian, who is supposed to be among men as one who serves, even to the point of sacrifice. It would seem that the genius of Christianity must become the spirit of secular society as well, unless the kingdoms of this world are to go on, as they are now going, from bad to worse.

We cannot pretend in America that our political and economic and industrial life is sacrificial. We are looking for markets after the war, for new customers, for more trade, for a greater share in the world's shipping. Many of our secular journals are exploring the prospects in these fields. As a result, our professed and idealistic war aims are in danger of being supplanted by the old familiar techniques of economic rivalry.

Thus, at a recent meeting of the American Academy of Arts and Letters, Mr Archibald MacLeish, the Librarian of Congress —himself one of our best poets—said to his fellows:

As things are now going, the peace we will make, the peace we seem to be making, will be a peace of oil, a peace of gold, a peace of shipping, a peace, in brief, of factual situations, a peace without moral purpose or human intent, a peace of dicker and trade, about the facts of commerce, the facts of banking, the facts of transportation, which will lead us where the treaties made by dicker and trade have always led.[1]

That is the sorry trend of which we are only too well aware in

[1] *The Herald Tribune*, 20 May 1944.

our own country. Yet, in so far as we can follow what is going on with you, you have not yet put such things behind you. You may not be prepared for the dissolution of the Empire—indeed we have it on the highest authority that you are not—but if your imperialism is to be once more consolidated and reaffirmed in its traditional form, your traders and ours will be at work the day the armistice is signed to out-outwit each other.

You ask us to abandon the mental habit and thus the practice of isolationism, which has been our national second nature for more than a century, and to abandon it for the sake of the wider world, rather than for the sake of our own profit. If we are to effect this change in our national character, we are not unwarranted in hoping that some remaking of your mental habits as a people may match that which you expect of us. Many Americans will not see why our isolationism should give place to a new sense of grave moral obligation to the world as a whole, if your imperialism is to persist unmodified. What the changes might be in either instance is by no means clear; how they could be effected is even less clear. But the fact remains that neither American isolationism nor British imperialism, doggedly reaffirmed after the conventional patterns of the past, holds out any sure promise of a better world hereafter. Plainly, acts of inner repentance and outer reform are asked of us both, if together we are to try to save civilization from the consequences of its present suicidal drift.

These sober second thoughts are much on the mind and conscience of Christians among us, as with you. Neither of us can deny the naked creature needs of the post-war years. Yet we cannot afford to allow the 'heavy and the weary weight' of economic necessity to defeat the good conscience of our common Christianity.

It is said that the Messianic hope of Israel shone most brightly when the times were darkest. We have lived through thirty years when the skies have been overcast. A second World War following that first World War which was to have been 'the war to end war' can best be described in the words of *Ecclesiastes*, 'And the clouds return after the rain'. In this overcast time we both need the good courage of the classical Messianic hope, 'Behold my servant. . . he shall bring forth judgment unto truth. He shall not fail or be discouraged, till he have set judgment in the earth.'

APPENDICES

Compiled by RALPH LAZZARO of the Harvard
Divinity School

A. NATIONAL ELEMENTS IN THE AMERICAN COLONIAL POPULATION

The problem of determining the population of the colonies in the pre-Revolutionary period and of establishing the number and extent of national strains in that population has been for long a difficult one. Inasmuch as there was no centralized government to hold the various colonies together before the Revolution, no general and comprehensive census was possible. True, the individual colonies periodically did count heads, but the work was not thoroughly done, nor have the records always come through to us. At best, only estimates can be given. The first all-inclusive American Census was taken in 1790, and of this we have a fairly complete record. On the basis of its figures, after much thorough investigation on rather sensible lines and improving on the conclusions reached by *A Century of Population Growth in America*, 1790–1900 (published in 1909 by the Department of Commerce and Labour, Bureau of the Census), the American Historical Association has worked out estimated maxima for the national elements that composed the American population in 1790.[1] In presenting the conclusions of this report, we hope that the reader may form some idea of the various national strains, and their extent, in the colonies at the time of the Revolution.

The major stocks in the American population of 1790 were four: English, Irish, Scotch, and German. The Dutch, the Swedes and the French represent the minor stocks. Contributions from other national groups are so slight that, even when they are all totalled, they do not amount to a considerable element worthy of separate mention.

A little has been said in the main text of this volume on the coming of the English, the Irish and the Scotch to the American shore. At any rate, the history of their migration to the colonies

[1] *American Historical Association*: *Annual Report, Proceedings*, vol. 1, 1931. Washington, D.C., U.S. Government Printing Office, 1932. From p. 126 on, Howard F. Barker and Marcus L. Hansen give an illuminating discussion of the national stocks in America in the Census of 1790.

is well enough known so that it requires no further statement here. As for the Germans: when the German or Teutonic contributions to 1790 America are mentioned, one understands, of course, that what is meant is the contributions of the 'German-speaking' people, for Germany was not at that time a unified nation but rather a geographical expression. The first shipload of Germans came in 1683, in the *Concord*, often called the German *Mayflower*. They first settled chiefly in Pennsylvania, but beginning with 1710 German settlements were established in New York and New Jersey and in small numbers in Delaware. From Pennsylvania there was then a considerable outpouring into Maryland, Virginia and the Carolinas. In 1734 some Austrian Salzburgers settled in Georgia, and thereafter the number of Germans in that state increased appreciably. New England received only a few of the German stock, but settlements of them are not unknown there after 1741.

We must remark here that, as Mr Hansen points out,[1] 'colonial population was not fluid. There was movement, but it was the movement of groups rather than of individuals.' Thus we see these various national stocks in America, both major and minor, moving about the colonies not as individuals, but in group-formations, bound by the ties of common language, religion, custom and tradition. The habits and *mores* of each group conditioned largely its choice of new settlement, for these national stocks, having a wide area from which to choose, migrated to and established themselves in those regions where conditions were best suited to their temperament, economic system, *et al*. In these new homes they settled most extensively, though they may also be found in scattered communities elsewhere in the colonies. The 1931 report of the American Historical Association gives some convenient charts of the distribution of the major stocks in the American colonies of 1790.

The other national groups which cut any appreciable figure in the American population of 1790 are the Dutch, the French and the Swedes. The French, like the Germans, had immigrated into the colonies only very rarely as individuals seeking economic fortune or adventure; they came most often as groups of religious refugees. The Swedes and the Dutch, on the other hand, were the residue of colonial empires established at an early date but later dissolved.

[1] *Annual Report of the American Historical Association*, 1931, p. 361.

I. ENGLISH POPULATION, 1790

Estimated maxima for numbers and proportions of English
in the white population of the United States, 1790

State	White population	% possibly English	No. possibly English
UNITED STATES	3,172,444	70	2,207,760
Maine	96,107	60	57,660
New Hampshire	141,112	61	86,080
Vermont	85,072	76	64,650
Massachusetts	373,187	82	306,010
Rhode Island	64,670	71	45,920
Connecticut	232,236	67	155,600
New York	314,366	57	179,190
New Jersey	169,954	58	98,570
Pennsylvania	423,373	40	169,350
Delaware	46,310	60	27,790
Maryland	208,649	72	150,230
Kentucky and Tennessee	93,046	75	69,780
Virginia	442,117	84	371,380
North Carolina	289,181	98	283,400
South Carolina	140,178	75	105,130
Georgia	52,886	70	37,020

II. IRISH POPULATION, 1790

Estimated numbers and proportions of Irish in the white
population of the United States, 1790

State	White population	% possibly Irish	No. possibly Irish
UNITED STATES	3,172,444	9·7	307,070
Maine	96,107	11·7	11,350
New Hampshire	141,112	7·5	10,580
Vermont	85,072	5·1	4,340
Massachusetts	373,187	3·9	15,550
Rhode Island	64,670	2·8	1,810
Connecticut	232,236	2·9	6,740
New York	314,366	8·1	25,460
New Jersey	169,954	9·5	16,150
Pennsylvania	423,373	14·5	61,390
Delaware	46,310	11·7	5,420
Maryland	208,649	12·3	25,670
Kentucky and Tennessee	93,046	12·2	11,350
Virginia	442,117	11·7	51,730
North Carolina	289,181	11·1	32,100
South Carolina	140,178	13·8	19,340
Georgia	52,886	15·3	8,090

III. SCOTCH POPULATION, 1790

Estimated numbers and proportions of Scots in the white population of the United States, 1790

State	White population	% possibly Scotch	No. possibly Scotch
UNITED STATES	3,172,444	8·3	263,330
Maine	96,107	4·5	4,320
New Hampshire	141,112	6·2	8,750
Vermont	85,072	5·1	4,340
Massachusetts	373,187	4·4	16,420
Rhode Island	64,670	5·8	3,750
Connecticut	232,236	2·2	5,110
New York	314,366	7·0	25,010
New Jersey	169,954	7·7	13,090
Pennsylvania	423,373	8·6	36,410
Delaware	46,310	8·0	3,700
Maryland	208,649	7·6	15,860
Kentucky and Tennessee	93,046	10·0	9,300
Virginia	442,117	10·2	45,100
North Carolina	289,181	14·8	42,800
South Carolina	140,178	15·1	21,170
Georgia	52,886	15·5	8,200

IV. GERMAN POPULATION, 1790

Estimated numbers and proportions of Germans in the white population of the United States, 1790

State	White population	% possibly German	No. possibly German
UNITED STATES	3,172,444	8·7	276,960
Maine	96,107	1·3	1,250
New Hampshire	141,112	0·4	560
Vermont	85,072	0·2	170
Massachusetts	373,187	0·3	1,120
Rhode Island	64,670	0·5	320
Connecticut	232,236	0·3	700
New York	314,366	8·2	25,800
New Jersey	169,954	9·2	15,640
Pennsylvania	423,373	33·3	140,980
Delaware	46,310	1·1	510
Maryland	208,649	11·7	24,410
Kentucky and Tennessee	93,046	14·0	13,030
Virginia	442,117	6·3	27,850
North Carolina	289,181	4·7	13,590
South Carolina	140,178	5·0	7,010
Georgia	52,886	7·6	4,020

THE DUTCH stock in America at the time of the 1790 Census was the product of the colonization, in the seventeenth century, of New Netherland. In the eighteenth century no new large groups came from the European Netherlands to swell the American number; scattered individuals did indeed arrive, but as far as the evidence goes, there was no 'immigrational' increase from sources outside of the colonies. The Dutch had stopped coming in 1664, when the English took over New Netherland from them. Their total maximum number by 1700 could not have exceeded 8650.

The Dutch had originally settled in those states which are now known as New York, New Jersey and Delaware. From these the first distinct waves of migration went into Pennsylvania, Maryland and Virginia. They increased at a fairly rapid rate, so that in 1790 there can be numbered, from the State estimates, 106,750 of them in the United States. The largest number of the Dutch, as is to be expected, was found in New York State, where they had originally settled for commercial and military reasons. Their influence in the 'Esopus', now Ulster County (the region between New York City and Albany), was great. When, for instance, a Huguenot settlement was made at New Paltz before the end of the seventeenth century, the church records were for fifty years kept in French; but after this, for the next seventy-five years, we find that the records of the 'French Church' at New Paltz appear in Dutch. Of the total white population of 314,366 in the state of New York in 1790, 55,000 were Dutch.

Agrarian expansion, starting about 1690, brought some Dutch to New Jersey (in and near Bergen) from New York. In 1790 there were in this State 35,000 Dutch out of a population of 169,954.

In Delaware a feeble Dutch colony clustered about the military post at New Castle. Here, approximately 2000 out of 46,310 were Dutch.

Early in the eighteenth century the Dutch expanded also into New England, where they tried to settle in the borderland between New England and New York. This region became debatable ground, for conflicts arose between the New Englanders and the Dutch over rival titles to the land; in these litigations the New Englanders were the most often successful. Nevertheless, by dint of hard work and persistence, the Dutch struck root in New England; intermarriage helped them in their struggle. In

1790 there were to be found about 600 Dutch in Connecticut; 600 in Massachusetts; 500 in Vermont; and 250 in Rhode Island. In Maine and New Hampshire there were hardly any.

In Pennsylvania, at the time of the first national census, they numbered 7000 out of 423,373; 1000 out of 208,649 in Maryland, where they were known as early as 1659; 1500 out of 442,117 in Virginia; 800 out of 298,181 in North Carolina; and 500 out of 140,178 in South Carolina. In Georgia there could have been no more than 100 Dutch at this time, and in Kentucky and Tennessee there were about 200.

THE FRENCH as a people are a non-migratory race; yet they came to the American colonies in various streams, exerting no inconsiderable influence on the history of the United States. The principal reason of their migration was, as we have said, religious persecution at home. Most of these French were Huguenots who had dispersed from their native land to Switzerland, Germany, Holland and Great Britain. From those countries of their exile they moved along with the regular tide to the American colonies, following the established lines of communication.

Their greatest numbers came to our shores around 1700; they scattered all over the land, settling in groups from Maine down to the Carolinas. The French adapted themselves easily to the manners and customs of their new home, and were apparently quietly happy here. In the years 1685–90, two distinct Huguenot colonies were established in New York State: New Rochelle and New Paltz. They remained Huguenot centres for a long time, and the descendants of these prolific settlements were not without power or honour in our land.

Huguenot settlements were founded also in northern New Jersey. From here and from southern New York the French came into Pennsylvania, where they took good root and were strengthened by additional arrivals. But these Huguenots had suffered a bitter and hard experience. Eager to forget the language and customs of the native land that had caused them so much pain, the Huguenots in Pennsylvania mixed early with the other elements in that state, and they began to lose their identity. Much the same thing happened in Maryland and Delaware. In Virginia the Huguenots are known as early as 1700, but here too they disperse and become denationalized. In the rest of the south, however, they managed to keep a more definite character. Several Huguenot centres in South Carolina, holding firmly

together, become the source of supply of French migrations into
Georgia, North Carolina and Tennessee.

In general, the French Huguenots were not welcome in the
colonies. They were often suspected of being French spies and
were irrevocably tied up in the minds of the other colonists with
the frontier massacres and disturbances of the period from 1689
to 1713. In fact, however, these outcast Huguenots had little
or no correspondence with the France that had spurned them.
At any rate, French religious emigration seems to come to a
definite standstill. And there is little trace of direct importation
from France of other than religious refugees to augment the
number of the French in the colonies. References to French
Catholics (probably of Canadian origin) are found quite early
(1697), but their number in the pre-Revolutionary colonies is
scant:

As to the number of Huguenots that sought refuge here, many
estimates have been given, covering the wide range of from a few
thousand to 50,000 before 1750. The American Historical
Association report of 1931, using very skilful methods, estimates
the total number of the French in the colonies in 1790 as approximately half that of the Dutch, or about 54,900.

THE SWEDES began their original settlement of the American
colonies in 1637; they came in twelve expeditions until 1655,
sent out by a trading company in Sweden. Thus, New Sweden
had been in existence for about twenty years when the Swedish
settlements along the Delaware[1] were conquered by the Dutch
in 1655. These united colonies were then in turn conquered by
the British in 1664. But by 1681, when the English finally made
comprehensive plans to establish colonies along the Delaware,
the Swedes were so firmly rooted that even up to the time of
the Revolution they still spoke their own tongue, maintained
their own churches, and kept up their traditional customs. Yet
there was dispersion among them; and this began quite early,
although it never reached the extent of the French scattering.
The Dutch, who wanted to break up Swedish concentration,
induced some of them to travel north to the Hudson valley. But
the greater movement was southward, proceeding from Wil-

[1] The original Swedish settlements were in three centres: (1) at
Christiana (now Wilmington, Delaware); (2) at Tinicum and Wicaco
(now parts of Philadelphia); (3) and at Raccoon Creek and Penn's Neck
(now Gloucester County, New Jersey).

mington into Newcastle County in Delaware and into Maryland, from Philadelphia down along the river banks and up the valley of the Schuylkill, and from Gloucester County in New Jersey into Burlington, Cumberland, Salem, and Cape May Counties. But the bulk of Swedish descendants remained in the region of the Delaware River.

A census of the Swedish inhabitants on the Delaware made in 1693 shows a Swedish population of 942—a total of 188 families. Israel Acrelius, who reports this census in his *History of New Sweden*, informs us also that before the close of the seventeenth century 'a newly arrived Swede was then a rare bird in the country'. For this reason, the number of Swedes in the colonial period never grew by leaps and bounds, but gradually and along natural lines, so that by 1790 their maximum in the United States may be estimated as 21,000, distributed as follows: 4100 in Delaware; 950 in Maryland; 3325 in Pennsylvania; 6650 in New Jersey; 2600 in Virginia; 700 in North Carolina; 325 in South Carolina; 300 in Georgia; 500 in Kentucky and Tennessee; 1500 in New York; 75 in Massachusetts; 50 in Rhode Island; 25 in Connecticut. Maine, New Hampshire and Vermont could lay claim to none.

REFERENCES

American Historical Association. *Annual Report*, 1931. In three volumes. Vol. 1: Proceedings. Washington (D.C.), United States Government Printing Office, 1932. Pp. 452.

Bureau of the Census: Department of Commerce and Labour. *A Century of Population Growth*. Washington (D.C.), United States Government Printing Office, 1909. Pp. x, 303.

Sutherland, Stella H. *Population Distribution in Colonial America*. N.Y., Columbia University Press, 1936. Pp. xxxii, 353.

B. RELIGIOUS DENOMINATIONS IN THE COLONIES BEFORE THE REVOLUTION

In the foregoing appendix we have seen how the various European elements came to the Atlantic seaboard of America, making permanent settlements here. It was inevitable that with their coming they should bring each group its particular religious system along with the other trappings. Thus was there introduced into the new land a motley assortment of religious practice and belief—an assortment which became the foundation of the 256 religious denominations of present-day America.

We propose in these next few pages to present a sketchy account of the different denominations that were brought to our shores until the time of the Revolution and in some measure to suggest the extent of the growth and development of this kaleidoscopic religious picture in the 150 years preceding the American declaration of independence.

I.   THE PROTESTANT EPISCOPAL CHURCH was introduced in Virginia first, by the Virginia Colony, when, on 13 May 1607, 105 English colonists arrived in Jamestown to settle there. In this state it became the 'Established' Church. At first Virginian Episcopalianism was under Puritan control, but after 1624 the new royal governors forbade all non-episcopal ministers from officiating in the colony.

Near the end of the seventeenth century, in 1692, Catholic rule was overthrown in Maryland, which then became a royal colony with an Episcopal establishment.

In New York the Episcopal Church was introduced after the Dutch surrender to the British in 1664 and from that time gained rapid ground.

Massachusetts had its first Episcopal service in 1686, in Boston's Old South Church. In 1686 'King's Chapel' was erected in the same city.

Connecticut received Episcopalianism fairly late—not until 1722.

From such centres as the above, this church spread, so that by the time of the Revolution it could be found in most of the colonies. Contributing strongly to its dissemination was the activity during the first half of the eighteenth century of the English Society for the Propagation of the Gospel in Foreign Parts, established in 1701.

II.   CONGREGATIONALISM came to the colonies with the landing of 102 Pilgrims in 1620 on Cape Cod. These radical Puritans, or Separatists, grew slowly in the Plymouth Colony.

Another group of Puritans, 'superior in wealth, station and capacity', backed by Puritan capitalists in England, arrived at what is now Salem in 1628. The Massachusetts Bay Colony was thus founded, and it is now estimated that from 1628 to 1642 between twenty and thirty thousand citizens came to New

England from the region in east-central England between the Thames and the Humber—the English stronghold of Puritanism. Of these, about one-fifth were professed Christians; and their ministers were Puritans. Originally the Massachusetts Bay Christians had no intention of separating from the Church of England. The direct occasion for Congregational foundation was the choice which the Salem congregation found necessary to make between Francis Higginson and Samuel Skelton for minister, on 20 July 1629. The manner of ordination was by the imposition of hands. Congregationalism hereafter became the State Church in Massachusetts. In 1631 the Massachusetts General Court decreed that the franchise be permitted only to 'Church' members.

In 1636 Thomas Hooker and John Warham transplanted two Massachusetts churches to Connecticut. This colony became less theocratic than Massachusetts. Under the leadership of the Reverend John Davenport and the merchant Theophilus Eaton, a group of Puritans came in the spring of 1637 directly from England to the southern coast of what is now the State of Connecticut, there establishing the New Haven Colony. In 1664 the Connecticut and New Haven colonies were united, and Congregationalism prevailed among them.

III. THE REGULAR BAPTIST CHURCH in America was not exactly a foreign 'importation'; it was the result of local circumstance. Roger Williams, who was not a Baptist before he went to Providence from Boston, formed in 1638 a new church in Rhode Island, based on the principle of separation of church from state and on general Baptist principles. This new group freely championed the idea of the liberty of the individual soul.

After this foundation in Rhode Island, Baptist views began to appear in the older Puritan colonies. A Baptist Church was reported in Newport, Rhode Island, in 1648; it is quite likely that this church, numbering fifteen members and headed by John Clarke when it was reported, was not Baptist at the time of its founding in 1638. Massachusetts saw its first Baptist Church established at Rehoboth in 1663; this congregation removed to Swansea, near the Rhode Island border, shortly thereafter. In 1665 a Baptist Church was founded in Boston. In general, Baptists were persecuted in Massachusetts until about the end of the seventeenth century. It was not until 1728 that Massachusetts passed an Act exempting Anabaptists, along with Quakers, from the payment of the tax imposed for the support of the Congregationalist clergy. In New York Baptist preaching and ordinances were reported as early as 1656, but they were here excluded by civil edict.

The Baptists gained ground slowly, nevertheless, and by 1740 there were at least eleven of them in Rhode Island, eight in Massachusetts, and four in Connecticut. Maine made a weak Baptist beginning in 1682. Connecticut permitted its first Baptist Church in 1705, New Hampshire in 1755, and Vermont in 1768.

Baptist polity, however, found its most favourable territory in the Middle Colonies. From Pennsylvania's first Baptist Church in 1684 the number grew steadily, so that in 1762 there were twenty-nine churches in the Philadelphia Association alone.

Important accessions of Baptists arrived from Europe to increase the American number, most of them from England, Wales and the Isle of Wight.

The first Baptist Church in South Carolina was organized in 1683; in New Jersey, 1688; in Delaware, 1701; in Virginia, 1714; and in North Carolina, 172.

IV. THE SIX-PRINCIPLE BAPTISTS date their origin to 1638 or 1639, in Rhode Island, claiming to be the original church founded by Roger Williams. At any rate, in 1653 a number of Baptists in Providence, Rhode Island, organized what was known as the General Six-Principle Baptist Church, distinguishing themselves essentially from the Particular (Calvinistic) Baptists in their acceptance of the necessity of the laying-on of hands as a qualification for church fellowship. Their foundation 'principles' are those found in Hebrews vi. 1, 2—repentance, baptism, faith, laying on of hands, resurrection of the dead, and eternal judgment. Conferences of Six-Principle Baptists were formed in Massachusetts, New York and Pennsylvania, as well as in Rhode Island.

V. THE SEVENTH DAY BAPTIST CHURCH was first introduced in America at Newport, Rhode Island, with the coming of Stephen Mumford from London in 1664. Mumford began observing the Sabbath on the seventh day; several members of the Newport church followed him in this practice and organized the first Seventh Day Baptist Church in America on 23 December 1671. The relations of this group with other Rhode

Island Baptists, however, remained amicable. It was not long before this doctrine and observance spread to Pennsylvania and New Jersey.

In 1723 a company of German emigrants settling in Germantown, Pennsylvania, brought into America the German Seventh Day Baptist Church.

VI. THE REFORMED (PROTESTANT DUTCH) CHURCH was planted on Manhattan Island in 1628. Ministers for this group were imported from the Netherlands, for this denomination depended upon the Classis of Amsterdam until 1771, when an independent organization was effected in America. Father Jogues, a French Jesuit Missionary, in writing of New Netherland (N.Y.) in 1640, says: 'No religion is publicly exercised but the Calvinist, and orders are to admit none but Calvinists. But this is not observed, for there are, besides Calvinists, in the colony, Catholics, English Puritans, Lutherans, Anabaptists,— here called Mennonists.' New settlers from the surrounding colonies brought in even a greater variety of sects into New Amsterdam during Stuyvesant's rule, being promised 'liberty of conscience according to the custom and manner of Holland'.

VII. THE QUAKERS (FRIENDS) first appear in New England about the middle of the seventeenth century. Almost everywhere they met with antipathy. Massachusetts drew up a string of cruel laws against them until 1661. Connecticut and New Haven, and even Rhode Island under Roger Williams, legislated against them. In New York they were persecuted until 1663. Undaunted, nevertheless, the Quakers gained a foothold and appeared in a majority of the colonies. They showed up in Virginia as early as 1656; in Maryland, 1657. George Fox himself established a settlement of Friends in Perquimans, North Carolina, in 1672. Another colony was founded in New Jersey in 1674, where by 1681 there were found nearly 1000 Quakers. The William Penn Colony settled in Pennsylvania in 1682, and this region, along with New Jersey and Delaware, became the centre of Quaker activity in the colonies.

Yearly Meetings were established in New England (Rhode Island) in 1661; in Baltimore, 1672. The Virginia Yearly Meeting dates from 1673; the Burlington, later changed to the Philadelphia, Yearly Meeting, was organized in 1681; the New York, in 1696; and the North Carolina, in 1698.

By 1760 the number of Quakers in the colonies was estimated at near 30,000.

VIII. PRESBYTERIANISM in America recruited its earliest members from several sources. In early New England there was a considerable Presbyterian Puritan element; the tendency of Congregationalists to turn Presbyterian as soon as they left New England was more widespread than historians of the religion of colonial America seem willing to admit. Along with this element must be listed the Scotch who made some definite contributions to early American Presbyterianism. The attempt to establish episcopacy in Scotland after 1662 forced many Presbyterians out of Scotland, bringing them to New England, Maryland, Virginia and South Carolina in considerable numbers. The French Huguenots also made their contribution to colonial Presbyterianism. By 1688 Presbyterians existed in large numbers in Pennsylvania. The first Presbytery, that of Philadelphia, was constituted in 1706, becoming a Synod in 1716.

But the greatest increase in American Presbyterianism occurred with the coming of the Scotch-Irish from North Ireland, whence they fled because of economic hardships suffered there. This migration began in 1710, starting as a trickle but increasing gradually in extent until the 1920s, when they poured in in great streams of from three to six thousand yearly. They continued coming in until well past the middle of the eighteenth century. From 1714 to 1720 they disembarked largely through the port of Boston and spread out into central Massachusetts, southern New Hampshire, Vermont and Maine. But finding that they did not mix well with the New England Puritans, they began to find their way into New York after 1720. The greatest number of them, however, came to central Pennsylvania, whence they gradually moved southward into western Maryland, Virginia, the Carolinas and Georgia.

They scattered very widely among the colonies, more so than any other racial group that had removed to our shores. By the beginning of the Revolution they were sufficiently numerous everywhere to make their influence felt, culturally, economically and politically. At this time there were seventy communities of them in New England; from 30 to 40 in New York; from 50 to 60 in New Jersey; 130 in Delaware and Pennsylvania; more than 100 in Virginia, Maryland, east Kentucky and Tennessee; 50 in North Carolina; and about 70 in South Carolina and Georgia.

IX. THE REFORMED PRESBYTERIAN group was made up of descendants of the persecuted Presbyterians in Scotland who refused to accede to the Erastian 'Settlement of Religion' at the Revolution of 1688. In America congregations of them were formed as early as 1752, but there was no regular organization until they united in a body in 1798, at Philadelphia.

X. THE ASSOCIATED REFORMED PRESBYTERIANS originated, in this country, from the union formed between the Reformed Presbyterian Church and a portion of the Associated Church on 13 June 1782. The Associated Presbyterian Church in the United States was organized in 1754.

XI. THE SCHWENKFELDERS originated in Silesia, as a group who followed the reformer Kasper Schwenkfeld von Ossig (1490–1561). The aristocratic Schwenkfeld held both anti-Catholic and anti-Lutheran views. His followers had no intention of becoming a separate sect, but owing to the rough treatment they received at the hands of both the recognized Catholic and Protestant Churches, they formed themselves into a new and distinct sect. When the Emperor Charles VI sought their extermination in 1720, they migrated in large numbers into Saxony, where Count Zinzendorf gave them refuge on his estate. From here, about 200 of them emigrated to America in 1733 and 1734, arriving in Philadelphia and settling in Pennsylvania in Bucks, Montgomery and Berks counties. In this country they had no official ministry, but left everything in the hands of elders or heads of families. They made no attempt to form a denomination until 1782, when the American Schwenkfelder Church was organized. Their first church building was erected in 1790.

XII. THE GERMAN REFORMED CHURCH in America was really founded by John Philip Boehm in 1720, even though Samuel Guldin, a German Reformed minister, had arrived in Pennsylvania in 1710. Guldin had organized no congregations; this task Boehm assumed in 1725, when he was persuaded by his fellow Germans to conduct services for them and administer the Sacraments to them at regular intervals, even though he was not an ordained man. The arrival in 1727 of a German Reformed minister, George Michael Weiss, with a group of Palatinates, slightly upset Boehm's plans. Boehm was denounced by the new arrival as unfit, because of his lack of ordination, to carry on the work of a Christian minister. Boehm's congregations came to his aid and appealed the case to the Classis at Amsterdam. The result was that Boehm's activities were approved, considering the circumstances. At the request of the Classis he was now ordained, and his work among the German Reformed continued uninterrupted. A happy relationship between the German Reformed in America and the Synods of Holland grew out of this incident, a relationship which remained warm for the entire colonial period. Large groups of this denomination arrived from Germany between 1727 and 1745; the American congregations thus increased, and the church spread from Pennsylvania into New Jersey, New York, Virginia and the Carolinas.

XIII. THE LUTHERANS, as far as numbers in colonial times are concerned, were the most important of the German religious bodies that came to America. Dutch Lutherans had already appeared on Manhattan Island as early as 1621, but without a pastor; religious liberty was granted these in 1664 by the English authorities, and in 1669 the Reverend Jacob Fabricius reached this country as the first Dutch Lutheran minister. The Swedes, too, had helped to introduce Lutheranism here (settling on the banks of the Delaware in 1638, with minister), so that when Lutherans began to arrive in large numbers from Germany about 1720, they did not come entirely among religious strangers. Like the German Reformed people, the German Lutherans arrived here with little economic resources, no ministers, and no educators. Pennsylvania became a true haven for them. They were organized into congregations by a succession of capable ministers, culminating with the eminent Henry M. Mühlenberg, whose arrival in 1742 marks the turning point in American Lutheranism. Mühlenberg began to bring organization into the widely scattered Lutheran congregations, and in 1748 a Synod was formed.

Between the years 1732 and 1741 four groups of Salzburger Lutherans arrived in Georgia, fleeing from the intolerance of the Catholic Archbishop of Salzburg, Austria. Their settlement at Ebenezer soon grew to sizable proportions; their piety and industry made them prosper. Though an isolated body of Lutherans on their arrival, these Salzburgers by the time of the revolutionary outbreak had already scattered and joined with other Lutheran congregations. It has been estimated that at the end of the colonial period there were some 75,000 Lutherans in Pennsylvania alone, though most of these were probably not active church members. In Maryland, Virginia, the Carolinas and Georgia there were at the same time about thirty-six Lutheran congregations.

XIV. THE TAUFERS or DUNKERS (also called German Baptists and Brethren) appeared in Pennsylvania early in the eighteenth century. A small settlement of them, about 120 in number, left Crefeld in Germany in 1719 under the leadership of a Peter Becker and established themselves in Germantown, Pennsylvania. In 1723 the first Dunker Church in America was formed, with Peter Becker as elder. Soon other congregations were formed in the German communities where Brethren were settling, and by the end of the colonial period nineteen congregations of them had been organized, twelve of them numbering 200 or more.

XV. THE MENNONITES were the first of the German settlers in America, thirteen families of them arriving in Pennsylvania on 6 October 1683. Here they laid out the important community of Germantown. These were direct descendants of the Reformation Anabaptists. By 1688 they had formed a Mennonite congregation in America, and twenty years later the first Mennonite church was erected. By 1712 they numbered 200 in Pennsylvania, and 100 of them, at least, were church members. New groups of them had arrived in 1698 and in 1711. Their number was further swelled by importations in 1717 and 1727. They seem to stop coming at the opening of the Seven Years' War (1756), but by the end of the colonial period, nevertheless, there were about 2000 families of Mennonites in America, most of them in Pennsylvania.

XVI. THE MORAVIANS as a religious group date back to 1457, when they were first formed into an association in Bohemia. At the beginning of the Reformation there were more than 400 Brethren churches in Bohemia and Moravia, and a membership of about 175,000 persons. Opposition caused them to scatter abroad on the continent. In 1722 a small company of Moravians was permitted to settle on the estate of Nicholas Louis, Count of Zinzendorf, in Saxony. Here they united with German colonists, and combined their own religious plans with those of Zinzendorf. In 1735 they established their society, which they called the *Unitas Fratrum*; in England and America this association has been known as the Moravian Church.

The first Moravian mission to the colonies was to Pennsylvania in 1734. A second settlement, in Georgia, 1736, met with numerous difficulties and removed to Pennsylvania to join the group there in 1740. The town of Nazareth was thus established at the Forks of the Delaware.

In December of 1741 Count Zinzendorf himself arrived in America to attempt to unify all the German religious groups, not in an external organization but into a 'Church of God in the Spirit'. The other groups distrusted him, supposing that he was carrying on a clever bit of propaganda for the Moravians. When his plan for unity failed, Zinzendorf did indeed turn his attention entirely to the Moravians, helping them to establish the Moravian communities at Nazareth and Bethlehem and laying the foundations for the extensive missionary work which this religious group carried on among the Indians. Moravian communities developed also in Lititz, Pennsylvania, and Salem, North Carolina, in colonial times, along the lines of their communities in the Old World. In their exclusiveness they prospered to the extent that they were able to send substantial financial contributions to their needy European Brethren. By 1775, there were some 2500 Moravians in Pennsylvania alone.

XVII. METHODISM was introduced to America about twenty-seven years after its origin in England. Religious services were held by Methodists in New York City in 1766—the result of spontaneous religious convictions within the Established Church. Gradually, however, Methodists began to withdraw from the establishment. Joseph Pilmore and Richard Boardman, the first missionaries sent here by John Wesley, organized the first Methodist societies in New York and Pennsylvania in 1769. An even greater influence, however, was exerted by the Anglican evangelical rector, Devereux Jarratt of Virginia. Under his leadership, Virginia in colonial times became the centre of the American Methodist movement. In 1777 there were six Methodist circuits in Virginia, and one in North Carolina. The total membership of these was 4379. In that same year the entire membership of all the Methodist circuits in America was in the vicinity of 7000.

XVIII. THE JEWS first came to the colonies to escape persecution elsewhere. Spanish and Portuguese Jews, fleeing the

Inquisition, sought their first refuge in Manhattan Island, where they are known from almost the very beginning of New Amsterdam. Peter Stuyvesant and the Reformed ministers opposed giving them protection, but the Jews were permitted to remain so long as they did not worship in public. New York granted them freedom of worship only at the end of the seventeenth century; their first synagogue in this state was erected in 1728. Other Jewish synagogues were established in Newport, Rhode Island, in 1658; in Richmond, Virginia, in 1719; in Savannah, Georgia, in 1733; and in Charleston, North Carolina, in the same year.

XVIII. THE ROMAN CATHOLICS in this country were throughout the colonial period the victims of strong anti-Spanish and anti-Catholic feeling. The Protestant crusade against Catholicism was never relaxed in this period. George Calvert, the first Lord Baltimore, who was converted to Catholicism while still in England, was the only Catholic to succeed in establishing a colony in Anglo-America. Not many of his fellow religionists came to Maryland, however, and yet the colony was branded as a hotbed of popery. Toleration and justice to all was the policy of Maryland, and here Protestants and Catholics might have lived side by side in mutual self-respect, had they wanted to. But there was much enmity and rivalry between them, the Protestants winning out with the establishment of the Church of England in Maryland in 1702. Only the Baptists and the Quakers in America made any show of courtesy to the Roman Catholics, but even these to no great extent.

As Maryland loses its appeal to Catholics, these moved into the neighbouring state of Pennsylvania, where they were relatively free to worship as they willed. Their numbers here were swelled by other Catholics that came in from Germany after 1700. The 6000 Acadians, furthermore, who were removed from Nova Scotia in 1755 and scattered throughout the thirteen colonies, were solidly Catholic.

In spite of difficulties, then, the Roman Catholic number in America grew during the colonial period. In the year 1756 the Superior of the Maryland mission, Father George Hunter, reported that there were some 7000 Catholic communicants in Maryland, and 3000 in Pennsylvania. At the outbreak of the Revolution there were in the colonies at least 26 priests, 52 churches, and about 20,000 Roman Catholics.

APPENDIX B

At the close of the colonial period, according to a report of the Society of the Descendants of the Colonial Clergy (incorporated in Lancaster, Massachusetts, on 9 February 1933), the number of churches in the American colonies was divided as follows:

1. *Congregational*, 800, with 750 or more in New England—Massachusetts, Connecticut and New Hampshire leading in that order.

2. *Presbyterian*, 502, of which more than 430 are in the Middle and Southern Colonies.

3. *Baptist*, 472, the majority of them again in the Middle and Southern Colonies.

4. *Episcopalian*, 408, the Middle and Southern Colonies claiming 332 of them, with Virginia far in the lead with 121.

5. *German Reformed*, 203, all in the Middle and South.

6. *French Reformed*, 16, with only 4 of them in New England.

7. *Dutch Reformed*, 126, with none in New England.

8. *Lutheran*, 243, of which 11 are distinctively Swedish Lutheran. Pennsylvania leads all the other states by a wide margin; there is only one in New England.

9. *Moravian*, 84, with only 1 in New England and 42 in Pennsylvania.

10. *Mennonite*, 68, with 63 in Pennsylvania, 5 of which are Amish Mennonite.

11. *Roman Catholics*, 57, with 20 in Maryland, 16 in Pennsylvania, 8 in New York, 4 in Delaware, and 3 in New Jersey. New England has 6, all of them in Maine.

12. *Methodist*, 16, with none in New England.

This report gives no figures for Quakers or Jews; under Miscellaneous it lists four Sandemanian churches (in New England), one Schwenkfelder (in Pennsylvania), one Labadist (in Maryland), one Universalist (in New Jersey), one Baumanite (in Pennsylvania), and one Weberite (in South Carolina).

REFERENCES

Dorchester, Daniel. *Christianity in the United States from the first settlement down to the present time.* New York, Hunt and Eaton, 1889. Pp. 799.
Sweet, W. W. *Religion in Colonial America.* New York, Scribner's, 1942. Pp. xiii, 367.
Sweet, W. W. *The Story of Religion in America.* New York, Harper, 1939. Pp. vi, 656.
Weis, F. L. *The Colonial Churches and the Colonial Clergy of the Middle and Southern Colonies, 1607–1776.* Lancaster, Mass., 1938. Pp. 140.

C. POLITIES IN THE AMERICAN CHURCHES

The 256 denominations in America fall chiefly into the three main types of church government: the Congregational, the Episcopal, and the Presbyterian. A few are best described as military in organization, and one is governed on the lines of a fraternal order. Some others defy classification in any one category and are best left in an unclassified list. The denominations line up as follows according to. polity:

Congregational	99
Episcopal	79
Presbyterian	52
Military	4
Fraternal	1
Unclassified	21
Total	256

CHURCHES ON CONGREGATIONAL POLITY: The American Census of 1936 reported the inclusive church membership as 55,807,366, a figure which, of course, would have been much larger had all churches furnished statistics. The 1943 edition of the *Yearbook of American Churches* gives in most instances more complete numbers, but here we find a lack of uniformity, for the figures given are not all as of one year, but range between the years 1936 and 1943, the latest-known figure being given for each denomination. This more recent authority gives the inclusive church membership in the United States as 67,327,719. Our observations, then, will be based on the listings found in these two sources, as being the best available at the present time. And if their figures cannot give us completeness or exactness, they will at any rate enable us to reach some broad conclusions that will afford us at least a fair likeness of the general picture, even though they cannot furnish us with the exact details of the situation.

The 99 denominations organized on a Congregational basis account, in 1936, for roughly 17 million church members whose government is strictly Congregational in form, and for 2 million more who have adopted a more modified Congregationalism. Their total of approximately 19 million is raised considerably by the 1943 *Yearbook of American Churches*, to 21 million under strict Congregational polity and 2½ million more under a modified Congregational system. These bodies thus account for about

32 per cent of the total church membership in 1936, and for 35 per cent in 1943. Some of the larger denominations included in this category are the numerous Baptist bodies, the Congregational Christian Churches, the Jewish congregations, the Disciples of Christ, the Churches of Christ, a good number of Lutheran bodies, the Quakers, and the Unitarian Churches.

CHURCHES ON EPISCOPAL POLITY: The 79 religious bodies that fall under the episcopal type of church government account roughly for 31 million church members in 1936, and 38 million in 1943—that is, approximately 57 per cent and 56 per cent of the inclusive church membership respectively according to both listings. Among the principal bodies in this class are the Eastern Orthodox churches, the Evangelical Church, the Evangelical Lutheran Joint Synod of Wisconsin and Other States, the Methodist Church, the African Methodist Episcopal Church, the African Methodist Episcopal Zion Church, the Coloured Methodist Episcopal Church, the Church of the United Brethren in Christ, the Protestant Episcopal Church, and the Roman Catholic Church.

CHURCHES ON PRESBYTERIAL POLITY: The 52 bodies under a Presbyterian form of government cover a membership of 5 million in 1936 and 5.9 million in 1943—that is, about 9 per cent of the total membership in the earlier census, and 8.7 per cent in the 1943 figuration. The American Presbyterial bodies include the Assemblies of God, General Council, the Evangelical and Reformed Church, the Evangelical Lutheran Augustana Synod of North America, the Norwegian Lutheran Church of America, the Presbyterian Church in the U.S.A., the Cumberland Presbyterian Church, the United Presbyterian Church of North America, the Presbyterian Church in the U.S., the Reformed Church in America, and the Christian Reformed Church.

OTHER FORMS OF GOVERNMENT: Those churches, like the Salvation Army, which function under a military type of government account for a membership of 128,000 in 1936 and 475,000 in 1943. The Church of the Living God (Christian Workers for Fellowship), which is organized on fraternal order lines, is listed with 4,525 members in the 1936 Census, and with 110 members as the 1942 figure given by the *Yearbook of American Churches* in 1943. The unclassified denominations represent 306,000 members in 1936, and 336,000 in 1943.

APPENDIX C

REFERENCES

United States Department of Commerce, Bureau of the Census. *Report on the Religious Bodies*, 1936. 3 volumes. Washington (D.C.), United States Government Printing Office, 1941.

Yearbook of American Churches (1943 Edition). Edited by Benson Y. Landis. Lebanon (Pa.), Sowers Printing Company, 1943. Pp. viii, 173.

D. RELIGIOUS BODIES WITH 50,000 MEMBERS AND OVER[1]

Name of religious body	Year of report	Number of churches	Inclusive church membership
Adventists, Seventh Day	1942	2,491	186,478
Assemblies of God	1942	4,840	222,730
Baptist Bodies:			
Northern Baptist Convention	1942	7,365	1,538,871
Southern Baptist Convention	1942	25,737	5,367,129
National Baptist Convention U.S.A., Inc. and National Baptist Convention of America	1942	24,575	3,911,612
American Baptist Association	1936	1,064	115,022
Free Will Baptists	1940	1,102	118,871
National Baptist Evangelical Life and Soul Saving Assembly of U.S.A.	1940	176	55,897
Primitive Baptists	1936	1,726	69,157
United American Free Will Baptists	1942	1,712	60,000
Church of the Brethren	1942	1,019	179,843
Church of Christ, Scientist	1936	2,113	268,915
Churches of God:			
Church of God	1942	1,686	82,462
Church of God (Anderson, Ind.)	1942	1,412	83,875
Church of the Nazarene	1942	2,898	180,243
Churches of Christ	1936	3,815	309,551
Congregational Christian Churches	1941	5,827	1,052,701
Disciples of Christ	1942	7,919	1,655,580
Eastern Orthodox Churches:			
Greek Orthodox Church (Hellenic)	1942	275	650,000
Russian Orthodox Greek Catholic Church of North America	1943	250	300,000
Serbian Eastern Orthodox Church	1942	45	110,000

[1] Landis, B. Y., ed. *Yearbook of American Churches*, p. 148. 1943.

Name of religious body	Year of report	Number of churches	Inclusive church membership
Evangelical and Reformed Church	1941	2,850	662,953
Evangelical Church	1942	1,983	248,475
Friends, Religious Society of (Five Years' Meeting)	1942	508	69,832
Independent Fundamental Churches of America	1943	435	50,000
International Church of the Four-Square Gospel	1942	408	250,000
Jewish Congregations	1936	3,728	4,641,184
Latter-Day Saints:			
Church of Jesus Christ of Latter-Day Saints	1941	1,598	816,774
Reorganized Church of Jesus Christ of Latter-Day Saints	1942	563	110,481
Lutherans:			
American Lutheran Conference:			
American Lutheran Church	1941	1,826	547,812
Evangelical Lutheran Augustana Synod	1941	1,126	352,571
Norwegian Lutheran Church of America	1941	2,477	569,112
Lutheran Synodical Conference of North America:			
Evangelical Lutheran Synod of Missouri, Ohio and Other States	1941	4,326	1,320,510
Evangelical Lutheran Joint Synod of Wisconsin and Other States	1942	745	315,560
United Lutheran Church in America	1941	4,046	1,709,290
Mennonite Church:	1942	445	51,879
Methodist Bodies:			
African Methodist Episcopal	1942	7,265	868,735
African Methodist Episcopal Zion	1936	2,252	414,244
Coloured Methodist Episcopal	1942	4,200	380,000
The Methodist Church	1942	42,206	6,640,424
Polish National Catholic Church	1936	118	63,366
Presbyterian Bodies:			
Cumberland Presbyterian Church	1942	1,088	72,591
Presbyterian Church in the U.S.	1942	3,500	546,479
Presbyterian Church in the U.S.A.	1942	8,511	1,986,257
United Presbyterian Church of North America	1942	850	190,724
Protestant Episcopal Church	1942	7,685	2,074,178

Name of religious body	Year of report	Number of churches	Inclusive church membership
Reformed Bodies:			
Christian Reformed Church	1942	306	126,293
Reformed Church in America	1942	727	163,835
Roman Catholic Church	1943	18,976	22,945,247
Salvation Army	1942	1,515	220,367
Unitarian Churches	1941	365	61,600
United Brethren in Christ	1942	2,788	425,337
TOTALS: 52 Bodies		227,463	65,415,047

These 52 bodies, having each 50,000 or more members, form over 97 per cent of the total national church membership. The remaining 3 per cent is spread out among the other 204 denominations.

E. THE NEGRO CHURCH IN AMERICA

STATISTICS

The following statement on the Negro Church in America is based upon the latest governmental Census, the 1936 report of the United States Department of Commerce, Bureau of the Census. The findings here reported represent at least a minimum, for the returns of 1936 were relatively incomplete on the part of some of the denominations.

Of the 256 religious bodies which sent in returns for the 1936 Census, 59 reported Negro Churches. 33 of these 59 denominations were exclusively Negro in membership. The remaining 26 reported Negro Churches, though they are primarily white in membership.

38,303 Negro Churches sent in returns in 1936; these were divided as follows:

Negro Baptist	23,093
African Methodist Episcopal	4,578
African Methodist Episcopal Zion	2,252
Coloured Methodist Episcopal	2,063
Methodist Episcopal [1]	1,730
Coloured Primitive Baptist	1,009
Church of God in Christ	772
Congregational and Christian	233
United American Free Will Baptist	226
Church of God and Saints of Christ	213
All others	2,134

[1] Negro churches of a denomination which is primarily white.

These churches make up a total Negro Church membership of 5,660,618, a figure which forms 10·1 per cent of the total American church membership reported. These numbers are an increase over the 1926 Census, but not an increase at the same rate as the growth in population.

The membership is distributed thus among the various denominations:

Negro Baptists[1]	3,782,464
African Methodist Episcopal	493,357
African Methodist Episcopal Zion	414,244
Coloured Methodist Episcopal	269,915
Methodist Episcopal	193,761
Roman Catholic	137,684
Northern Baptist	45,821
Coloured Primitive Baptist	43,897
Church of God and Saints of Christ	37,084
Church of God in Christ	31,564
All others	210,827
Total	5,660,618

The sex ratio for Negro Church membership is 60·5 men for every 100 women, as against the ratio of 78·5 men per 100 women for all churches.

The 1936 Census shows a decrease in the number of Negro churches when compared with the Census of 1926: the later report shows 38,303 churches against the 42,585 of 1926. This decrease is probably due to the disintegration of some of the churches at the migratory movements of population and, as well, to the consolidation of some of the churches for economic reasons.

An increase in the number of churches, however, is shown by the Negro Baptists, the United American Free Will Baptists, the Roman Catholic Church, the Church of God and Saints of Christ, and some of the smaller denominations. A sharp decrease is noticed in the Churches of Christ and in the Disciples of Christ.

Fourteen new bodies among the Negro denominations were reported for the first time in 1936. Among these are the United Holy Church of America (162 churches and 7535 members), the National Baptist Evangelical Life and Soul Saving Assembly of the United States of America (28 churches and 2300 members), and the Fire Baptized Holiness Church of God of the Americas (59 churches and 1793 members).

[1] This figure amounts to 66·8 per cent of all Negro Church membership.

APPENDIX F

F. CONSCIENTIOUS OBJECTORS[1]

This world war, like the last, has produced an appreciable number of conscientious objectors both here and in England. These are a wartime minority, to be sure, but they are a minority which both the public and governments must take into serious account when military conflict breaks out among the nations. The following is an outline of the method of procedure followed by England and the United States in the matter of conscientious objectors. The problem in both countries has been the same, but the handling of it in each has followed a different course.

Six per cent of England's professed conscientious objectors have been granted total exemption from any form of service under conscription. The United States has not seen fit to provide such complete exemption for objectors, but it has granted them some concessions under the Selective Service Act of 1940. This congressional legislation required two conditions of conscientious objectors: first, that the registrant be opposed to 'participation in war in any form'; and second, that his scruples be founded on 'religious training and belief'. The requirement of church membership, on which the American draft law of 1917 insisted, has been dispensed with in this war.

It is not an easy matter, however, for a draftee in our country to claim exemption 'for conscience sake'. The red tape involved is almost beyond description, and the lack of uniform procedure has led to various difficulties. The American conscientious objector must first register like all other draftees. When this is done, he then fills a detailed questionnaire, on the basis of which his draft board decides on his sincerity and evaluates the claim of exemption. If the draft board cannot, from the questionnaire, grant him an objector's classification, the draftee may appeal and appear before a Hearing Officer of the Department of Justice after a thorough investigation by the Federal Bureau. It is then for the Hearing Officer to recommend the claimant to the final tribunal, the Board of Appeal.

Those conscientious objectors who are approved under Selective Service are then classified in two categories: (a) those who object only to combatant service; (b) and those who object to all military service. The first group are assigned to the Army

[1] Cf. Cornell, Julien, *The Conscientious Objector*, pp. x, 158. John Day and Company, New York, 1943.

Medical Corps; and the second 'to do work of national importance under civilian direction'.

The British Statute, 'National Service (Armed Forces) Act',
which went into effect on 3 September 1939, was constructed
with a little more care than its American counterpart, at least in
regard to the treatment of conscientious objectors. The result has
been that there is less friction in England than there is here on
that account. Unlike the procedure in this country, British
conscientious objectors do not register for military service, but
apply immediately to a separate register which is provided for
them. After tests of the applicant's sincerity, this first provisional
registration is approved, and the registrant becomes permanently
classified as a conscientious objector. Any who refuse to sign a
military register have in England hearings before the tribunals.
But not so in America: our draft law has made no such special
provision, and consequently we have on record a number of
cases of men who have been imprisoned for refusing to be put
on the military register 'for conscience sake'.

The qualification made by the American law on the kind of
objection it will permit, i.e. only when it proceeds from 'religious training and belief', has been a source of discontent and
confusion here, because it allows of varied interpretation and
leads to varying results in procedure. Humanitarian philosophical
and political objectors, for instance, have in this country no claim
to exemption. The British law, on the other hand, has left no
room for such difficulty by recognizing all kinds of objection, so
long as they are based on conscience.

A number of Americans have been critical of our local draft
boards, as having been selected in haste, without particular discrimination and without concern for the qualifications of the
personnel who make up these boards. Mismanagement on the
part of the local boards in several cases regarding the conscientious
objector has not helped to reduce their reputed incompetence.
The local tribunals for England, Scotland, and Wales are believed, on the whole, to be much more efficient groups, being
fewer in number and having been appointed with greater care
than our own here. To prejudice further the argument in favour
of the English tribunals, they have the added advantage that any
hearing at the local tribunal must be public and that the applicant
may be represented by a lawyer or a friend. The American
system is less prone to air itself, and hearings, when they are
granted, are private, with the right to counsel expressly denied.

APPENDIX F

The case of a conscientious objector in England may be decided in one of four different ways:

1. The applicant may be accorded unconditional exemption, with no requirement to perform any kind of service. He is registered without condition in the Register of Conscientious Objectors.

2. The applicant may be registered as a conscientious objector of whom work of a certain general nature, public or private, is required. Such work, determined by the tribunal, must be civilian in character and under civilian control, and may be for wages or for maintenance only.

3. The applicant may be removed from the provisional Register of Conscientious Objectors and placed on the Military Service Register for non-combatant duty.

4. The applicant may be registered on the Military Service Register for combatant duty.

The lists published by the Central Board of Conscientious Objectors, London, as of 1 January 1943, give some 45,000 English objectors who have been granted exemption. This figure is relatively high when compared with the mere 6000 who at about the same time had been granted conscientious exemption in America. Of the English number, about 6 per cent, i.e. 2700, received unconditional exemption. Some 20,000 men have been granted conditional exemption; many of these work in private industry, while others engage in civilian defence. 15,000 objectors or so have been assigned to non-combatant duty with the military services, and as many more have been denied any exemption and have been placed on combatant duty.

The English penalties for Conscientious Objectors who become involved in the law courts are less severe than the American. Though the original English fine of £100 or one year imprisonment for delinquents has been doubled, it is still far below the American requirement of $10,000 or five years' imprisonment. Not a few conscientious objectors in this country have come to grips with the law, civil and military, and have been convicted. Several hundred pacifists are now in prison for opposing all military conscription. Also confined are many objectors who were willing to serve under civilian direction but, being denied that classification, felt a compulsion to refuse induction into military service. The Department of Justice (1 July 1943) disclosed that under the draft 2701 conscientious objectors, out of a little more than 12,000 who had claimed exemption, had been convicted. This number, which is considerably higher than similar convictions in America during the first World War, is also relatively far greater than the number of imprisonments in England, where out of the 60,000 who have claimed conscientious exemption, only 3000, about 5 per cent, find themselves in prison. The American figure, however, is perhaps swelled by the Jehovah's Witnesses, who demand complete exemption, not permitted by our law. They form two-thirds of the American imprisonments.

Some 7000 American pacifists are found in the Civilian Public Service Camps and Units, the aim of which is to protect and conserve natural resources and to engage in other special services. Of these, two-thirds come from the 'historic peace churches', the Mennonites, Friends, Brethren, Christadelphians, and Molokans. Without pay, these men perform such civilian tasks as draining swamps, building dams, fighting forest fires, tending patients in mental hospitals, serving as 'guinea-pigs' in medical research, constructing rural sanitation facilities, and producing food and milk. Like their friends in the armed services, these men in the Civilian Public Service units will serve throughout the war and six months thereafter. Their schedule is rigorous, requiring at least fifty-one work-hours a week; free time is permitted them on Sunday and a furlough of thirty days once a year. CPS men are not uniformed; each supplies his own clothes. They are not paid, except for a bare monthly pittance ranging from $2.50 to $15.00, depending on the project in which the objector is engaged.

The churches on the whole have supported the right to exemption from military service for those who oppose participation in war on grounds of conscience. Three major non-pacifist churches have made the following statements:

1. The Methodist General Conference, 1940.

We ask and claim exemption from all forms of military preparations or service for all conscientious objectors who may be members of the Methodist Church. Those of our members who, as conscientious objectors, seek exemption from...military service...have the authority and support of their church.

2. The Northern Baptist Convention, 1940.

We lay upon the conscience of our people the responsibility to maintain our bond of fellowship in Christ despite differences of opinion,

APPENDIX F

and to give moral support and protection to those who follow the voice of conscience either in personal participation or refusal to participate in war.

3. The Presbyterian (U.S.A.) Assembly, 1942.

We reaffirm past deliverances of General Assembly on the equal standing within the fellowship and support of the Church of those who for conscience sake either object to, or participate in, war. We urge the continuance of the government's recognition of the right of conscientious objection and its extension into all aspects of participation in the war effort.

Most of the CPS camps and units are administered, at the request of Selective Service, by church agencies. The government, however, operates some camps directly. It provides the basic camp equipment, project supervisors and maintenance for those men in the camps which it administers directly. The rest of the CPS burden lies on the churches, who finance the nation-wide service almost entirely by voluntary contributions. Part of the expense is paid by the men themselves, when they can.

Many denominations are represented in the CPS camps. Of the non-pacifist churches, the Methodists have contributed 577 men to Civilian Public Service; Jehovah's Witnesses, 202; Presbyterians, 172; Baptists, 162; Congregational-Christians, 144; Church of Christ, 108; Catholics, 104; Lutherans, 73; Disciples of Christ, 55; Evangelical and Reformed, 54; Episcopalians, 52; Evangelicals, 50; Jews, 33; Pentecostals, 27; Unitarians, 26; Assemblies of God, 12. Ninety-seven other denominations account for 397 men. The number of conscientious objectors in CPS camps who have no church affiliation is 431. The Historic Peace Churches have offered 2477 Mennonites; 911 Brethren; 579 Friends (Quakers); 68 Christadelphians; and 23 Molokans. The total on 30 November 1943, was thus 6737 men.

APPENDIX G

G. DENOMINATIONAL COLLEGES AND UNIVERSITIES IN THE UNITED STATES, Organized 1800–1900

(Accredited by national and regional accrediting associations)

No.	Institution	Year of organization	Location, by State	Denomination
1	Moravian College	1807	Pennsylvania	Moravian
2	Mount Saint Mary's College	1808	Maryland	Catholic
3	Allegheny College	1815	Pennsylvania	Methodist
4	Colby College	1818	Maine	Northern Baptist
5	Saint Louis University	1818	Missouri	Catholic
6	Centre College	1819	Kentucky	Presbyterian (U.S. and U.S.A.)
7	Colgate University	1819	New York	Northern Baptist
8	Maryville College	1819	Tennessee	Presbyterian (U.S.A.)
9	Hobart College	1822	New York	Protestant Episcopal
10	Trinity College	1823	Connecticut	Protestant Episcopal
11	Kenyon College	1824	Ohio	Protestant Episcopal
12	Centenary College	1825	Louisiana	Methodist
13	Lafayette College	1825	Pennsylvania	Presbyterian (U.S.A.)
14	Furman University	1826	South Carolina	Southern Baptist
15	Mississippi College	1826	Mississippi	Southern Baptist
16	Georgetown College	1829	Kentucky	Southern Baptist
17	Illinois College	1829	Illinois	Presbyterian (U.S.A.)
18	Lindenwood College	1830	Missouri	Presbyterian (U.S.A.)
19	Randolph-Macon College	1830	Virginia	Methodist
20	Spring Hill College	1830	Alabama	Catholic
21	Denison University	1831	Ohio	Northern Baptist

22	Wesleyan University	1831	Connecticut	Methodist
23	Xavier University	1831	Ohio	Catholic
24	Gettysburg College	1832	Pennsylvania	United Lutheran
25	University of Richmond	1832	Virginia	Southern Baptist
26	Haverford College	1833	Pennsylvania	Friends
27	Kalamazoo College	1833	Michigan	Northern Baptist
28	Mercer University	1833	Georgia	Southern Baptist
29	Franklin College of Indiana	1834	Indiana	Northern Baptist
30	Wake Forest College	1834	North Carolina	Southern Baptist
31	Albion College	1835	Michigan	Methodist
32	Alfred University	1836	New York	Seventh-Day Baptist
33	Emory University	1836	Georgia	Methodist
34	Wesleyan College	1836	Georgia	Methodist
35	Davidson College	1837	North Carolina	Presbyterian (U.S.)
36	De Pauw University	1837	Indiana	Methodist
37	Guilford College	1837	North Carolina	Friends
38	Muskingum College	1837	Ohio	United Presbyterian
39	Duke University	1838	North Carolina	Methodist
40	Emory and Henry College	1838	Virginia	Methodist
41	Greensboro College	1838	North Carolina	Methodist
42	Judson College	1838	Alabama	Southern Baptist
43	Boston University	1839	Massachusetts	Methodist
44	Erskine College	1839	South Carolina	Associate Reformed Presbyterian
45	Loras College	1839	Iowa	Catholic
46	Southwestern University	1840	Texas	Methodist
47	Bethany College	1841	West Virginia	Disciples
48	Fordham University	1841	New York	Catholic

No.	Institution	Year of organization	Location, by State	Denomination
49	Howard College	1841	Alabama	Southern Baptist
50	Manhattansville College of the Sacred Heart	1841	New York	Catholic
51	Iowa Wesleyan College	1842	Iowa	Methodist
52	Mary Baldwin College	1842	Virginia	Presbyterian (U.S.)
53	Ohio Wesleyan University	1842	Ohio	Methodist
54	University of Notre Dame	1842	Indiana	Catholic
55	Villanova College	1842	Pennsylvania	Catholic
56	Willamette University	1842	Oregon	Methodist
57	Clarke College	1843	Iowa	Catholic
58	College of the Holy Cross	1843	Massachusetts	Catholic
59	Hillsdale College	1844	Michigan	Northern Baptist
60	Baldwin–Wallace College	1845	Ohio	Methodist
61	Baylor University	1845	Texas	Southern Baptist
62	Limestone College	1845	South Carolina	Southern Baptist
63	Mary Hardin–Baylor College	1845	Texas	Southern Baptist
64	Wittenberg College	1845	Ohio	United Lutheran
65	Bucknell University	1846	Pennsylvania	Northern Baptist
66	Carroll College	1846	Wisconsin	Presbyterian (U.S.A.)
67	Mount Union College	1846	Ohio	Methodist
68	Saint Vincent's College	1846	Pennsylvania	Catholic
69	College of Mount Saint Vincent	1847	New York	Catholic
70	Earlham College	1847	Indiana	Friends
71	Lawrence College	1847	Wisconsin	Methodist
72	MacMurray College	1847	Illinois	Methodist

73	Otterbein College	Ohio	1847	United Brethren
74	Saint Francis College	Pennsylvania	1847	Catholic
75	Geneva College	Pennsylvania	1848	Reformed Presbyterian in North America
76	Muhlenberg College	Pennsylvania	1848	United Lutheran
77	William Jewell College	Missouri	1849	Southern Baptist
78	Capital University	Ohio	1850	American Lutheran
79	Dayton University	Ohio	1850	Catholic
80	Heidelberg College	Ohio	1850	Evangelical and Reformed
81	Illinois Wesleyan University	Illinois	1850	Methodist
82	Carson-Newman College	Tennessee	1851	Southern Baptist
83	Catawba College	North Carolina	1851	Evangelical and Reformed
84	College of the Pacific	California	1851	Methodist
85	Northwestern University	Illinois	1851	Methodist
86	Saint Joseph's College	Pennsylvania	1851	Catholic
87	University of Santa Clara	California	1851	Catholic
88	Wofford College	South Carolina	1851	Methodist
89	Loyola College	Maryland	1852	Catholic
90	University of Dubuque	Iowa	1852	Presbyterian (U.S.A.)
91	Westminster College	Pennsylvania	1852	United Presbyterian
92	Central College	Iowa	1853	Reformed Church in America
93	Cornell College	Iowa	1853	Methodist
94	Culver-Stockton College	Missouri	1853	Disciples
95	Manhattan College	New York	1853	Catholic
96	Roanoke College	Virginia	1853	United Lutheran
97	Westminster College	Missouri	1853	Presbyterian (U.S.)
98	Evansville College	Indiana	1854	Methodist
99	Hamline University	Minnesota	1854	Methodist

No.	Institution	Year of organization	Location, by State	Denomination
100	Huntington College	1854	Alabama	Methodist
101	Butler University	1855	Indiana	Disciples
102	Saint Mary's College	1855	Indiana	Catholic
103	University of San Francisco	1855	California	Catholic
104	Albright College	1856	Pennsylvania	Evangelical
105	Birmingham-Southern College	1856	Alabama	Methodist
106	Monmouth College	1856	Illinois	United Presbyterian
107	Newberry College	1856	South Carolina	United Lutheran
108	Niagara University	1856	New York	Catholic
109	Seton Hall College	1856	New Jersey	Catholic
110	Wilberforce University	1856	Ohio	African Methodist Episcopal
111	Central College	1857	Missouri	Methodist
112	Lake Forest College	1857	Illinois	Presbyterian (U.S.A.)
113	Queens College	1857	North Carolina	Presbyterian (U.S.)
114	Baker University	1858	Kansas	Methodist
115	Linfield College	1858	Oregon	Northern Baptist
116	Saint Benedict's College	1858	Kansas	Catholic
117	Susquehanna University	1858	Pennsylvania	United Lutheran
118	Columbia College	1859	South Carolina	Methodist
119	Saint Bonaventure College	1859	New York	Catholic
120	Augustana College	1860	South Dakota	Norwegian Lutheran
121	Augustana College and Theological Seminary	1860	Illinois	Lutheran (Augustana Synod)
122	Bard College	1860	New York	Protestant Episcopal
123	Simpson College	1860	Iowa	Methodist

124	Luther College	Iowa	Norwegian Lutheran	1861
125	North Central College	Illinois	Evangelical	1861
126	Gustavus Adolphus College	Minnesota	Lutheran (Augustana Synod)	1862
127	Saint Mary's College	California	Catholic	1862
128	Bates College	Maine	Northern Baptist	1863
129	Boston College	Massachusetts	Catholic	1863
130	University of Denver	Colorado	Methodist	1864
131	Loyola University	California	Catholic	1865
132	Ottawa University	Kansas	Northern Baptist	1865
133	Shaw University	North Carolina	National Baptist	1865
134	Hope College	Michigan	Reformed Church in America	1866
135	Lebanon Valley College	Pennsylvania	United Brethren	1866
136	Drew University	New Jersey	Methodist	1867
137	Johnson C. Smith University	North Carolina	Presbyterian (U.S.A.)	1867
138	Morehouse College	Georgia	National Baptist	1867
139	Saint Augustine's College	North Carolina	Protestant Episcopal	1867
140	Western Maryland College	Maryland	Methodist	1868
141	University of the South	Tennessee	Protestant Episcopal	1868
142	Ursinus College	Pennsylvania	Evangelical and Reformed	1869
143	Canisius College	New York	Catholic	1870
144	Carthage College	Illinois	United Lutheran	1870
145	Clark College	Georgia	Methodist	1870
146	College of Wooster	Ohio	Presbyterian (U.S.A.)	1870
147	Loyola University	Illinois	Catholic	1870
148	Syracuse University	New York	Methodist	1870
149	Thiel College	Pennsylvania	Evangelical Lutheran	1870
150	Wilson College	Pennsylvania	Presbyterian (U.S.A.)	1870

APPENDIX G

No.	Institution	Year of organization	Location, by State	Denomination
151	Benedict College	1871	South Carolina	National Baptist
152	Elmhurst College	1871	Illinois	Evangelical and Reformed
153	Ursuline College	1871	Ohio	Catholic
154	Maryville College	1872	Missouri	Catholic
155	Valparaiso University	1872	Indiana	Lutheran (Missouri Synod)
156	Blue Mountain College	1873	Mississippi	Southern Baptist
157	College of Notre Dame of Maryland	1873	Maryland	Catholic
158	Shorter College	1873	Georgia	Southern Baptist
159	Texas Christian University	1873	Texas	Disciples
160	Wiley College	1873	Texas	Coloured Methodist Episcopal
161	Saint Olaf College	1874	Minnesota	Norwegian Lutheran
162	Brigham Young University	1875	Utah	Latter-Day Saints
163	Knoxville College	1875	Tennessee	United Presbyterian
164	Southwestern College	1875	Tennessee	Presbyterian (U.S.)
165	Parsons College	1875	Iowa	Presbyterian (U.S.A.)
166	Calvin College	1876	Michigan	Christian Reformed
167	Juniata College	1876	Pennsylvania	Church of the Brethren
168	University of Detroit	1877	Michigan	Catholic
169	Ashland College	1878	Ohio	Brethren (Progressive Dunk.)
170	Creighton University	1878	Nebraska	Catholic
171	Duquesne University	1878	Pennsylvania	Catholic
172	Saint Peter's College	1878	New Jersey	Catholic
173	Union College	1879	Kentucky	Methodist
174	Bridgewater College	1880	Virginia	Brethren

300

APPENDIX G

175	University of Southern California	1880	California	Methodist
176	Bethany College	1881	Kansas	Lutheran (Augustana Synod)
177	Bishop College	1881	Texas	National Baptist
178	Drake University	1881	Iowa	Disciples
179	Marquette University	1881	Wisconsin	Catholic
180	Spelman College	1881	Georgia	National Baptist
181	Findlay College	1882	Ohio	Church of God
182	Hastings College	1882	Nebraska	Presbyterian (U.S.A.)
183	Lane College	1882	Tennessee	Coloured Methodist Episcopal
184	Livingstone College	1882	North Carolina	African Methodist Episcopal Zion
185	Saint Ambrose College	1882	Iowa	Catholic
186	Huron College	1883	South Dakota	Presbyterian (U.S.A.)
187	Jamestown College	1883	North Dakota	Presbyterian (U.S.A.)
188	Seton Hill College	1883	Pennsylvania	Catholic
189	Tarkio College	1883	Missouri	United Presbyterian
190	Wagner Memorial Lutheran College	1883	New York	United Lutheran
191	Hendrix College	1884	Arkansas	Methodist
192	Houghton College	1884	New York	Wesleyan Methodist
193	College of Saint Thomas	1885	Minnesota	Catholic
194	Dakota Wesleyan University	1885	South Dakota	Methodist
195	Macalester College	1885	Minnesota	Presbyterian (U.S.A.)
196	Morris Brown College	1885	Georgia	African Methodist Episcopal
197	Southwestern College	1885	Kansas	Methodist
198	Florida Southern College	1886	Florida	Methodist
199	John Carroll University	1886	Ohio	Catholic
200	Ouachita Baptist College	1886	Arkansas	Southern Baptist
201	University of Chattanooga	1886	Tennessee	Methodist

No.	Institution	Year of organization	Location, by State	Denomination
202	Alma College	1887	Michigan	Presbyterian (U.S.A.)
203	Catholic University of America	1887	District of Columbia	Catholic
204	Gonzaga University	1887	Washington	Catholic
205	John B. Stetson University	1887	Florida	Southern Baptist
206	McPherson College	1887	Kansas	Brethren
207	Mount Angel College	1887	Oregon	Catholic
208	College of Puget Sound	1888	Washington	Methodist
209	Nebraska Wesleyan University	1888	Nebraska	Methodist
210	University of Scranton	1888	Pennsylvania	Catholic
211	Agnes Scott College	1889	Georgia	Presbyterian (U.S.)
212	College of Saint Elizabeth	1889	New Jersey	Catholic
213	Missouri Valley College	1889	Missouri	Presbyterian (U.S.A.)
214	Saint Anselm's College	1889	New Hampshire	Catholic
215	Whitworth College	1890	Washington	Presbyterian (U.S.A.)
216	College of Idaho	1891	Idaho	Presbyterian (U.S.A.)
217	Concordia College	1891	Minnesota	Norwegian Lutheran
218	Hardin-Simmons University	1891	Texas	Southern Baptist
219	Lenoir-Rhyne College	1891	North Carolina	United Lutheran
220	Union College	1891	Nebraska	Seventh-Day Adventist
221	Keuka College	1892	New York	Northern Baptist
222	Millsaps College	1892	Mississippi	Methodist
223	Seattle College	1892	Washington	Catholic
224	University of Chicago	1892	Illinois	Northern Baptist
225	Walla Walla College	1892	Washington	Seventh-Day Adventist

226	American University	1893	District of Columbia	Methodist
227	Aurora College	1893	Illinois	Advent Christian Church
228	Hood College	1893	Maryland	Evangelical and Reformed
229	Randolph-Macon Women's College	1893	Virginia	Methodist
230	Seattle Pacific College	1893	Washington	Free Methodist
231	Upsala College	1893	New Jersey	Lutheran (Augustana Synod)
232	Morningside College	1894	Iowa	Methodist
233	Texas College	1894	Texas	Coloured Methodist Episcopal
234	Manchester College	1895	Indiana	Church of the Brethren
235	Saint Martin's College	1895	Washington	Catholic
236	Our Lady of the Lake College	1896	Texas	Catholic
237	Nazareth College	1897	Michigan	Catholic
238	Trinity College	1897	District of Columbia	Catholic
239	De Paul University	1898	Illinois	Catholic
240	Saint Norbert College	1898	Wisconsin	Catholic
241	Meredith College	1899	North Carolina	Southern Baptist
242	Virginia Union University	1899	Virginia	National Baptist
243	Incarnate Word College	1900	Texas	Catholic
244	Samuel Houston College	1900	Texas	Methodist

(*Note.* The above list is compiled from *The Year Book of American Churches*. It does not include colleges which were Congregational in their origin or early connection, presumably because the polity of that denomination does not give ecclesiastical control of the colleges. The total list would be, however, incomplete and misleading without mention of those institutions, cited in the Year Book of the Congregational and Christian Churches as having had historical connection with these bodies, though now listed as nondenominational.)

No.	College	Year organized	Location, by State
1	Middlebury College	1800	Vermont
2	Amherst College	1821	Massachusetts
3	Oberlin College	1833	Ohio
4	Knox College	1837	Illinois
5	Mount Holyoke College	1837	Massachusetts
6	Olivet College	1844	Michigan
7	Beloit College	1846	Wisconsin
8	Grinnell College	1846	Iowa
9	Rockford College	1847	Illinois
10	Pacific University	1849	Oregon
11	Milwaukee-Downer College	1851	Wisconsin
12	Ripon College	1851	Wisconsin
13	Whitman College	1859	Washington
14	Washburn College	1865	Kansas
15	Carleton College	1866	Minnesota
16	Fisk University	1866	Tennessee
17	Atlanta University	1867	Georgia
18	Talladega College	1867	Alabama
19	Tougaloo College	1869	Mississippi
20	LeMoyne College	1870	Tennessee
21	Wellesley College	1870	Massachusetts
22	Smith College	1871	Massachusetts
23	Doane College	1872	Nebraska
24	Drury College	1873	Missouri
25	Colorado College	1874	Colorado
26	Tillotson College	1877	Texas
27	Yankton College	1881	South Dakota
28	American International College	1885	Massachusetts
29	Rollins College	1885	Florida
30	Schauffler College	1886	Ohio
31	Pomona College	1887	California
32	Elon College	1890	North Carolina
33	Piedmont College	1897	Georgia

H. 'A JUST AND DURABLE PEACE'[1]

STATEMENT OF POLITICAL PROPOSITIONS

which underlie a Just and Durable Peace
and which the United States ought now
to accept for itself and begin forthwith
to realize in cooperation with others.

I. The peace must provide the political framework for a continuing collaboration of the United Nations and, in due course, of neutral and enemy nations.

II. The peace must make provision for bringing within the scope of international agreement those economic and financial acts of national governments which have widespread international repercussions.

III. The peace must make provision for an organization to adapt the treaty structure of the world to changing underlying conditions.

IV. The peace must proclaim the goal of autonomy for subject peoples, and it must establish international organization to assure and to supervise the realization of that end.

V. The peace must establish procedures for controlling military establishments everywhere.

VI. The peace must establish in principle, and seek to achieve in practice, the right of individuals everywhere to religious and intellectual liberty.

[1] Formulated by The Commission to Study the Bases of a Just and Durable Peace instituted by the Federal Council of the Churches of Christ in America. March, 1943.

INDEX

Abbott, Dr Lyman, 125
Abyssinia, 185
Abyssinian Baptist Church, 189
Adams, Henry, 194
Adams, James Truslow, 27, 131
(note 1)
Adams, John, 42, 55
Adams, Samuel, 41
Adler, 154, 191
Adventists, 83, 104
Africa, 186
Agape, 121
Alabama, 98, 100
Albania, Church of, 97, 227
Alcott, 43 .
Amana Society, 100
American Academy of Arts and
Letters, 262
'Americanism', 218, 222
Americans, characteristics of, 4, 10,
11, 12, 69, 124, 149, 150, 153,
156, 172, 217, 231, 237, 238–9,
262
Anabaptism *and* Anabaptists, 49,
95, 97, 107, 178
Anderson, South Carolina, 72
Andros, Sir Edmund, 32
Anglican Church (Church of Eng-
land), 6, 7, 33, 49, 65, 110,
132, 161, 242, 243
Anglicans (in American colonies),
31, 32, 36, 37, 39, 40, 50 (n. 1),
51, 79, 188, 203, 206
Anglo-Catholics, 90, 110, 123,
127, 242
Anti-Catholic movement, 214
Anti-clericalism, 68, 165, 178, 195,
255
Anti-Semitism, 109, 235
APA, 214
Apocalypse, 197
Apostles' Creed, 132, 136
Appalachian Mountains, 35, 107

Architecture, 116–19, 240
Arians, 87
Armageddon, 104
Army of U.S.A., 185
Arnold, Matthew, 155
Articles, XXXIX, 136
Atheism, 165
Atlantic City, 95
Atlantic Monthly, 151
Atlantic seaboard, 76, 107, 162,
164, 166, 205, 213
Attucks, Crispus, 181
Augsburg Confession, 136, 238
Peace of (1555), 48
Augustana Synod, 3
Axis countries, 62

Baltimore, the Lords, 30, 36, 201,
203
(U.S.A.), 87, 209, 212 (n. 1)
Bishop of, 207
Baptisms, 122
Baptists, 3, 34, 37, 41, 53, 75
(statistics), 76, 78, 80, 98, 107,
138, 176, 177, 188, 189, 190,
192, 211, 230, 232, 236, 246,
Appendix B
Barry, Bishop, 256
Barth, Karl, 153, 156
Benson, Hugh, 240
Bible, 57, 81, 83, 104, 119, 138,
139, 162, 163, 169, 171, 178,
188, 193, 217
Biology, 254
Birth control, 63, 199, 219
Bishops, 39, 40, 41, 71, 78, 206,
207, 208, 209, 211, 212
Black-shirt agitation, 109
Blasphemy, 63
Boston, 31, 34, 40, 53, 85, 90, 91,
112, 113, 212 (n. 1)
Massacre, 181
Boston Daily Globe, 224

Bradley's *Appearance and Reality*, 86
Bresee, Rev. Phineas F., 98
British, the, 41, 43
BBC, 147
British Empire, 140–1, 263
Broadcasting, 67, 68
Broadway, 95
Browning, Robert, 102, 160, 165
Bryce, Lord, *The American Commonwealth*, 8, 9, 128; 253 (*The Hindrances to Good Citizenship*)
Buchmanism, 161
Bulgaria, Church of, 97, 227
Bunyan, John, 194
Bushnell, Horace, *Christian Nurture*, 170–1

California, 91
Calvert, Cecil *and* Sir George, *see* Baltimore, Lords
Calvinism *and* Calvinists, 15, 17, 33, 52, 55, 87, 88, 90, 98, 143, 144, 146, 149, 150, 151, 159, 232, 250
Cambridge (England), King's College Chapel in, 116, 118
Tripos, 169
Cambridge (U.S.A.), 61
'Camp meeting', 98, 99, 190
Campbell, Reginald, *New Theology*, 252
Campbell, Rev. Thomas, 81
'Campbellites', 81
Canada *and* Canadian, 81, 107, 113, 205, 210, 216
Cane River (in Chilhowee Mountains), 98
Canterbury, Archbishop of, 65
Carlyle, Thomas, *Heroes and Hero Worship*, 206
Carolinas, the, 90
Carroll, Charles, 40, 206
Carroll, John, 206–9
Carthage (Illinois), 83
Cartwright, Peter, 99

Catechism, Heidelberg, 238
Luther's Smaller, 238
Cathedral Chapter, 168
Cather, Willa, *Death Comes to the Archbishop*, 2
Catholics, *see* Roman Catholics
Celibacy, 99
Celt, The, 215
Census of 1936, 66–7, 71, 72, 74, 86, 94, 108, 176, 187, 227, 246
Channing, William Ellery, 57, 87, 88, 89, 252
Chaplains, Army, 60, 69, 217, 233, 259
Charleston (South Carolina), 208
Constitution, 208
Chesterton, G. K., 220
Chicago, 183
Choirs, 125–6
Christ, The American, 150
Christ, Divinity of, 88
Christian Endeavour Society, 120
Christian Ethic, 256
Christian Reformed Church, 108
Christian Science *and* Scientists, 82, 85–7
Christian Science Monitor, 86
Christianity, 20, 21, 58, 60, 65, 68–70, 80, 102, 133, 136, 137, 138, 142, 148, 151, 193, 232, 234, 238, 258, 261, 262, 263
Early history of, 46–7
Church and State (separation of), 42–3, ch. iii, ch. iv, 115, 116, 133, 146, 162, 221
'Church, the', 8, 9, 10, 18, 65, 81, 94, 114, 132, 133, 148, 170, 226, 229, 243, 244
'Church of God and Saints of Christ', 72
Church buildings, 116–19, 121, 125–6, 187, 190, 191, 207, 211, 213, 214
Church-going, 16–18, 131
Church membership, 74–75, 94, 131, 153, 171
Church property, 60, 61, 187, 207

INDEX

INDEX

MacLeigh, Archibald, 262
McPherson, Aimée, 71
Madison, James, 45, 54, 71
Maine, 35, 36, 100, 201, 212
Manhattan Island (New York), 108, 113, 183
Manichaean dualism, 87
Maréchal, Ambrose (Archbishop of Baltimore), 207, 208
Marine City, St Clair County, Mich., 72
Maritain, 21
Maritime Provinces (Canada), 113
Marriages, 213 (mixed): *see also* Civil marriages
Martineau, Harriet, 195
Martineau, James, 88, 127
Maryland, 3, 30, 35, 40, 91, 181, 201, 202, 203, 204, 206, 222, 244
Mass (Roman Catholic), *see* Sacrament
Massachusetts, 3, 34, 35, 36, 45, 52, 87, 88, 90, 143, 145, 179, 181, 201, 202, 203, 229, 244
  Bay Colony, 27, 28, 31-2, 33, 34, 122
  Council of Churches, 233-4
Mather, Cotton, 33
Mathers, the, 135
Maynard, Theodore, *The Story of American Catholicism*, 200-17 *passim*, 220-1
Mays, Benjamin E., *The Negro's God*, 193
Medium, 102
Meiklejohn, Alexander, *Education Between Two Worlds*, 60
Mennonites, 4 (Amish), 38, 76, 97, 102, 259, Appendix B
Merchant adventurers, 30, 31
Messianic hope, 251, 263
Methodism *and* Methodists, 37, 75 (statistics), 76, 78, 80, 96, 98, 107, 177, 189, 190, 211, 219, 226, 230, 236, 237, 243, 259, Appendix B

Methodist Episcopal Church, South, 19, 189
Metropolitan Catholic Almanac, 211
Mexico, 204
Michigan, 108
Milan, Edict of (313), 46, 47
Military training, 165
Millennium, the, 104
Ministers, *see* Clergy
Minnesota, 3, 108, 227
Missionaries *and* Missions, 28, 29, 78, 82, 84-5, 90, 111, 114, 120, 140, 141, 142, 187, 211, 222, 234
Mississippi Valley, 83, 237
  State, 182
Mobile (Alabama), 100
Modernism, 137, 170, 195, 197, 225
Monk, Maria, 214
Montefiore, Claude, 110
Montessori method, 172
Moody, Dwight L., 160, 179
Moore, George Foot, 110
Morality, Religion and, 58, 63, 149-50, 153
Moravians, Appendix B
Morison, Professor Samuel Eliot, 27
Morley, John, 256
Mormons, 3, 82-5
'Mount Moriah Fire Baptized Church of Knoxville, Tenn.', 72
Mount Vernon, 51
Mussolini, 185
Myrdal, Gunnar, *An American Dilemma*, 198
Mysticism, 10, 134-5, 150, 217, 218

NAACP, 197
'Nativism', 199, 213, 214, 222
Nature, Temple of, 57
Navy of U.S.A., 185
Nazarene, First Church of the, 98, 226
Nazis, 232

313

INDEX

Negroes (*see* also Slavery), 95, 100–1, 106, 176, 177, ch. x, Appendix E

New England, 3, 9, 25, 31, 33, 34, 41, 42, 50, 52, 88, 112, 113, 122, 143, 203, 204, 212, 236, 250, 252

New Hampshire, 35, 45
New Haven, 32
New Jersey, 36
New Netherlands, 30
New Orleans, 195
New Testament, 76, 217, 238
'New Thought', 105
New York, 30, 50, 57, 60, 69, 75, 83, 99, 108, 112, 113, 164, 175, 183, 212, 223, 231
  Archbishop of, 200
Newman, Cardinal, 113, 142, 216
Newport (Rhode Island), 91
Newspapers, 11
  New York Times, 11, 19
Nicene Creed, 136
Niebuhr, Richard, *The Social Sources of Denominationalism*, 96; *The Church Against the World*, 148
Nonconformity and Dissent, 7, 242, 243
Non-Trinitarians, 52, 88, 203
Norfolk (Virginia), 207, 208
North, the, 3, 77, 78, 79, 80, 180, 183, 184, 189, 192, 195, 236, 243
North Carolina, 91
Northampton (U.S.A.), 143, 145
Norton, Charles Eliot, 19
Norway, 108
Novena, 199

Oglethorpe, General, 38
Ohio, 83, 91, 108, 230
Old Testament, 55, 149, 193, 238, 248
Oneida Community, 99
Optimism, 12–15, 248, 250, 251
Oxford, 168, 169, 191

Oxford Conference on Life and Work (1937), 46, 232
  Groups, 145, 160–1

Pacific, the, 107
Pacifists, 38–9, 92–3, 101, 102, 230, 259, Appendix F
Page, Walter Hines, 124
Papacy, the, 111, 206, 222, 242
Parishes, 111, 112, 113, 116, 129, 207
Parker, Theodore, 89
Pascal, Blaise, 144, 151
Peabody, Francis Greenwood, 88, 89
Peace, 262
  'A Just and Durable', Appendix H
Pearl Harbour, 147, 259
Péguy, Charles, 220
Penn, William, 30, 90, 97, 202
Pennsylvania, 4, 30, 35, 36, 38, 53, 81, 90, 91, 97, 108, 112, 187, 203, 204, 209, 211, 237, 244
Perfectionism, Political, 13–15, 88
  Religious, 98, 103, 254
Persecution, 36, 83, 90–1, 92, 203, 205, 213–14
Personalities, cult of, 11–12
Philadelphia, 87, 237
Philippines, 141
'Piedmont', the, 35
Pilgrim Fathers, 30, 31, 49, 177, 236
'Piskys' (Episcopalians), 112
Plymouth (U.S.A.), 28, 31, 33
Plymouth Brethren, 76
Politics, Religion and, 63–6, 77, 80, 208, 218, 219, 232
Polygamy, 82, 99
Pope, the, 111, 208, 221, 223
  Leo XIII, 218
Population, 216, Appendix A
Portuguese, 28, 107, 212
Pragmatism, 153
Prayer, Lord's, 67, 68, 123

314

INDEX

INDEX